Best Technologies for Public Libraries

Best Technologies for Public Libraries

Policies, Programs, and Services

Christopher DeCristofaro, James Hutter, and Nick Tanzi

An Imprint of ABC-CLIO, LLC
Santa Barbara, California • Denver, Colorado

Library of Congress Cataloging-in-Publication Data

Names: DeCristofaro, Christopher, author. | Hutter, James, author. | Tanzi, Nicholas, author.
Title: Best technologies for public libraries : policies, programs, and services / Christopher DeCristofaro, James Hutter, and Nick Tanzi.
Description: Santa Barbara, California : Libraries Unlimited, 2020. | Includes bibliographical references and index.
Identifiers: LCCN 2019039224 (print) | LCCN 2019039225 (ebook) | ISBN 9781440869280 (paperback ; acid-free paper) | ISBN 9781440869273 (ebook)
Subjects: LCSH: Public libraries—Technological innovations. | Public libraries—Information technology. | Three-dimensional printing services in libraries. | Drone aircraft. | Virtual reality—Library applications. | Public libraries—United States—Case studies.
Classification: LCC Z678.9 .D39 2020 (print) | LCC Z678.9 (ebook) | DDC 027.4—dc23
LC record available at https://lccn.loc.gov/2019039224
LC ebook record available at https://lccn.loc.gov/2019039225

ISBN: 978-1-4408-6928-0 (paperback)
978-1-4408-6927-3 (ebook)

24 23 22 21 20 1 2 3 4 5

This book is also available as an eBook.

Libraries Unlimited
An Imprint of ABC-CLIO, LLC

ABC-CLIO, LLC
147 Castilian Drive
Santa Barbara, California 93117
www.abc-clio.com

This book is printed on acid-free paper ∞

Manufactured in the United States of America

Contents

Acknowledgments

Together, the authors would like to thank the following individuals, whose assistance made this book possible:

Michael Bartolomeo

Melanie Davidoff

Brandon Faucett

Scott Kalogris

Jane Kauzlaric

Keith Klang

Chad Mairn

Alison Mirabella

Dean Meyer

P. J. Novak

Katy O'Grady

Nicole Parisi

Steve Patti

Nils Reardon

Georgina Rivas-Martinez

Janet Scherer

Ian Sloat

Noah Thielke

Andrew Tricket

Sally Turbitt

Angela Zimmermann

Christopher DeCristofaro

I would like to thank the following people:

My wife, Kim, and my daughters, Julia and Courtney, for their gracious understanding and support while I worked on this endeavor.

Anthony Bliss and Alexander Boris, my colleagues and "partners in crime," who have been great sources of knowledge, wisdom, and guidance.

Colleagues both near and far, who would lend an ear and donate an idea that, many times, would become inspiration for content in this book.

Neely McCahey, for always listening, understanding, and inspiring.

James Hutter

I wish to thank the following people:

Jamie, for providing the patience and understanding during this project that only a fellow author could. I get to now return the favor as you complete your novel!

Mina, for doing her best to provide Jamie and me with at least five hours of sleep each night and for sharing valuable insights into cutting-edge technologies that only a four-month-old baby could.

My Port Washington Public Library family, for being courageous enough to experiment with many of these technologies and for supporting my efforts to share our knowledge and experiences with the world.

. . . and I thank the reader. Remember to experiment! Fail! Then, succeed and teach the rest of us!

Nick Tanzi

I would like to thank the following people:

My wife, Kristine, for enduring many extra hours of Play-Doh hamburgers, *Dora the Explorer* marathons, and Laurie Berkner dance parties with our daughter so I could get away to write. The next year of letting out our dog, Bear, at 4:00 a.m. are on me.

Sara Roye, for pretending to be surprised when I told her I needed some help creating graphics for a book, and for not surprising me when she selflessly agreed to do it.

My friends, for feigning interest in a conversation on emerging technologies in libraries while we're at a restaurant on a Saturday night.

My colleagues, for their encouragement, support, and dedication to serving the public. It's dangerously liberating when you have a team behind you that will always figure things out.

My editor, Jessica Gribble, for her attention to detail, calming influence, and scary-fast responses to emails.

Introduction: Why Read This Book?

"Emerging technology" is a term that can inspire excitement or dread in equal measure among library staff. While new technologies offer tremendous opportunities for the development of programs and services, they also present multiple challenges to your organization. This book examines four technologies—3D printing, drones, virtual reality, and augmented reality—and their place in the public library. In doing so, it addresses several critical issues.

STAFF TRAINING

When introducing a new technology to the library, it is only natural that a large percentage of your staff will be unfamiliar with it. Unless this unfamiliarity is addressed, it can quickly lead to staff anxiety. Training is, of course, essential. Any training you offer, however, should never be one-size-fits-all! Rather, it should be developed around specific staff roles. Consider the use of computers within your organization. You don't simply require that every library employee be a computer expert capable of troubleshooting and repair!

Using the example of computers, a more reasonable approach to training is to ensure that all staff members are aware that the library has computers available for public use. You require that a sizeable portion of library staff understand the basics of using a computer. Continuing on, a somewhat smaller percentage of staff will have been shown how to utilize specific software. Finally, the smallest group of users are trained in the troubleshooting and repair of your hardware, software, and overall computer network.

In a similar fashion, this book addresses training by first creating roles within an overall workflow and then determining what skills are necessary in each. This approach will allow your organization to engage in targeted staff development that matches how individual employees will interact with each technology. By creating role-specific training, your organization will save both time and money.

IMPLEMENTATION

After coming to know and understand a new technology, a library must next move toward implementation. The many possibilities offered by each is overwhelming and can paralyze an organization with indecision. This book seeks to address this issue using a multi-pronged approach, including the elements listed below.

Equipment Selection

Within each technology, options abound! We'll discuss what's out there in the marketplace and just what it's capable of. Far from just rating individual pieces of equipment, we will provide you with the tools needed to perform your own evaluations. Although there is no true way to future-proof a book on technology, this approach will serve you well into the future. Ultimately, the goal is to identify not just the best equipment but also the best fit for your unique organization.

Software Options

Many of the technologies we will discuss are driven as much by software as they are by hardware. With that in mind, this book provides specific options for both traditional computers and mobile devices, where both exist.

Developing Programs and Services

Public libraries are built on serving our communities; it is therefore critical that a library's investment in an emerging technology pays dividends in the form of programs and services for our patrons. Acknowledging this, a substantial portion of this book concerns itself with just that.

In each technology covered, we describe specific library programs. Descriptions include necessary equipment, setup, age-appropriateness, and time required. Occasionally, a manufacturer's requirement may result in some inflexibility; barring that, if a program is scalable or can be adjusted to reach a younger audience, that option is provided. In addition to formalized programs, we identify services you can extend to your patrons using the technologies covered. These offerings are varied and range from virtual reality headset-lending programs to 3D printing/scanning services. When detailing these services, we outline suggestions for workflow that can be tailored to your own organization.

Policy

As you look to incorporate new technologies into the library's service model, it is essential that you develop effective policy. Ideally, policies should be clear and practical while also flexible enough to avoid becoming burdensome. This book addresses policy writing in two ways. First, we examine all the considerations you should take when formulating policy. We outline concerns, liabilities, and desired goals. By doing so, we aim to equip the reader with the information necessary to build a policy from the ground up, if they so choose. Second, an appendix to this book offers sample policies that we believe best encapsulate our research. These policies can be reviewed and adapted as desired.

HOW TO USE THIS BOOK

Though the authors enthusiastically agree that this book should be read cover to cover multiple times, it has been written with browsing in mind. Comprising individual chapters devoted to exploring 3D printing, drones, augmented reality, and virtual reality, you, the reader, can easily dive into your topic(s) of interest using the information we've provided, you can make an informed decision on the best fit for your library, individual departments, and the patrons you serve. This format should allow you to select ideas à la carte, adapting them as necessary. A final chapter examines the synergy between these four technologies and explores the growing opportunities to combine two or more of them within library programming and services.

Part of the groundwork for this book involved seeking out innovative uses of each technology within public libraries. We conducted interviews with library professionals at institutions large and small, gleaning valuable information. The results of these conversations are a series of case studies that reveal both the potential of the technology and a blueprint for its application. We remain grateful to our colleagues for sharing their ideas; this book is the better for it.

In total, the content contained within should provide you with a roadmap for incorporating 3D printing, drones, virtual reality, and augmented reality into your library. By completing such planning, you can proceed with a destination already in mind. Early successes are essential to building organizational confidence and can help alleviate any staff resistance to change that may emerge. Ultimately, we hope this book provides you with a strong foundation; we cannot wait to see what you will build! If you'd like to share your stories, please feel free to contact the authors at:

Chris DeCristofaro:
cdecris2@gmail.com
Twitter handle: @cdecrist

James Hutter:
james.hutter@gmail.com
Twitter handle: @james_lead

Nick Tanzi:
nicktanzi@gmail.com
Twitter handle: @techie_lib

ONE

3D Printing

3D Printing is an exciting technology that is being rapidly adopted by libraries. Despite its seeming newness, the technology has in fact existed since for several decades! In 1983, Chuck Hull created the first 3D printer, the SLA-1. The process he patented was known as stereolithography, which created solid objects "by successively 'printing' thin layers of ultraviolet curable material one on top of the other" ("What Is 3D Printing?," 2019). Hull's SLA-1 is the forerunner of today's modern liquid resin printers, such as those manufactured by Formlabs.

Although stereolithography printers may have been the first, the technology now encompasses other processes, namely selective laser sintering (SLS) and fused deposition modeling (FDM). Despite their technical-sounding names, the processes themselves are fairly simple. SLS printing refers to a process in which a laser heats powdered plastic material into a solid structure based on a 3D model ("An Introductory Guide to Selective Laser Sintering (SLS) 3D Printing," 2017). FDM printers, on the other hand, build a 3D object by extruding melted material layer by layer along a path, based on a file, most often an STL ("Varotsis," 2019). Today, FDM and SLA are the most common desktop 3D printers in use.

HOW IS 3D PRINTING BEING USED?

Operating as a sort of self-contained manufacturing process, 3D printing is widely used in a number of industries. These are discussed below.

The Medical Field

Some 3D printers are being utilized to assist with organ transplants. Scaffolds are printed in the shape of organs onto which living cells are added (Chowdhry, 2013). At present, there are efforts to print directly using cells! In addition to organ transplants, 3D printers can create high-quality and cost-effective prosthetic limbs.

The Aerospace Industry

The precise nature of 3D printing and its ability to perform rapid prototyping allows for the creation and testing of scale models. This is especially useful in aerodynamic testing (Artley, n.d.). 3D printing is also being explored by NASA. Given the cost of moving supplies into space, the agency has determined it to be far more economical to send a 3D printer and manufacture tools as the need arises! (Rainey, 2015).

The Automotive Industry

Prior to investing in expensive molding tools, engineers are able to rapidly test and modify designs, shortening the development cycle to days instead of months ("3D Printing in Automotive," n.d.).

This, of course, brings us to libraries. Later in this chapter, we will outline numerous programs and services you can deliver to your patrons using a 3D printer. Before that, however, let us focus on equipment selection. When choosing a 3D printer, we're often inclined to look for the best printer that we can practically afford. While those are sensible parameters, what you should truly be seeking is the printer that is the *best fit* for your library. In order to do that, you must evaluate your organization and begin to outline the intended use of your printer.

EVALUATING YOUR LIBRARY WHEN PURCHASING A 3D PRINTER

What Are Your Values?

Every library (hopefully) is guided by a set of values. Most libraries have established a mission statement. Now consider where 3D printing fits in at your organization. For example, imagine a library that has made a commitment to sustainability. ABS plastic is a petroleum-based filament commonly used by 3D printers. ABS plastic is not accepted at many recycling facilities (Leigh, 2011). Left in a landfill, printed objects and leftover filament could take approximately a thousand years to biodegrade! Clearly, using such a printer would be at odds with that library's values.

So, what might a values-driven approach look like for such a library? A library committed to sustainability may wish to invest in a printer that prints using more ecofriendly materials, such as PLA plastic, which is compatible with many FDM printers. PLA (or polylactic acid) is derived from sugar cane or corn starch, both of which are renewable resources (Rogers, 2015). Even then, PLA is only biodegradable under very specific conditions, which are not met by simply throwing it into a landfill. To truly meet the values this library aspires to, it might be necessary to choose a printer that is compatible with more exotic plant and wood-based filaments, such as bioFila.

In addition to sustainability, a library might be driven by the desire to purchase domestically or within its town/state. Perhaps it has adopted a do-it-yourself creed that drives it to build its own printer, so that it seeks a manufacturer that sells assembly kits. In short, be sure to review your library's values prior to making a purchase and see how they may inform your decision making.

What Is the Size and Skill Set of Your Staff?

Staff, is of course, your library's greatest asset. It is therefore important that you consider your staff while seeking a printer that is the best fit for your organization. Evaluate how "techie" your staff is. Many 3D printers embrace a real do-it-yourself mantra, requiring a lot of tinkering and experimentation, whereas others are more of the plug-and-play variety. Selecting a printer that requires constant adjustments, swapping of extruders, and other maintenance can intimidate your non-techies. On the other hand, if you have a very technical staff, you can dive into the realm of more flexible printers. Furthermore, a technical staff might consider purchasing a printer kit and then assembling the 3D printer at a substantial discount.

Aside from the makeup of your staff, consider how well-staffed you are. Some printers require varying degrees of attention. If you are short-staffed, the reliability of a printer may be one of your primary requirements. Additionally, some printers offer an onboard camera or online monitoring of a print job, allowing staff members to keep an eye on the printing while they multitask.

What Are You Planning to Do with Your Printer?

Clearly, how you intend to use your printer is going to be a driving force in your decision making. Speaking broadly, consider the following:

Will You Be Using It in Programming? 3D printers hold tremendous programming potential, which we will explore in depth a bit later. A printer that sees regular use in programs may need to produce a large volume of prints, ideally with a short turnaround time. Whether your library charges for programs or not, the print material should be a prime consideration. Printing in liquid resin can be very expensive, whereas PLA is generally much more affordable. For that reason alone, I recommend an FDM printer for general programming.

Will You Be Using It in Prototyping? As defined by *Merriam-Webster Dictionary*, prototyping refers to "the creation of an original model on which something is patterned." Prototypes can run the gamut and may or may not be scale models. Although 3D printing is a precise technology, the level of precision does vary. For a prototype that may be small in size or have many interlocking parts requiring the highest print resolution and exactness, an SLA printer may be required. At the same time, some FDM printers, while less precise, can utilize a wider range of material types, including flexible materials like nylon.

Is Mobility Important?

Oh, the places your printer will go!—or perhaps not. Ease of travel may factor heavily into your decision making. Consider whether your printer will be used in outreach. A standard printer can weigh between 20 and 30 pounds. One printer may require an attached laptop or computer, or process prints wirelessly, while others are capable of printing off of a USB drive or SD card. The combined weight of a printer and its peripherals can factor heavily (no pun intended) in how practical it will be to move it. One strategy for increasing the mobility of your hardware is to invest in a lighter printer, including miniaturized versions of some of the more popular models.

Beyond the weight of your printer, other factors will impact mobility. For instance, 3D printing is a precision technology, requiring the careful calibration of your build plate and extruders. Moving a printer can disturb a finely tuned machine. The process for leveling your printer may be automatic, or it may require hand-tuning. A printer that requires labor-intensive hand-tuning may be a poor fit for travel. Conversely, a printer that features auto-leveling can remove this concern. Consider also the physical layout of a printer. A boxier, self-contained printer generally travels better than one that is more open-air and sprawling. In summary, picture yourself having to pack up and move a printer to another location, and then determine how practical and impractical that would be given your preferred device.

Where Will You Be Leaving Your Printer?

Where you choose to house your printer should also affect the selection process. At the very least, determine if your device will sit in a public or staff area. While making that determination, also consider the issues discussed below.

Sound and Smell

Research into the microparticles emitted by 3D printers is still in its infancy; however, one should always err on the side of caution. As such, any printer, whether FDM or SLA, should be placed in a well-ventilated area. FDM printers can give off a slight smell of burning plastic, especially if printing in ABS filament, and the alcohol rinse associated with SLA printing can be quite strong (and messy). With regard to sound, printers can run the gamut from silent to quite loud, and you should be aware of where on this scale a printer under consideration will land. While these factors should immediately eliminate the possibility of housing a printer in a cramped office or study room, consider the impact it could have adjacent to the reference desk or study area!

Safety and Security

A 3D printer can draw a lot of interest from your community. Even the best of signage may not prevent little hands from trying to touch a printer while it is in operation. For added peace of mind, libraries can invest in an enclosure for their printer (or build their own); however, there are also passive manufacturing decisions that can increase or reduce the chance of injury. A printer that has a door in front of the build plate is less accessible to tampering than one that is open-air. All SLA printers and many FDM printers are enclosed this way. Additionally, a door can easily be reinforced using a piece of tape or Velcro. In FDM printing, the extruder is very hot and can burn at a touch. Some model printers utilize an additional heated build plate, which are generally more accessible than an extruder, and can represent an added liability in an unattended printer.

Visibility

As was previously noted, a 3D printer can draw a lot of interest from your community. As a device that patrons will directly interact with, the ability to "see" the process can factor into your decision making. As an additive process, your 3D printer, whether SLA or FDM, will create an object layer by successive layer. In the case of an SLA printer, this process will happen behind an ultraviolet (UV) protected enclosure, which can make viewing in any detail difficult at best. At the other extreme, an open-air FDM printer presents a good view from nearly any angle.

GETTING RECOMMENDATIONS

Having evaluated your organization and considered all the different variables that may factor into your decision making, you can now seek recommendations from an informed position. Sources of printer recommendations are discussed in the following sections.

Recommendations from Other Library Professionals

It is our habit, as library professionals, to seek the advice of our peers. It may then surprise you that it is the opinion of the authors that while you should indeed ask for recommendations from other libraries, it should not be the primary factor in your decision making. The reason is this: experiences may vary.

Your peers will undoubtedly have printers that they recommend wholeheartedly. Conversely, there will be printers that have earned their ire. These are individual experiences. What is lacking in any review a peer will give you is statistical significance. An individual person's experience with a single printer or handful of printers is simply not enough data to render an informed decision as to whether a printer is good or bad. An individual library could conceivably have an excellent experience with an unreliable printer—or a terrible experience with a reliable one. They simply lie within the margin of error.

This is not to say the experiences of other library professionals should have no bearing on your decision making. Other libraries can speak to a printer's ease of use. They can weigh in (again, no pun intended) on how easy a printer was to move. Of essential importance, they can inform you as to how responsive a manufacturer's customer service department was, particularly in the event they needed to utilize a warranty.

Ultimately, in seeking the advice of your peers, you should identify libraries that are using their printers in ways that closely mirror your own intentions. These will be the reviews with the most applicability to your own organization.

Customer Reviews

Anyone who has shopped online has undoubtedly perused the review section of a product they were considering purchasing. Customer reviews can be a good source of information when purchasing a 3D printer, if using the same caveats and criteria given in the "professional recommendation" section. To maximize and authenticate the information you are gleaning from customer reviews, it is best to seek consistency within a large number of reviews. For example, if customers commonly complain about their printer jamming, it seems clear that there may be an issue with the extruder! A review associated with a verified purchase should always be given more weight than an unverified one. During this process, be sure to differentiate between criticisms directed at the manufacturer versus the reseller. A more common complaint regarding many purchases (not just 3D printers) can involve shipping. These include the cost of shipping, damage or delays in delivery, and other associated issues. These should be held against the reputation of the reseller and not the manufacturer. As such, you can ignore these complaints, provided a trustworthy reseller can be identified.

3D Hubs Best 3D Printer Guide

Self-described as "the world's largest network of manufacturing hubs," 3DHubs.com maintains an annual "Best 3D Printer Guide" that represents an excellent, invaluable source of reviews. This guide acts as a review aggregator—a Rotten Tomatoes for 3D printers, if you will. The advantage of this approach is that you are able to examine individual reviews that represent the consensus opinion of many users and experts. The 2018 edition of the Best Printer Guide was developed based on 10,154 reviews and 1,482,614 print jobs made on reviewed printers ("2018 Best 3D Printer Guide," 2018).

Aside from the depth of information within the Best 3D Printer Guide, reviews are arranged into categories of printers. Their descriptions on the website are provided below.

Prosumer

Printers in the Prosumer category are for professionals looking for a 3D printer with exceptional build quality that can produce high-quality parts, reliably. These are highly advanced desktop machines with a variety of applications. Printers in this category are best suited for professional designers and small businesses.

Workhorse

Printers in the Workhorse category are for users looking for robust machines that can print nonstop with minimal print failure. These are printers manufactured with reliability in mind and are open to slight modifications and tinkering.

Budget

Printers in this category are all about value and bang for your buck. These machines offer good print quality for money along with a supportive community and are open to modifications and tinkering, with a reasonable degree of reliability.

Plug 'n' Play

Printers in the Plug 'n' Play category are capable of printing straight out of the box with minimal setup. These are considered to be the easiest to use and are characterized by consistent print quality and great customer support. Tradeoffs include limited modification abilities and little room to experiment with tinkering.

Other Review Sources

As the adoption of 3D printing continues to increase, so to do professional review sources. Digital Trends, *PC Magazine*, CNET, and others now provide useful reviews of current-model printers. Libraries with databases such as *Consumer Reports* can view these as additional review sources.

A FINAL WORD ON EQUIPMENT SELECTION

The key to making an informed decision is information! Understanding the strengths and weaknesses of your organization, your goals and intended use are the foundation you will build on. Armed with that knowledge, you can then consult the aforementioned sources of reviews and recommendations, making a selection that aligns with your library.

POLICY CONSIDERATIONS

Once you have a 3D printer, it might be tempting to immediately move on to building programs and services around the technology. This would be the wrong approach. To understand the importance of policy, let's look back to the summer of 2018, when some libraries in possession of 3D printers found themselves in a crisis situation. During this time, it came to the public's attention that a law preventing the publication of 3D schematics for firearms was set to expire on August 1, 2018 (Cullinane & Criss, 2018). Suddenly, libraries found themselves inundated with questions from patrons, advocacy groups, members of the press—and members of their own staff—as to whether one could print a gun at the library. In some cases, library administration was caught flat-footed and raced to adopt policy and understand their legal responsibility. Ultimately, a federal judge issued an injunction, and plans to publish the schematics were shelved (Bellisle & Daley, 2018).

If there is a lesson to be learned from that experience, it is the importance of developing appropriate library policy governing your 3D printer(s).

Effective policy will create clarity for your staff and patrons, ensure consistency in service, and help mitigate the risks of inappropriate use. Later in this chapter, we will provide sample policies that can be adapted. These aside, what are the policy considerations your organization will need to decide upon?

Conformity with Local, State, and Federal Law

Consider this the low-hanging fruit in policy development. Simply put, the library should make plain that its printers are not meant to facilitate a crime! However, as recent events demonstrate, technology often outpaces the law necessitating further detail. Conformity with the law trumps any other policy consideration listed below.

Prohibition against Weapons

While the library seeks to provide access to information, it need not position itself as a DIY arms manufacturer. A prohibition should be flexible; rather than being firearms specific, it should include items that are unsafe, dangerous, or posing a threat to others.

Respect for Copyright

In many ways, this is covered under the "conformity with the law" provision. However, as copyright represents a significant area of concern for a 3D printer, it is worth stating explicitly. Such a policy is doubly important if your library owns a 3D scanner, as copyrighted materials can be digitized and then uploaded as a schematic online.

Security of Data

Some patrons may wish to use your printer to create a prototype of an invention. As such, they may have concerns about their idea being "stolen". Can you/should you guarantee privacy? If you printer is in the public space, this may prove difficult. Consider the files themselves. Do you delete them after printing? Do your computers wipe after a session has ended?

Appropriate Use

What constitutes proper use? Is there a time or size limit to prints? A monthly limit? How much assistance can/should staff reasonably provide? It's best to be upfront about these things, both to manage patron expectations and to ensure that staff provides consistent service.

Handling Cost

How much, if at all, does your library intend to charge for prints? Two schools of thought are charging by weight or by print time. Weight is a good method for offsetting material costs. If your printer(s) use material types with noticeably different costs, you may need to set your pricing accordingly. In the case of charging by print time, this is an excellent method for preventing monopolization of printers and easing potential logjams.

Hold Harmless

Consider what happens if a 3D printed object fails to perform. Does the library intend to reimburse a patron if the phone case they had printed results in a cracked screen? What if a 3D-printed mounting bracket gives out and their expensive urn shatters on the ground?

Library's Discretion Clause

This is a final, catch-all provision that states the library's right of refusal for prints it may find inappropriate or unwarranted. This clause can help deal with matters that may outpace explicitly written policy. In any refusal, you may wish to have a mechanism for petitioning the library's director and board. The nature of technology is change. As these changes often outpace our laws, library policies that are thoughtful—and, as importantly, flexible—can provide an important safety net for your organization.

Appeal Process

When your library refuses a request, what recourse does your patron have? Policy terms such as "appropriate use" are often subjective in nature. Inevitably, there will be areas of disagreement. Ensure that there is a clearly delineated process for patrons to petition the library's administration or board of trustees, if they feel their print job has been rejected in error.

STAFF TRAINING

Once you have your printer and policy, it's time to move on to training your staff. When conducting training, it's important to remember that not everyone needs to know everything! By deciding upon a division of labor, you can develop a curriculum that is more focused and therefore cost and time effective. While each organization will decide upon the best approach, below are some suggested categories for training.

All Staff

With a constantly expanding list of programs and services, it can often seem like a herculean task to keep your patrons abreast of them all. Consider how much more difficult this work becomes if a portion of your own staff is unaware of them. For that reason, all staff should be given a basic orientation on your printer(s). Such a curriculum should cover what equipment you have, a general description of how it works, and how it will be used at your library. Provide staff with any marketing materials you intend to use for the public. Finally, impart to them the basic 3D printer workflow, specific to your own organization, namely which staff will perform what particular functions in service to your 3D printer(s).

Handlers

Your handlers will be the frontline staff who will interact with your printer. Handlers should know the basics of your printer, as outlined above. Additionally, the handler should be trained in the normal operation of a printer. This means understanding how to turn the printer on and off, how to begin a print job, how to monitor the equipment for signs of trouble, and cancel an in-progress print if it becomes necessary. A handler should be able to engage in casual conversation about how the printer works and guide a patron to further resources. Further resources might take the form of upcoming library classes, library computers with software, or third-party referral information. If your library offers a 3D printing service for the public, a handler can instruct a patron on how to submit a print request.

Jobbers

A jobber will perform all of the work that your handler does. Additionally, jobbers will be the ones who moderate printing requests (staff or patron) and prepare files to be printed. This will require familiarity with the library's policy and training on the slicing software used by your printer(s). Staff in this role will account for completed prints, ensuring they are delivered to the intended recipient. A jobber should be trained on basic troubleshooting of a misprint or other error, in the event that one occurs.

Printer Technicians

Printer technicians represent the highest level of involvement with your 3D printer; being responsible for its long-term health and operation. As it is the most technical position, staff who fill this role should be tech-savvy, or at the very least comfortable learning new things. Indeed, your first technician may need to be self-taught or rely on a third-party resources when you initially introduce a new printer. Your technicians will need to learn the full operation of a printer, including maintenance, calibration, and advanced troubleshooting. If your printer has a warranty, it should be accessible by these staff members, as they will be the ones communicating with the manufacturer.

These categories are meant to represent general responsibilities that will need to be shouldered by staff. Each library should decide upon the best division of labor for their own unique organization. Depending on the size and composition of a library's staff, these roles may be modified or even combined.

DEVELOPING SERVICES

Once your library has written and adopted a 3D printing policy, you can begin the exciting work of developing programs and services! What follow are different ideas that are flexible with regard to audience and budget. They can be modified to fit your organization and taken en masse or à la carte, as is your preference!

A Public 3D Printing Service

At its most basic, a public 3D printing service allows your community to make use of your library's printer. That said, there are many ways of molding such a service to best fit your library. Will your patrons interact directly with the printer, or will you instead have a staff-moderated process? Let's first explore a moderated approach.

In a staff-moderated 3D print service, your patrons will submit their requests to staff. As such, you will need to decide how you'd like to receive submissions, namely, online or in person. Online submissions can be as simple as providing an address to email requests or as involved as an embedded web form. If you'd prefer to take requests in person, you'll need to create an intake form. Whether the format is print or digital, your intake form should include the following:

- **Contact information:** A full name and either a phone number or email address should be provided to allow staff to follow up on a request.
- **Barcode:** A library barcode is a necessity if you restrict access to library patrons.
- **Description of the project:** This is an opportunity for patrons to describe what they're planning on printing. This can act as a self-reporting tool for any conflict with policy. More importantly, it ensures that patrons have attached the correct file.
- **Material requested:** If you have multiple filament/material types or colors, this gives patrons the opportunity to select their preference.
- **File type accepted:** Generally speaking, you'll want to require open-source file types like STL and OBJ while avoiding proprietary ones. This will help ensure you can print the files as-is without utilizing a 3rd-party conversion software.
- **Acceptance of the library's policy:** As a prerequisite to completing any job, patrons should acknowledge that they have read and understand the library's 3D printing policy.

The Review Process

Once a request has been formally submitted, staff will need to review the file to ensure it complies with the library's 3D print policy. If it does, you can then open it in your printer's associated slicing software and confirm that it is printable, that it fits within the build plate, and that the software deems it error-free. This is also an opportunity to confirm the print time and weight, which will determine the cost, if you charge for prints.

The 3D Printing Reference Interview

Once a request is submitted, it is incumbent on staff to engage in a reference interview with the patron. Depending on their preference, this may take place in person, over the phone, or via email. If a print is going to be rejected, you will use this conversation to explain the reasons why, and determine if there is a solution. If the print remains in noncompliance with the policy and the patrons wishes to contest, provide them with information on your appeals process. If, on the other hand, the file is approved you'll want to go over a few items before officially printing.

Like any good reference interview, you'll want to engage in a discussion with your patrons. Listen to them and do your best to determine their needs. Does their intended use of a print line up with the file itself? For example, if a patron has designed an object they plan to use as an iPhone case, is the print size consistent with the manufacturer's specifications? A file that is only three inches long is clearly not suited for this task. Perhaps they have designed a fork or bowl. Is the filament they requested food-safe? Ultimately, just because a file is printable and consistent with your policy does not mean it is going to meet your patron's true needs.

Beyond these items, you'll want to discuss the print cost. If the price is an issue, consider solutions such as a reduced print size, higher infill percentage (a more hollow print), or an alternative material, if this is an option. After settling on price, share with your patron when they can expect to receive their print and where they can pick it up once it's ready.

Delivering a Completed Print

After a request has been submitted, reviewed, and confirmed with your patron, it is time to actually produce and deliver a 3D print. As always, a library is free to pursue a process that works best for them. That being said, below is a suggested workflow.

Once a print has been completed, the patron should be contacted. A finished print can be placed within a Ziploc bag (or other inexpensive container) along with a receipt. The receipt should indicate the patron's name, contact information, barcode number, and the total cost of the print. The date the patron was notified should also be indicated, particularly if you are enforcing a deadline for pickups. Be sure to include instructions if a print requires further processing, such as painting (particularly important when using liquid resin) or the cleanup of rafting/supports.

Generally, your print, receipt, and instructions can then go to your circulation department or other public service desk, provided they process paid transactions. Unless you find yourself processing a large number of prints, you need not come up with a true filing system, other than a bin with your "past due" prints. This bin can be used as a final stop while you attempt to contact the tardy patron. The aforementioned library barcode on your receipt gives you an easy lookup if it becomes necessary to add a fine on a patron's card for failure to pick up a print. If you choose to develop a filing system, this can be a simple as chronological order or by patron last name.

Open Access to Printers

If you prefer to allow more open access to your 3D printers, you will want to ensure that patrons are certified on your printers. Such training should cover the basic operation of the printer, including how to use slicing software, how to send a print job, how to cancel a job, and how to change materials. Describe any library procedures that need to be followed. In-person instruction can occur by appointment, or it can be offered at regular intervals. For user-directed training, consider recording an orientation video followed by an accompanying quiz. Regardless of how patrons become certified, you'll want to document their achievement. Consider keeping a logbook or adding a note to a patron's record to indicate that they've been certified.

3D Scanning

When patrons utilize your print service, these files are sourced from one of several places. They include objects they have designed themselves, as well as third-party sites, such as Thingiverse and MyMiniverse. A third option is digitizing a physical object using a 3D scanner. Investing in a 3D scanner can be a valuable addition to your 3D printing service, as it delivers a range of possibilities for your patrons. While there is some diversity within 3D scanning, desktop scanners or mobile/handheld scanners are among the most common and practical to be found within a public library.

A desktop scanner occupies a fixed space and generally requires an attached computer to assist in the processing of a scan. An object is placed on a turntable, where it slowly rotates while being scanned by a laser or structured light (Arrighi, 2018). A digital representation of the object appears within the scanning software. Upon completion, a scan can then be downloaded in a variety of file types compatible with a 3D printer. With a higher-end scanner, this process can be quite precise.

In mobile scanning, the capture and processing take place on a scanner that is intended to travel, which may be handheld or mounted on a tripod. Occasionally, an attached computer may be necessary to aid in the processing, though this is not always the case. In the case of mobile scanning, it is the user who moves around the object, capturing a scan at multiple angles. Such a process can capture a very small object, such as a game piece, or a large object, such as a room! With the aid of an attached peripheral, a phone or tablet is also capable of becoming a mobile 3D scanner. For example, Occipital manufactures the Structure Sensor, which is an iPad attachment that allows the tablet to capture and process a scan using its high-definition video camera.

As a final option, there are a number of mobile apps that can also convert a phone or tablet into a 3D scanner. Qlone is one such app. Available for both iOS and Android, it is capable of scanning a small object placed on a printed black-and-white grid. In the case of mobile apps, performance varies widely and often correlates to the capabilities of the device you are using.

By either providing a 3D scanner to the public or referring them to apps they can use themselves, you are opening another avenue for exploration. A high-quality scanner is capable of accurately replicating intricate objects, which is essential for replacement parts. Patrons seeking to recreate unique screws, brackets, gears, and wheels generally prefer using a scanner over attempting to design their own object, if an open-source file is unavailable. For the creative types, they can draw inspiration from the world around them by scanning an object and incorporating it into a new design. Indeed, a mobile scanner is even capable of scanning people!

Giveaways, Promotions, and Demonstrations

When a library first debuts its 3D printer, there is a certain novelty attached to it. Sites like Thingiverse, My Mini Factory, and others offer large repositories of free, open-source files. Inevitably, if all you're doing is printing the same designs, this novelty will eventually wear off. Staff and public may come to question the point of having a 3D printer. If this

Case Study: 3D Scanning and William Floyd's Birthday Celebration

For several years running, the Mastics-Moriches-Shirley Community Library had celebrated the birthday of William Floyd in partnership with the school district that bears his name. Floyd was a signer of the Declaration of Independence and is considered a local hero. In 2016, the planned festivities included a birthday cake baked by culinary students, essay readings, and the display of student art. This year, however, the library's 3D scanning capability would add a new and exciting dimension to the celebration.

In the lead-up to the birthday celebration, staff struggled to come up with a memento to distribute to attendees. While William Floyd is a popular figure within the district, there was a distinct lack of merchandise available to purchase for giveaways. In the absence of a ready-made solution, staff would need to craft their own!

Within the library was a bust of William Floyd that was donated by a local artist and resident of the community named William Lauer. After reaching out to Mr. Lauer, the library asked and received his permission to 3D scan the bust so they could create keychains for attendees of the celebration. Permission in hand, the process of digitizing the bust began.

Using a NextEngine Laser 3D Scanner, the bust was digitized into an STL file. Next, this file was imported into TinkerCAD. Within TinkerCAD, the bust was resized to roughly two inches tall, and a simple loop was added to the top to form a simple keyring. This new model was exported as a new STL file to be 3D printed. In all, approximately one hundred keychains were made over the course of one week (see figure 1.1), using a single spool of PLA filament. The total cost was just under $50.

Figure 1.1 A 3D-printed William Floyd keychain distributed to attendees of his birthday celebration.

This particular story showcases the strengths of both 3D scanning and 3D printing. Using 3D scanning technology, the library was able to digitize a unique physical object for manipulation. With simple computer-aided design software, the object was repurposed into a prototype giveaway for a specific event. Over the course of a week, a small manufacturing run of 100 items was able to take place. From concept to production, the library was able to manage the entire process!

sounds like an argument against printing off of these sites—it's not! When you do use these sources, however, it is essential that you do so in ways that maximize the capabilities of your printer. These capabilities are discussed below.

Quick Turnaround Time

One of the reasons 3D printing technology is considered advantageous in prototyping is its ability to rapidly turn an idea into a physical product. Whenever possible, you should consider this strength when printing. Take, for instance, pop-culture phenomena. We are living in a meme-driven era. Examples of meme culture, such as Left Shark and Salt Bae, are flash-in-the-pan moments that experience incredible, albeit fleeting, popularity. Indeed, by the time of this book's publication, their moment will have passed! By designing your own file or locating an open-source model, your 3D printer allows you to produce a meme-inspired object while it's at the height of its popularity. As their fame rapidly wanes, such creations rarely find their way to commercially available products; a 3D printer bypasses the vacuum.

Personalization

With a little editing in computer aided design (CAD) software such as TinkerCAD, you can quickly personalize an open-source file to better suit your needs. Take, for example, customized trophies. If your library offers game tournaments, reading clubs, trivia nights, or other contests, a customized, 3D-printed trophy makes for a low-cost, unique award! Using a generic file, you can quickly add details including the recipient, the date, and the event. This same concept can be applied to personalized name plates for library clubs and committees, such as teen advisory groups, book clubs, anime clubs, and ad hoc committees. Consider personalizing any tchotchke the library prints! With a very small investment in time, you can add library branding and/or contact information to your print, which itself can help promote 3D printing at the library.

Teachable Prints

As you seek to maximize the value of your prints, consider print jobs that are instructional in nature. Terms like "infill percentage," "number of shells," "rafts," and "supports" are unfamiliar to the layman. Happily,

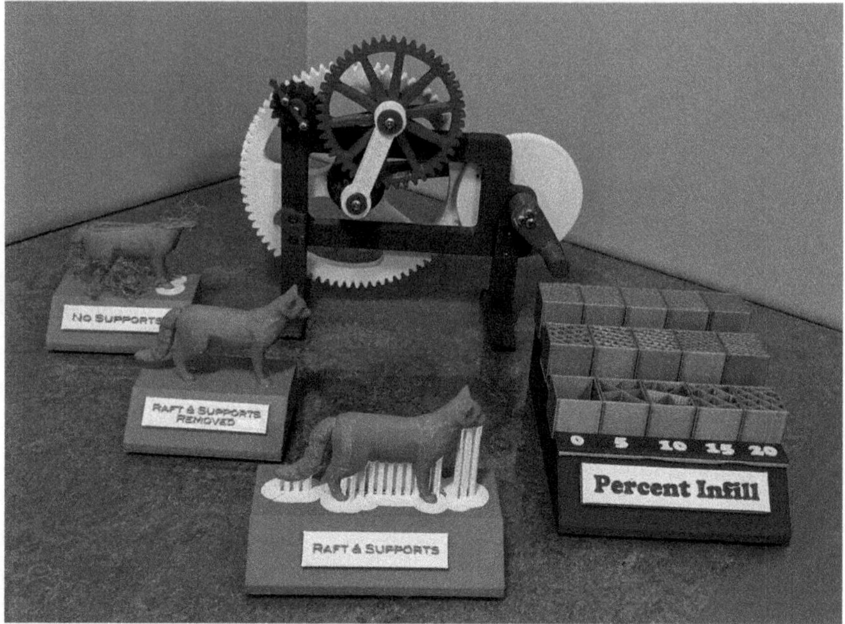

Figure 1.2 An example of instructional prints, demonstrating infill percentage, rafts, supports, and interlocking parts.

there are printable teaching tools available. A simple search on repository sites like Thingiverse for an "infill percent display" returns a number of helpful display models (see figure 1.2). Likewise, models exist to demonstrate rafts and supports. Any time your tchotchkes can double as an instructional tool, you are extracting maximum value from your printer!

LECTURE-STYLE PROGRAMS

When developing programs around your 3D printer, it is important to remember that the more advanced your offerings are, the smaller the potential audience will be. Likewise, classes with more of a beginner to intermediate difficulty will naturally be suitable for a larger audience. Assuming that a large swath of your public is unfamiliar with the technology, it is in your interest to initially offer basic classes to build the competencies of your public. You can then pursue a ladder of engagement, offering increasingly advanced classes to a more technologically literate audience. With that in mind, let's look at some program offerings.

Popup 3D Printer Demonstration

Audience: School Age Children to Adult
Budget: Variable. The material cost of a two-hour print will run between 5 and 25 dollars, based on filament type and infill percentage. Small, tchotchke-sized giveaways will cost around 50 cents each.

A drop-in class is a great way to let your public know that the library has a 3D printer. Your goal should be to get the technology in front of people and get them excited about it. This type of programming is very informal, and it can be scheduled in advance or run on the fly; in either case, it is best to aim for periods of heavy foot traffic. At its core is a 3D printing demonstration, with a staff member available to answer any questions the public may have. Staff should have flyers available detailing a schedule of upcoming classes, the library's 3D print policy, and any other print resources. When running this type of program, you should consider the following.

Who Is Your Audience?

Is your program for children, teens, adults, or a mixed group? As much as possible, you'll want to develop an experience that matches this audience. For example, a print demonstration is far more engaging to children if the object is age-appropriate, such as a popular cartoon character. The questions asked by an adult or teen may be more technical in nature than those of a young child. Additionally, libraries strive to build relationships with their communities. As such, a patron may be far more likely to approach if they see a trusted staff member whom they've interacted with in the past.

What Is Your Location?

Carefully consider the location of your 3D printing demonstration. Depending on the visibility of your printer, you may need some directional signage, particularly for a printer that's tucked away in a meeting room.

What Are You Printing?

Depending on what you're printing, the print time may vary from a half hour to a full day! Patrons tend to be genuinely interested in what is being created. For a larger print, you may wish to have one already printed so patrons will be able to see the finished product, similar to the format of many cooking shows. Alternatively, you can simply print a smaller object to increase the likelihood of patrons witnessing a completed print.

Will You Be Distributing Giveaways?

Library-branded 3D-printed giveaways are a great way to get the word out. If engaging in giveaways, you'll want to pre-print an appropriate number. Generally, something small and functional, such as a bookmark corner, works well.

Introduction to 3D Printing

Audience: Adults
Time: 1½–2 hours
Budget: $5–$150

Introduction to 3D printing is a lecture-style program that is one step up from the "3D Printer Demonstration" on the ladder of engagement. Much like the demonstration, your intent is to introduce the technology to your public, only this time in much greater detail. The general curriculum should be as described in the following sections.

What Is 3D Printing?

Take some time to discuss just how 3D printing works. Cover the different types of printers, including fused deposition modeling, stereolithography, and selective laser sintering.

A Brief History

Give a brief history of 3D printing, like the one given at the start of this chapter. Explain the origins of the technology. Companies like 3D Hubs and Autodesk maintain an easily digested timeline on their websites.

Discuss How the Technology Is Used

Giving real-world applications of 3D printing in the medical, automotive, and aerospace industries can help students better conceptualize the technology. With a little searching, you can tie in a recent news story, perhaps a local one that deals with 3D printing.

Explore Open-Source and Paid Repositories

One common question you will likely receive is, "Where do 3D print files come from?" Be sure to give patrons a quick tour of sites like MyMiniFactory, Thingiverse, and commercial alternatives. Show how they are organized and how to search them. Spend a little time on how to evaluate a file, including reading the print instructions, viewing the schematic, and seeing how others have fared by viewing the community's prints and feedback.

Demonstrate the Slicing Software

As you explore 3D printing file repositories, it's a useful exercise to download a file and drop it into the slicing software that is used with your printer. This allows your patrons to see the next step toward turning a file into a completed print. If your procedures allow patrons to interact directly with your printer, this step represents essential information.

Explore Sources of Free CAD Software

Beyond repositories of existing 3D files, patrons should be shown how they might create their own objects. Some of the better free options include TinkerCAD, SketchUp, and Blender. Additionally, AutoCAD provides a free organizational license for educators. If your library has purchased software for public use, be sure to let your patrons know!

Discuss How 3D Printing Works Specifically at Your Library

This is perhaps the most important ground for you to cover, as it lays the groundwork for attendees to become long-term users of your 3D printing service. Give a quick rundown of your 3D printing policy and answer any questions that may arise. Describe the general process for submitting and receiving a print, as well as an approximate printing cost.

Show and Tell

Your show-and-tell portion of the presentation includes a printer demonstration. Additionally, it is an opportunity for users to view the different filament or resin types you offer and examine objects that have been printed with them. If you've printed any teaching tools, such as infill or support samples, they can be distributed among attendees.

DESIGN PROJECTS

As patrons become familiar with your 3D printer(s) and their capabilities, some will begin to express an interest in learning to design their own objects. CAD software can have a very steep learning curve, with a user interface that some will find difficult to navigate. There are software options that appeal to the casual user; chief among them is TinkerCAD.

TinkerCAD is simple, yet powerful, web-based CAD software, appropriate for ages eight and up. It has several features that make it useful within library programming, starting with its cost: free. As it is web-based and utilizes a cloud save feature, it can be used on public computers that utilize Pharonics or other system restore software without worry. TinkerCAD's only true hard requirement is a modern web browser, such as Microsoft Edge, Google Chrome, or Firefox. Chrome compatibility also means TinkerCAD can be run using an inexpensive Chromebook.

TinkerCAD Workshop

Audience: Ages 8–12, Teens, Adults
Cost: Variable. Approximately $10–$100 in materials.
Time: 1–2 hours

Advance Work

Your instructor will, of course, need to create a TinkerCAD account and achieve a basic familiarity with the software. Happily, TinkerCAD has a number of lessons designed to build the core skills you'll need to teach an introductory course! As with any library program, the instructor should be comfortable with the source material and the time it will take to teach. You'll also want to test each of your computers well in advance to ensure there's no issue with its web browser. During your program, attendees will need to be logged into TinkerCAD; here you have options, the details of which are available at www.tinkercad.com/teach.

- You can log into each computer in advance using the instructor's TinkerCAD account, provided no two users access the same exact design.

This will remove the requirement for individual account creation, which can slow down a class. You will have access to your attendees' designs and manage them as necessary.

- Individuals ages 13 and up can create their own free accounts using a personal email address. While they can follow along, the instructor will not have access to their designs.
- You can set up the instructor account as an educator (teacher account) and generate a teacher's code to send to your students. Patrons under 13 will provide a parent's or teacher's email during sign-up, as well as the teacher's code. Your instructor will then be able to moderate their account and manage their designs. Patrons ages 13 and older may also provide this code when creating their own free TinkerCAD accounts; this will add the instructor as a moderator of the account.

Requirements

A class will require one computer, laptop, or Chromebook with an attached mouse for each attendee. A projector or large screen will allow attendees to follow along with your instructor. All computers will need internet access.

Curriculum

Your goal for this class is to familiarize patrons with the basics of TinkerCAD software. To do that, you'll go through a series of exercises demonstrating the basic controls, before creating a simple design to be printed later. You should cover core skills, including the following:

- **Understanding the Basic Layout:** Give a general orientation of the design page. Identify the different panels they will be using, and have students name their design.
- **Navigating the Work Plane:** Demonstrate how to use left-click-and-drag to move about the work plane. Show how right-click can be used to pan your view around the plane and any objects within. Finally, cover zooming in and out using the mouse's scroll bar.
- **Adding an Object to the Work Plane:** At its core, TinkerCAD is a geometric editor. Demonstrate how to drag and drop a simple object onto the work plane.

- **Manipulating an Object:** Demonstrate how to move an object on the work plane. Show how to resize, rotate, and change its height. Detail how the "snap grid works." Duplicate an object.
- **Merging and Unmerging:** Take two or more objects and merge them together to form a new one. Demonstrate the difference between a "hole" and a "solid" object. Teach students how an object can be used to add or subtract from a design.
- **Correcting Mistakes:** Patrons should be shown the "undo" function, how to select and delete objects individually, and how to clear the work plane entirely.

As you go through these different skills, set aside a few minutes for patrons to try them out. Observe their progress and answer any questions that arise. It can be helpful to have an assistant, particularly if your class is large or may need more guidance. Once your students are comfortable with these concepts, plan on having a half hour set aside to design a simple object that will engage these newly learned skills. Whatever design you decide upon, ensure that it is functional, prints well at a small scale, and is customizable. A keychain, in particular, meets these requirements.

Once your students have completed their designs, you'll need to download their STL files for printing. If they were completed using an account you have access to, this can be done at a later date. If they were designed on a patron's personal account, the STL file can be downloaded to a flash drive or emailed to the instructor. Individually managed patron accounts also have the ability to "publish" their designs, making it publicly accessible to other TinkerCAD users, including your instructor.

At the conclusion of a class, you'll want to let patrons know that you will contact them when their prints are ready for pickup. It is strongly recommended that this process mirror your public print service, although you may decide to waive any print charge. By using the same process as your public print service, you are educating your patrons on the process, keeping your staff trained, and removing the need to develop an additional workflow around your 3D printer.

Starting a 3D Printing Club

[*A version of this section originally appears as "Starting a Teen 3D Printing Club" in VOYA Magazine, February 2017. Volume 39, issue 6.*]

Audience: Ages 8–12, Teens, Adults
Cost: Variable

A 3D printing club is an excellent way to ensure steady, continuous use of your library's 3D printer(s). Participants in a club that meets regularly have the opportunity to build a deeper proficiency in CAD software over time, rather than haphazardly taking and retaking various introductory classes or courses focused on specific projects. The skills learned in a club may then be applied to each individual's particular interest.

Setup

Your setup should largely resemble that of a design class, meaning one computer, laptop, Mac, or Chromebook with an attached mouse for each attendee. An instructor should be connected to either a projector or two-way monitor to facilitate demonstrations.

Your Inaugural Meeting

For your first club meeting(s), you should focus on both 3D printing and 3D design. Have your 3D printer on hand so you can go over its anatomy before giving a printing demonstration. Explain the basics of the technology. Show participants the materials used in 3D printing and some sample printed items.

Aside from the hardware, you should next tackle the software. In the case of TinkerCAD, you can have your patrons work on one of the curated lessons or choose to teach the software basics yourself. If you're vastly outnumbered, premade lessons will allow you the flexibility to assist anyone who is struggling, while still keeping the group moving. It is also important that you establish some ground rules early on. These include the following:

- **How Often Are You Printing?** Printing can be a time-consuming process! Even a small chess-sized print could take 45 minutes to an hour. Multiply that by the number of club members, and you can see a potential logjam! Your club may meet weekly, monthly, and so forth. It is important that you come up with a schedule that can accommodate your patrons' creativity and the workload of your staff and printer.

- **<u>What Are the Specifications of Your Prints?</u>** Often, when it comes time to print, your patrons will want to "make it as big as possible." In terms of time and material, this is impractical at best. You may wish to define some limits for your prints, using either print time or the amount of material. Aside from managing workflow, this will also allow you to accurately budget for your filament. A secondary consideration is whether your patrons will have the option of choosing their material types and/or colors. Swapping material can be time-consuming, and material types can vary dramatically in price.
- **<u>What Is Appropriate to Print?</u>** Familiarizing patrons with the basics of your 3D print policy will allow you to be transparent and consistent. It's better to have a set of clear rules to point to than make it up as you go!
- **<u>Will You Be Charging for Prints?</u>** Depending on the age of your audience and your library's preference, you may wish to waive print costs for items designed during print club. Rather than a hard yes or no determination, you could consider a material allocation (ex: one hundred grams of filament per month), after which a patron would need to pay.

Regular Activities

Generally, your club can be run in a "less-structured environment." In this format, participants simply design what they want to. The instructor of the class is present to offer advice and otherwise troubleshoot as patrons create their designs. You can run the entirety of your club in this format, or you can use it as a break from more formalized sessions. When a participant has finished a design, the instructor gives it a look-over, ensuring it is a printable object that adheres to your club's guidelines. If it checks out, the design is downloaded as an STL file, which can be formatted for printing in whatever design software your printer runs on (Cura, Makerbot Desktop, etc.). Most often, this printing will take place outside of the club, given time constraints.

Even after a design is printed, there's often more to do. Designs commonly have excess material that serves as a support structure while they are printed. Beyond that, prints can have rough edges or "fuzz" that requires cleaning. Depending on the size and intricacy, excess material can be removed by hand, sanded away, or clipped with simple tools such as scissors and needle-nosed pliers. Cleanups may be time-consuming, but they can also be fun!

These postprint sessions are also an opportunity to see what went wrong or, at least, what can be improved. An ideal design is one that takes into account the limitations of a 3D printer. As your patrons examine their printed works, they may discover design flaws that lead to poor prints—too much overhang, weak connections, not enough contact points with the build plate, etc. Many times, a design session is actually spent reworking a prior design to make it more printable. This is exactly the benefit of the club—it represents an ongoing learning process!

Beyond your club is a greater community of 3D printing enthusiasts. Sites like Thingiverse allow designs to be uploaded and shared with others, who can then print them or even incorporate them into new designs. Creating a Thingiverse site for your library is a great way to collect and showcase these works online. Depending on the age of your audience, they may also create their own sites, which can follow or be followed by the library. Set aside some time for your club members to upload their proven (successfully printed) models if they wish. These designs can be added to a collection within Thingiverse, allowing you to organize by club, project, or any other criteria you wish to use.

Mixing It Up!

If your club ever feels like things are getting stale, it may be time to mix things up! Try one of the following to keep things fresh:

- **Challenges:** In a challenge session, you simply confront the group with a task. You might say, "Create a new utensil," or "Design a phone case!" These are ways of getting the creative juices flowing. As patrons view each other's designs, they may draw inspiration from one another.
- **Collaborations:** This type of format is one where the whole is greater than the sum of its parts. You might have the class design a chess board. Each patron would work on the different parts, from the game board to the pawns, rooks and other pieces. This format works well when you have an established club whose members know each other.
- **Demonstrations:** A demonstration is an opportunity to check out a new piece of equipment or introduce a speaker or concept. Perhaps you have someone in the industry who is willing to talk to the group. Maybe there is an opportunity to have a new printer on loan or a

complementary piece of equipment, such as a 3D scanner! You can also introduce a new piece of design software.

- **Remix:** A remix session is one where you rework an existing design. Your patrons can download a model from an open-source site (always check the licensing permissions); open it in TinkerCAD or other design software; and then add on, combine, or otherwise rework it to create something new. They can even use each other's files!

Wrapping Up Your Club with a 3D Print Expo

While a club can run indefinitely, your child and teen patrons will eventually age out of their clubs. For this reason, it is nice to have a culminating event, namely, a 3D print expo! A 3D expo is a chance to showcase the good work your patrons have been doing during the club, particularly if the club is oriented more toward expression than practicality.

As your patrons create their designs, they will accrue quite a portfolio over time. Have them each select a favorite design, one that has already been printed in miniature and perfected. This print will be rendered in a size fit for display—likely a 6–10 hour print. In addition to your display piece, you can also print their designs in the traditional sense. This means saving the image itself (in TinkerCAD or your design/printer software) and then printing it on paper and mounting it to foam board, cardboard, or another material. This will allow participants to feature multiple works, including some designs that could have proven difficult to print. You can then add each patron's name to the exhibit by adding a label or name plate, or simply by having them sign their work. A 3D expo can be scaled to taste. It can be done as an annual or semiannual event. It can operate as a stand-alone event, or exist as an exhibit within a general art show. It also acts as a great recruitment event for new members, so you can fill your ranks and plan for another year of printing!

3D SCANNING PROGRAM: ME IN 3D!

Cost: Onetime cost for the scanner is approximately $350
Material cost: $5 per participant for a 2-hour print
Time: 1½–2 hours
Ages: Tweens, Teens, Adults

We value 3D printing's ability to produce a one-of-a-kind creation—and what's more unique than you? Using a handheld scanner and some free software, you can quickly digitize a person and then 3D print their likeness!

Requirements

A mobile 3D scanner, Wi-Fi, once or more computers with mesh processing software, one computer or Chromebook per attendee with 3D modeling software.

Digitization

The top of your program will be spent doing an initial capture of your participants, using a mobile 3D scanner. While 3D scanners can be quite costly, you may achieve good results using relatively inexpensive options, such as the Structure Sensor iPad attachment or, potentially, a smartphone with a 3D scanning app. Using your device, you will need to complete one or more passes around your subject, focusing on the waist up (see figure 1.3). As you do so, a digital representation will come to completion. This scan can be done by an instructor or any of the participants.

Cleanup

Once you've finished scanning an individual, you will need to export the STL file. More often than not, this file will require further adjustment. A quick cleanup can be done in Meshmixer or another mesh processing program. This final STL file may then be placed in the 3D modeling software of your choice; TinkerCAD is a good free option.

Customization

Once participants have their scans in the modeling software, they can incorporate them into an overall design. For an easy project, focus on creating a bust. This requires the construction of a simple base, to which the scan is mounted. A name, nickname, or message can then be added. Other straightforward options include bookends and keychains. For the truly adventurous, the sky's the limit! In one 3D scanning program at the

Figure 1.3 Staff member 3D scanning a patron using a Structure Sensor iPad attachment.

Mastics-Moriches-Shirley Community Library, teen participants "monsterfied" their creations, adding horns, fangs, and other Halloween-inspired touches.

Ending a Class

Once you have possession of the final finished STL files of your participants, you may end the class. As the prints will take some time to complete, you may wish to request contact information, or instruct patrons where and when they can expect to pick up their prints.

3D PRINTING CHILDREN'S PROSTHETICS HANDS

3D printing is seeing increasing adoption in the medical field, particularly with regard to prosthetics. Libraries now have the opportunity to engage with their community and collaborate with non-profit organizations to manufacture low-cost prosthetic hands for children! To that end, let us examine two potential partners.

e-Nable: http://enablingthefuture.org/

Nonprofit organization e-Nable describes itself as "an amazing group of individuals from all over the world who are using their 3D printers to create free 3D printed hands and arms for those in need of an upper limb assistive device" (Owen, 2017). This community is made up of everyone from educators and engineers to students and tinkerers. This community offers a wealth of resources, including tutorials on prosthetic assembly, forums to discuss questions and concerns, and the means to connect donors and those in need. It also contains open-source files for 3D-printed prosthetic limbs and accepts donations of both unassembled and fully assembled prosthetics.

Prosthetic Kids Hand Challenge: http://www.handchallenge.com/

The Prosthetic Kids Hand Challenge is dedicated to instructing people how to successfully assemble a 3D-printed prosthetic limb and source it to a person in need. The site contains excellent, easily digestible information. It is important to check to ensure they are accepting donations, as they can occasionally become overwhelmed.

Getting Involved

There are many ways to involve your library in the production of 3D-printed prosthetics, including making your printer available for use. In many ways, you may have already accomplished this with a public print service. The difference here, is that you can have your printer listed on e-Nable's website to indicate its availability for the purpose of printing prosthetics. To do so, simply complete a brief intake at www.amandagoodman.com/3d/. Doing so will make your library appear on a map, increasing the likelihood of discovery by both individuals interested in creating a prosthetic limb on one of your printers and those who may be in need of one.

If your library is interested in further involvement, you can register to become a Community Chapter of e-Nable. These Community Chapters function as local hubs, bringing different stakeholders together. At your request, your library may offer to adopt schools and other organizations, providing equipment, supplies and expertise to underserved communities ("e-NABLE Chapters," n.d.).

Hand Challenge Program Idea

Audience: Ages 12 and up, Families, Adults
Cost: Approximately $25 per set of tools, $30 per assembly kit, $25 filament cost
Time: 3–5 hours for assembly

The goal of this class is to have participants assemble a completed prosthetic hand for a child. You may achieve this goal through a variety of formats; this can even be done without a formal instructor.

Preparation

Your first action will be to go to EnablingTheFuture.org and choosing what design you will be assembling. Design types include wrist-powered and elbow-actuated ("Which Design?," 2018). Among those types, there will be specific models to choose from. Ensure that your printer is capable of producing the model, namely that your build plate is large enough, your material type is appropriate, and you can meet the technical specifications, such as infill percentage. For demonstration purposes, we will assume the Phoenix Hand was the model chosen.

As with any program, you will want to prepare a full working model ahead of time. In this case, that means downloading the files and assembly instructions and then printing all the required parts. This will take between ten and fifteen hours to complete, though a reliable 3D printer won't require your constant attention during this time. A completed prosthetic will require more than just 3D printed parts; an accompanying kit will also need to be purchased. Kits include screws, cordage, foam inserts and Velcro that will be used in conjunction with your 3D-printed parts, and will cost roughly $30 each. The e-Nable website provides links to these kits.

With all your parts printed and purchased, you can move on to assembly. The necessary tools can vary slightly; they will be indicated on the instructions associated with your model. In the case of the Phoenix Hand, the suggested list includes:

- Pair of 8" slip joint pliers
- 2 pairs of small needlenose pliers
- Small flat file
- Small round file
- Medium half round file
- Small hammer
- Pair of side cutters
- #2 4" Phillips screwdriver
- Pair of scissors for cutting card template and foam

For safety, you should also invest in inexpensive protective eyewear and a first aid kit. During the process of assembly, eyewear will guard against a stray part snapping off and striking you, as well as any irritation that might occur while sanding. A first aid kit should be available during any program, regardless of the type; have it available for minor cuts and scratches when handling tools.

Once you've assembled your first prosthetic hand kit (see figure 1.4), use the experience to draw some conclusions. You should now know how long your printer takes to produce the parts, and the amount of material

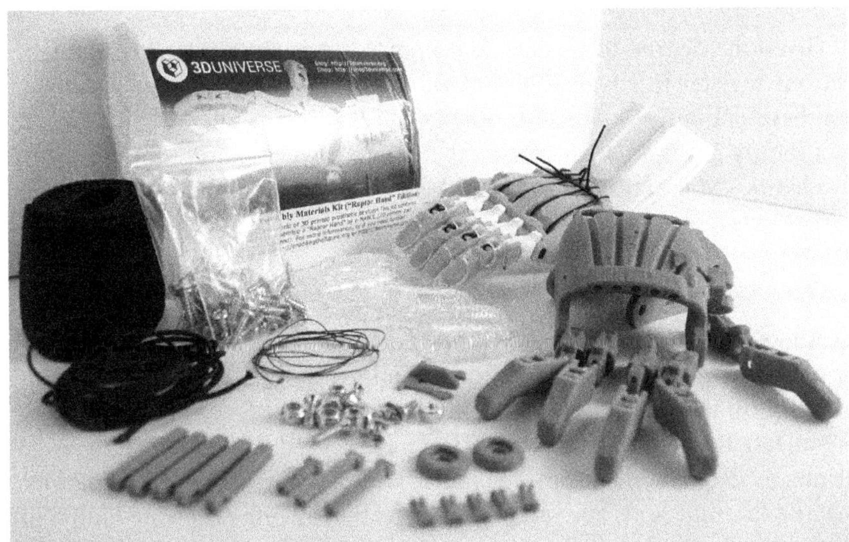

Figure 1.4 A picture of a prosthetic hand kit and 3D-printed parts. Photo by Sara Roye.

needed. These details will allow you to accurately predict your cost per prosthetic. Finally, gauge the difficulty of the project and assess the time it takes to fully assemble.

Preparing Prosthetic Projects

Once you are confident in your ability to produce a completed prosthetic hand, you can move on to prepackaging projects for use in a class. Although any of these projects can be completed by an individual, it can be quicker and more cost-effective to work in groups of two to five people. To start, repeat the process of 3D printing your files in advance of a program—one full set for each package. Small parts, such as pins and joints, should be kept together in a Ziploc bag to prevent pieces from going missing. Next, add the associated kit to your package (i.e., the Phoenix kit for a Phoenix Hand). A program will require a full set of tools for each working group, so a class for 15 students could be conducted with as few as three sets. Finally, provide printed assembly instructions; each package should have enough for each program attendee.

Registration

Given the degree of preparation required, it is strongly suggested that patrons register in advance of a class. When determining your audience, you have options. Prosthetic assembly can be done by teens, by adults, or as a family program. Considering the length of such a program—three to five hours—you may wish to offer it as a two-part workshop.

Conducting a Class

At the start of a class, you will need to organize attendees into groups, or allow them to do so on their own. Following this, show them a completed prosthetic and demonstrate how it functions. Discuss your partner organizations and how the prosthetics may be used. If possible, have a 3D printer available in the room. This serves several purposes. Not all patrons may be familiar with how a 3D printer works; having preprinted all your parts has removed them from this process. Additionally, you can set the printer to work making extra parts, either for future use or in the event that there is some breakage. In particular, the pins and swivels can snap if too much pressure is exerted on them.

Once the work of assembly begins, at least one staff member will need to be present to supervise the process. Each group will work at their own pace, so your staff member(s) need not teach the process to the group; rather, they will facilitate the process by moving between groups. If you have laptops available, how-to videos exist for assembling the prosthetic. These can provide a better visual aid to attendees, as well as ease the burden on staff. If you are offering the program in multiple parts, you will need to label the partially assembled prosthetics so that, in the following session, the teams can pick up where they left off.

When the prosthetics are completed, staff should examine them and exert quality control. Occasionally you will discover a prosthetic that may need slight adjustments, particularly to the tension on the cords. Once you are satisfied with the work, they can be packaged and delivered to your partner agency in accordance with their instructions.

Alternate Idea: Community Service Program

If the students in your service area have a community service requirement, you should consider making kits available on an ongoing basis. Rather than a formal program, preassembled kits can be kept in your youth services/young adult department until needed. Within this service, you'll need to make the following decisions:

- **Take Home or Assemble In-House:** As a prepackaged model, these prosthetic hands could be "checked out" and then assembled at home. There are several advantages to this approach: it removes the need for staff supervision, patrons may use their own personal tools, and the assembly process may take place on the patron's own time. However, a take-home prosthetic is generally assembled by an individual, not a group. Patrons may not have the proper tools to complete a prosthetic. If you lend these necessary tools, or a prosthetic kit itself, there is the potential that they may not return. Checking out a kit or having a user agreement may decrease this liability.
- **Level of Staff Involvement:** In the case of in-library assembly, you will need to determine how much staff assistance you are able to provide. If a staff member will be working on assembly with students, you may wish to carve out specific days and times when this service will be available to better manage staff time. If, on the other hand, you would like this process to be student-guided, you will likely want to provide a computer or laptop with a video tutorial.

In the case of home assembly, staff involvement will include checking out kits, as well as performing an inventory on their parts before checkout and upon their return. A staff member should also inspect completed prosthetics to exercise quality control before they are sent to a final destination.

Distributing Community Service Hours

Part of any community service program is documenting volunteer hours. While the most straightforward approach is to simply award the five or so hours it will take to complete a prosthetic, there are reasons to decide against this. Understanding that your prosthetic kits are a finite resource, you should seek to design a program in a way that offers the most service hours to as many volunteers as possible. Allowing people to work in groups is among the more practical ways to achieve this. Another is by widening the scope of volunteerism. Consider expanding your community service program to include not just assembly, but also its day-to-day operation.

To do this, you can structure your program as something resembling a train-the-trainer. To start, have your participants undergo an orientation where they learn about your partnering organization(s) and the need for upper limb prosthetics. Involve your volunteers in the printing and sorting of parts into kits. Once this is complete, they can complete the assembly in groups and can even assist in the packaging and delivery of their prosthetic. After they've completed the process, they can earn further hours by onboarding the next group of volunteers and overseeing prosthetic assembly. This full process can easily earn 10 to 15 hours of community service for a sizable group, with the added benefit of reducing the burden on staff in the long term.

MARKETING YOUR 3D PRINTER

3D printing at your library will be doomed to failure if your patrons are unaware you offer it and uninformed on how it works. An effective marketing strategy is therefore key to a successful adoption of the technology. There are a number of approaches you can take in marketing your printer that include both the traditional and the technical.

Developing a 3D Printing Guide

A 3D printing guide is an essential resource for a library to have. A guide is both staff and public-facing and can exist in both print and digital format. Your guide should resemble much of the content you would cover in an "Introduction to 3D Printing" program, and as such, it should include the following:

- A brief description of how 3D printing works, its history and common uses of the technology.
- A list of open-source marketplaces for 3D files, including Thingiverse, MyMiniFactory, YouMagine, and Shapeways.
- A list of free options for CAD software, including TinkerCAD, Sketchup, and Blender.
- A glossary of common 3D printing terms, including infill, shells, supports, raft, and brim.
- A list of the library's available 3D printers that includes their basic specifications. This includes the size of the print bed/maximum print size.
- A list of the materials a patron may print in. The individual properties of the various print materials should be outlined.
- Resources for further information. If regularly occurring training takes place at your library, you should list it. If your library subscribes to online learning software (such as Lynda.com) that offers lessons in 3D printing and CAD software, be sure to include this information as well!
- Your 3D print policy and the procedure for submitting print requests.

Once your 3D printing resource is complete, you can make it available to your staff to serve as a ready-reference guide to 3D printing at your library. For the public, you'll want to have it available on your website, as well as in print. Print copies can be kept at your public service desks and may also be housed in your makerspace or in close proximity to your 3D printer, if possible.

Creating a 3D Printing Display

Creating a 3D printing display can provide your patrons with an experience that is both promotional and educational. The core purpose of such a display is to get your patrons excited about 3D printing, while at the same time providing understanding and context to the technology. Such a display should include:

- **Your 3D Printer:** While its inclusion may seem obvious, you will also need to make some additional provisions. An unattended printer in the public space can be a liability. In an FDM printer, the extruder becomes very hot and can easily burn someone who reaches in. Print jobs can be started, stopped, or otherwise interfered with. For these reasons, you should ensure a printer has some basic safety measures in place. Some of these approaches can be passive in nature. For a printer with an enclosed bed, this can be as simple as velcroing shut the door. For more open-air printers, sitting a printer further back on a higher surface can mitigate the risk of little hands and fingers reaching it. For a more involved approach, 3D printer enclosures are available for purchase. Some are model-specific, while others are generics able to accommodate a variety of printers of a certain size. Finally, you may wish to consider building your own by making a simple acrylic box to place over an active printer.

- **Sample Materials:** Provide some samples of the raw materials used by your 3D printer. In the case of an FDM printer, you can provide spools, or several lengths of filament in a variety of colors. As your patrons would be unable to handle the liquid resin of an SLA printer, simply provide a few cubes of the hardened material, postprint.
- **Instructional Prints:** Have sample objects that demonstrate the unique properties of your available printing material. This could simply be color options, or it may include material types such as flexible, glow-in-the-dark, or other exotic categories. Have some teaching tools demonstrating infill, brim, supports, rafts, shells, and other specifications. You may wish to tape, tie, or otherwise affix these prints to avoid theft, although a missing item can always be easily reprinted.
- **Handouts:** Supply some information your patrons can take with them. Ideally, provide the aforementioned 3D printing guide. A list of upcoming 3D printing classes, copies of your policy, and a point of contact for further information are all useful additions to your display.

Utilizing Social Media and Time-Lapse Video

Effective social media marketing can greatly increase the utilization of your 3D printer by your patrons. As a general rule, you will want to favor approaches that are highly visual. On a platform like Facebook, posts which utilize photos draw 53 percent more likes and 104 percent more comments than those using text alone (Pollard, 2017). Video on Facebook produces even greater results, receiving, on average, 135 percent more organic traffic than a photo! (Ross, 2015). With this in mind, consider crafting posts which use time-lapse video.

Simply put, time-lapse video is a method of filming very slow actions by taking a series of single pictures over a period of time and then putting them together to show the action happening very quickly. As 3D printing is generally slow, your patrons rarely see the entire process start to finish. By utilizing time-lapse, you can record the entirety of a print job and present it to your public in an easily digestible minute or less!

The process for creating a time-lapse video is fairly simple. First, you will need to select a device to record your video. Modern iOS devices such as the iPad and iPhone offer time-lapse as a built-in camera feature, as do some Androids and digital cameras. Regardless of your device, you will want to ensure that your equipment remains steady throughout the video capture. An inexpensive tripod is the most straightforward way to ensure stability. If a tripod isn't an option, you can repurpose a book stand or even 3D print a stand specific to your device! Ensure that a stand placed on the same surface of your printer doesn't wobble when your printer is in motion.

When shooting your time lapse, choose a well-lit area. If you are relying on daylight, consider the duration of your print. As the hours pass, a bright area could fall into darkness, or a shadow may be cast by an object in the room—including your recording device. Finally, select a place where your printer can operate unobstructed—if people continually walk or gather in front of your printer, there won't be much to see in your final video!

Once you've captured your video, it is time to perform some light editing. In the case of a smartphone or tablet, this can likely be done directly on your device. An excellent option for the iPhone or iPad is iMovie. If using a Windows 10 machine, you can use the Photos app (Hoffman, 2018). Cut out any slack at the beginning or end of your video, such as setup or the printer sitting idle after printing has ceased. Finally, take a brief, five-second video that pans the final print. Alternatively, you can snap a few photos from multiple angles. Facebook will loop any video thirty seconds or shorter, so adding this final footage will allow your viewers to get a good look at the finished print ("Video Length and Loops on Facebook," n.d.).

Engage with Hobbyists

3D printing's ability to create unique objects, or produce hard-to-find replacements, makes the technology especially useful to hobbyists. As such, you should actively seek to identify and connect with these communities. Interested parties may include the individuals described below.

Tabletop RPG Gamers

Games like Dungeons & Dragons, Pathfinder, and others utilize representative miniatures during gameplay. Additionally, some may also incorporate terrain, such as tiles and even three-dimensional structures. These game pieces are often very expensive. 3D printing offers an alternative and more affordable option for patrons who either design their own pieces or download pre-existing files. Indeed, Thingiverse.com offers many free options, and Miguel Zavala, one hobbyist on Shapeways.com, has made a collection of 300 models available for download! (Zavala, n.d.).

Model Train Collectors

Online repositories are full of HO scale (1:87 real-life scale) model train sets ("Model Train Scale and Gauge," 2019). These include trains, carts, cargo, people, buildings, and even the tracks themselves!

Cosplayers

The *Merriam-Webster* dictionary defines cosplay as "the practice of dressing up as a character from a work of fiction (such as a comic book, video game, or television show)." By definition, many cosplayers take a do-it-yourself approach to their costumes, particularly when a costume isn't commercially available. 3D printing offers an excellent option for masks, equipment, and other accessories. Interest naturally increases during local and national or international comic conventions.

Robotics Teams

Files for entire robots exist online. Additionally, designs covering chassis, battery enclosures, mounts for circuit boards, and more are also available. Individuals may also wish to utilize your printers to create custom designs.

Many of these groups have an active presence on Facebook or Meetup. Extend invitations to the library and provide relevant information to them. Within your building, display works that showcase a printer's capabilities; examples might include a set of Dungeons & Dragons–inspired miniatures or a model train. Pictures and videos of the process can similarly be shared with online communities. As individuals begin to use your 3D printer, they will often share information with others within the hobbyist community, increasing your printer's reach. As such, outreach to small, niche groups can still result in a deep level of engagement and substantial use of the library's equipment!

LOOKING TO THE FUTURE

Where Is 3D Printing Heading?

So just where is 3D printing heading in the coming years? Like many emerging technologies, costs will continue to drop over time, while the overall capability and performance of printers will climb. Future 3D printers will utilize new, high-performance materials, including metal alloys, creating new possibilities for the technology (Reichental, 2018). More than ever, fields including medical, automotive, aerospace, and architecture will further incorporate 3D printing into their business models as it establishes itself as a mainstream manufacturing process (Yeap, 2019).

With the increased affordability of 3D printers, you can expect to see a growing consumer market, with increasing prevalence in households. Creative types will put the technology to use in fields like art and fashion. For more practical users, having a 3D printer in the house could make it far easier to source replacement parts. For example, a missing or damaged screw, joint, or hinge could be downloaded directly from a manufacturer and then printed onsite, removing the need to visit a store or have the item shipped (Karin, 2018).

Where Do Libraries Come In?

When we look at technology, we see that libraries have a long history in leveling the playing field, providing access and training to our patrons. Take the example of the computer. When the personal computer first became widely available to consumers, libraries incorporated the technology into their organizations to better serve our patrons. With the high early cost of PCs, libraries provided critical access to those unable to afford one. For those patrons who owned a computer, libraries were still able to assist by providing training on both hardware and associated software. Even as computers have become more ingrained in society, there has remained a need to assist our patrons through changes, such as a new or updated operating system.

In a future where more of our patrons have access to their own printers, the library will continue to provide access to those who are left out. Among owners of 3D printers, the need for access to library-owned equipment will still exist if their device lacks features such as build size or the ability to print in their required materials. We should expect to see a growing need for high-quality 3D scanning. As 3D printing hardware and software undergo changes, libraries will need to step in and offer classes to our patrons.

Finally, there is the content itself. While repositories of free 3D files exist on sites like Thingiverse and MyMiniFactory, there is a large number that must be purchased. Will the library offer free or discounted access to these materials, much as we do with our digital collections of eBooks, streaming movies, and so on? Would this be on a per-file basis, or more akin to subscription access of a database? Will libraries facilitate patron-created collections within our communities, as the 3D printing equivalent of self-publishing? The possibilities are as exciting as they are endless!

TWO

Drones

Although drones have been adopted by hobbyists and are used by a number of industries, they are relative newcomers to libraries. Their introduction into a library environment may, at first glance, seem an odd fit, but in actuality it aligns with our mission to educate and entertain our public. From use by hobbyists to applications in business, science, engineering, piloting, and job exploration, offering drones of all types for patron use fits the model of libraries quite nicely.

According to *Merriam-Webster*, the term "drone" refers to "an unmanned aerial vehicle (UAV) guided by remote control or onboard computers." However, drones are not necessarily limited to flight; they can also be associated with undersea exploration or even space exploration. Remote controlled vehicles, such as a child's remote-controlled car or boat, also fall into the category of "drone," and even the robots that vacuum our floors or clean our pools fall into the category of drone.

Drones are widely known for military purposes. We see how effective they are in engaging enemy targets with the pilot being thousands of miles away. There are also examples of ground "bomb robots" that can be driven by an operator at a safe distance. We have seen drone exploration under the sea with unmanned subs equipped with cameras that explore the sea bed or shipwrecks like *Titanic*, and NASA has also been using rolling drones on the surface of Mars. The expansion of drone development, production, and civilian commercial and private use has grown since 2006 when the Federal Aviation Administration (FAA) first required operators to acquire permits. Permit requests averaged two per year over the following eight years. In 2013, when Amazon CEO Jeff Bezos announced that the company was considering drone delivery, permit applications skyrocketed to 3,100 in 2016 (Ford, 2019).

There has always been a hobbyist market for scale model planes, helicopters, remote-controlled cars, and off-road vehicles. As of 2015, the flying consumer drone industry has been growing at an estimated 15–20 percent annually (LaFay, 2015, pp. 17–18). Drones are attractive to the consumer market because of their versatility. Drones are available in many shapes and sizes. They can fly, drive, or be submerged for longer periods of time and, in some cases, be autonomous of their operator.

As with all technologies, the cost of implementing drone technology has decreased and become affordable for various government agencies and even the average consumer. Today, it is becoming increasingly common to see local news stations utilizing drones instead of helicopters to provide viewers with aerial footage. Firefighters use drones to quickly survey wilderness areas to assess wildfires. Hikers and outdoor adventurers have taken to drones to capture amazing footage of remote locations. Even real estate professionals have utilized this technology to better photograph and feature properties. Drones can be small enough to be packed into a bag and hiked in to a remote location. Many drones will have small "onboard" cameras or have the ability to carry popular outdoor cameras from brands such as GoPro, which are lightweight, waterproof, and able to absorb the shock of being dropped—even from a great height.

LIBRARY DRONE POLICY

Policy Considerations

In order to have sound drone policies in place, you will first need to determine what equipment you intend to purchase, as well as how you intend to use your drones. Making these determinations will facilitate a policy specifically tailored to drone use within your organization. That aside, key factors that need to be considered include the following:

- Conformity with the library's mission statement
- Safety
- Adult and parental/guardian consent and waivers
- Privacy implications

Conformity with Your Mission Statement

Before making a purchase for use in any program no matter the scope or reach, consideration should be given to why it is being offered and how it fits the mission of the library. Libraries have always been a place where people have come in search of knowledge and entertainment. The library is further evolving into the maker movement. The purpose of making is to spark the imagination and further educate all who walk through the doors of the library. Whether 3D printing, learning about virtual reality, or even flying drones, the purpose for these types of programs is clear. Libraries are about education and training. Drones are part of the future, and exposing library users to that technology can only further advance the mission of the library. Drone flying has already revolutionized aviation and the transport of goods and services, and it will continue to do so into the future.

What does the library want to accomplish with the addition of drones to its inventory of maker/educational items? Beyond classes, what is the "return on investment" for your patrons? Will they learn a skill? Will what they are doing have a practical application for future use? What is the *raison d'etre*? Generally, the goal of a library is to inspire, engage, and educate. Although drones are fun, they also can teach many lessons, from simple hand/eye coordination, to general aviation and career exploration, to inspiration and innovation. In considering these goals, drones have a place in libraries.

Safety

Policies that protect both the patron and unintended victims of misused drones should be taken into account in addition to the regular policies that cover most programs. With regard to guided programming taking place in the library (or a library-sponsored program outside the library), participant safety should be the staff's primary concern. Drones have many moving parts that can potentially cause injury to hands, fingers, and other extremities. Additionally, if drones are not operated properly or responsibly, they have the potential to get out of control and potentially strike participants, observers, or passersby. In the case of a supervised library program, a library staff member should always not only be trained in the proper operation but also be prepared for the possibility of an incident in which injuries can occur. Aside from being aware of the safety of participants, staff must have a working knowledge of not just the operation of the drone but also of syncing the controller to the drone and the procedures for battery replacement of both the controller and drone. Staff should have a general knowledge of quick repairs for common problems or issues if the drone makes a hard landing. Providing robust training for staff members will only help to enhance the drone-flying experience.

Adult and Parental/Guardian Consent and Waivers

Many programs center on the use of drones for children or teens. As can be expected with this age group, the levels of excitement and maturity play a factor in instruction and programming. For elementary-age students, starting second grade through sixth grade, small, nano-sized drones are most appropriate because of their size, range of travel, and weight (many of them fall below the FAA weight requirements for registration). They also have a breakaway type of propeller, which has a very low likelihood of causing injury.

When conducting training and programming with middle and high school-aged participants, nano and, in some situations, small drones should be considered, depending on the maturity level of the group participating. Larger-sized drones should be used in programming after participants in this age group have first had training and experience with nano drones. Work with nano drones can allow staff to determine whether or not teens have adequate hand-eye coordination and are responsible enough to handle a larger drone.

Parental or guardian consent for patrons under the age of 18 who are involved in the operation of library-owned drones, whether in a library-sponsored class environment or lending, should be secured in the form of a consent or waiver of liability. Whether the parent or guardian signs the waiver/consent at registration or on the date of the program/class, securing consent and raising the awareness of the risks inherent in operating drones will allow them to make a determination regarding whether their child is responsible enough to take part in the program/class. The library's goal is to provide robust programming that will inspire, engage, and educate in an environment that is safe for all participants. Library administration should always consult their attorney with regard to any type of consent/waiver form language, but in general, the document should be brief and contain language that will inform the parent or guardian about the potential hazards involved, including potential injuries that may occur to both the operator and spectator. Although the library will take precautions to ensure that injury will not occur, there are unforeseen circumstances in which accidents do arise. Libraries will make every attempt to mitigate these hazards with safe flying environments, but the risk still exists. Depending on the type of library program that is being offered, a constant parental presence during the program may be required as well.

For programs that are centered on adult participants, similar considerations must be taken into account with regard to consent. Considerations for the type of drone, the location that the drone will be operated in, and its durability to hard landings or mishaps must be taken into account. Nano drones or small quadcopter drones with breakaway propellers are likely the best option for beginners. It is not in anyone's best interest to have a first-time operator fly an expensive, high-powered drone that cannot tolerate first-time-user abuse. Additionally, training patrons in the use of the drone that will be used is critical, not only to the safety of the individual who will operate the drone, but also to avoid any damage to it during its operation. Libraries should always place the safety of the patron first, but it is also critical avoid damaging any piece of equipment that the library lends. Patrons should complete training and then sign a waiver/consent form that makes the user very aware of their responsibilities as an operator of a drone, the risks involved in its operation, and the possible risks of injury if the craft is not operated in a safe manner and in conformity with FAA regulations. Language in these disclaimers should include:

- Consent to the training
- Acknowledgment that the patron has received, been instructed in and has read the FAA regulations with regard to the operation of the drone
- Understanding that unsafe operation is in violation of the rules of the library
- A "Hold Harmless" for the library

A strong policy in place that will protect the safety of participants, observers, passersby and the library will not only protect the library in the case of an incident or accident, but also sends a strong message to the user that safety is the library's primary concern.

Privacy Implications

In the case when operation of drones take place outside the building, there are certain rules that the FAA have put in place regarding safe operation. Although the regulations do not explicitly state that operators cannot operate over the property of others, many libraries are located in or around residential areas, and many drones are equipped with cameras. When operating drones during library instruction, those drones should never be operated out of eyesight of the operator and they should never be operated over an area of land that is not within the boundaries of the library (Federal Aviation Administration, 2019). Even if a drone operated by the library is not equipped with cameras, residents who live in and around libraries or the areas that libraries have secured for the operation of the drone may still feel that their privacy has been violated by a flyover of their property. Having a "Good Neighbor" policy in place will ensure that local residents will not object to the library operating drones near their homes or places of business.

FAA REGULATIONS

Of all the types of drones available in the marketplace, the type that is most heavily regulated is the flying type. With the easy availability of drones in physical stores and online, usage issues have arisen. In light of those issues, the FAA created and fine-tuned regulations for hobbyist drone flying. If your library is considering flying drones, you must adhere to FAA rules, located online at https://www.faa.gov/uas/getting_started/. They include the following:

- If your drone weighs more than .55 of a pound and less than 55 pounds, you can register your drone online at https://faadronezone.faa.gov/#/.
- Drones may not fly higher than 400 feet.
- Keep your drone within your line of sight.
- Be aware of FAA airspace restrictions: https://www.faa.gov/uas/recreational_fliers/where_can_i_fly/airspace_restrictions/.
- Respect others' privacy.
- Never fly near other aircraft, especially near airports.
- Never fly over groups of people, public events, or stadiums full of people.
- Never fly near emergencies such as fires or hurricane recovery efforts.
- Never fly under the influence of drugs or alcohol.

When considering if drone programming and/or lending is something your library should consider, be aware of the FAA rules, especially those regarding restricted airspace within your library district. It is always helpful to remind patrons who wish to operate a library owned drone about any no-fly areas and the FAA regulations concerning safe operation. The FAA has created an app, B4UFLY, which is free and easy to use that will assist in assessing where drones can safely be flown.

As mentioned earlier, flying drones over 0.55 pounds and under 55 pounds must be registered with the FAA and also must have its registration number marked either by engraving, permanent label or permanent marker. There is a $5.00 fee associated with the registration and once registered, the license is valid for three years. Also, if patrons are interested in registering their flying drones, the owner must be 13 years of age (or a parent or guardian must register it under their name).

FLYING DRONE TYPES

Flying drones are initially classified by usage. The three basic classifications are as follows:

1. *Hobbyist Drone:* This type of drone is used for recreational purposes, for fun and sports. Such as drone racing, taking flying selfies, hobbyist photography, etc.
2. *Commercial Drone:* These drones are meant for business use, such as aerial photography and video recording, terrain inspection, real estate usage, package or pizza delivery, etc.
3. *Military Drone:* Military drones are manufactured for specific purposes by specific companies, for example, spy drones, attack drones, riot control drones, etc. ("Drone Classification and Types," 2017).

For the purpose of use in a library, the focus will be on the hobbyist category because this platform is the most cost effective and regulations with regard to this type are simple for libraries to conform with.

Size Classifications

Within the classifications mentioned above, there is further classification with regard to frame size. Regarding size, there are four classifications:

- **Nano:** averages 4 inches/10cm in diameter (most drones are square-shaped quadcopters)

- **Small:** larger than nano but can range from 12 inches/30cm to 6 feet/2 meters in length, which is the size of most consumer-based drones.
- **Medium:** Smaller than light aircraft and usually need to be carried by more than one person.
- **Large:** size of a small aircraft, traditionally used in military or surveillance applications (Abdullah, n.d.).

Frame Types

A sub category within size is "frame type" for which there are three classifications:

- **Fixed Wing:** These types of drones use a method of flight and lift very similar to an airplane. This type of drone can glide and uses wings for lift with motors propelling the drone forward. These types of drones cannot hover or stay in a fixed position.
- **Single Rotor:** Designed much like traditional helicopters, these drones rely on a single large propeller to lift and navigate. It is considered a single rotor design in spite of there being a tail rotor (which does not aid in propulsion, but is there purely for stability). These types of drones use gasoline motors as a source of fuel.
- **Multirotors:** Drones with more than one rotor are generally classified as multirotor. This simply means that the drone relies on a series of rotors for lift and maneuverability. No one rotor is primary and all work in unison to fly the unit. Most all of these types are battery powered electric motored. The name of each type of drone is based on the number of rotors:
    - **Dual Rotors:** These have a set of two rotors mounted to the airframe.
    - **Trirotors:** Three rotors are mounted to the airframe and positioned in a triangular configuration.
    - **Quadrotors:** Also known as "Quad-copters": there are four rotors mounted in a square or diamond configuration. This is the most common type of drone because of its ability to be piloted with ease.
    - **Pentirotors:** Drones with this configuration have five rotors mounted to the airframe.

- **Hexarotors:** This airframe is supported by six rotors which give very tight air control. Hexarotors can fly higher and longer distances than the quadcoptors. This type of vehicle can safely fly even if three of the six rotors fail.
- **Octorotors:** Drones with this particular configuration have eight rotors. They have greater power, speed and maneuverability in windy conditions. This vehicle type can lift heavier loads, but it has less battery life than the quadcopter ("Drone Classification and Types," 2017).

DRONE PURCHASING

Making the initial investment in drone platforms takes on many facets. Before considering the size, number or rotors, or other factors, the first question that should be considered is relevance. What are the programming needs and goals of the library? What are the library's expectations regarding the outcome of a drone program? How can the library adhere to FAA guidelines? What are the populations that you expect to attend the classes? How will the programs evolve and will there be further classes for users who become proficient in the basic classes or come to classes with an already established and advanced skill set? Will the library hire outside clubs or experts to conduct classes? If the in-house staff are being considered as programmers, then having a coordinated initial plan will be helpful in making a decision regarding purchases.

When making that final decision regarding purchasing drones, having a focus on size is crucial to be in compliance with FAA regulations. Without that compliance, usage cannot proceed. There are other factors that must also be considered. These include ease of use, compatibility with programming, space, and cost. Because of these factors, the types of drones that are most suited for library use are the nano- to small-sized quadcopters. They are easier to control, conform to FAA guidelines without further licensing, and lend themselves toward easier user training.

Nano drones are more affordable but are fragile because of their size. Many nano drones are approximately four to five inches (approximately 100mm) in size and have a cost ranging from $15–$30. Most quadcopter nanos are square. They have a higher probability of being damaged from accidental crashes, being stepped on, or having propellers fail. Nano drones are excellent for flying inside a building because of size and ease of use. This type of drone can be operated outside so long as there it is not a windy day. Although operating a nano drone still requires its user to follow FAA guidelines, many nano types fall below the 0.55-pound weight classification for registration, thus making it easier for library and patron use. Operation of this type of drone can be challenging because many designs are square, so unless the drone has a particular marking to allow the operator to identify which side is considered the front, it may be challenging to properly operate. Rotors on this size of drone are usually very safe for young users as they are designed to break away and have no sharp edges. Replacement rotors are also inexpensive to purchase, and in some cases, replacement rotors can be 3D printed. Flight time can also be challenging with nanos. Most drones of this size have a flying time of approximately 5–10 minutes, so having additional batteries and a rapid charger will help maximize flight times within the program setting.

Small drones are larger than the nano classification and may require FAA registration. They can be in the same size and weight range as a nano or as large as six feet/two meters in diameter. These drones are the most versatile because they are the bulk of the consumer market. Drones of this type that are on the smaller side can be operated indoors, but they will have a substantial amount of rotor noise. Although not as inexpensive as the nano class of drone, having a more robust airframe allows for more versatility with programming. This size of drone is more durable and less prone to damage from rough landings or being stepped upon. They also lend themselves to a more realistic flight experience because of their size and the ability to fly more easily outdoors. Battery life, depending on the size of the small drone, can have advantages over the nano because it increases flight time for the user and gives greater flexibility to do more. Depending on the model, spare parts are often easy to obtain.

These small-sized drones also have features that lend themselves towards programming and lending for specific uses. If the library has a slim budget, focusing on drones with fewer bells and whistles will still give the user a sound experience, but many of the features that once were pricey extras are now affordable, the biggest being a camera.

Features List

Here is a list of several features to consider when researching which drone or set of drones is right for your facility. Be mindful of long-term goals when considering additional drone features that can turn into new programming as patron skills develop:

- Flight time/battery capacity
- Still Camera vs. no camera
- Video Camera vs. still camera
- LED lights
- GPS
- Attachments that allow drones to lift and transport
- Availability or replacement parts/rotors
- Breakability factor

When considering any of the above features (or other features not listed), always keep in mind the budget available, the number of drones needed to have a successful program, the types of programming the library is trying to create and what features will be necessary for it, and the availability of spare parts. Probably the biggest consideration is battery life, recharging time, and ease of swapping out those batteries. There are many drones on the market that are very affordable but may only have a 5-minute flight time that require 20 minutes to recharge. So if you are doing a program, and you have 5 minutes of flight time for 20 minutes of charge time, it may be a good idea to price out a charger and 5 batteries for every drone (assuming 5 minutes flight time and 20 minutes of charge time), so there is a continual opportunity for quick battery swap-out, providing a continuous flight experience for the patron.

Review Sources

There are many resources available online to initially learn about the types of drones. Some are commercial, and others are from academia. Recommendations from colleagues at other libraries can also be a valuable asset in formulating what types of drones will work at the library. In conducting research on which drones are the best fit for the library, sites that are reliable sources are CNET, Techradar, Digital Trends, Tom's Guide, and *Consumer Reports* (although *Consumer Reports* may not rate drones as frequently as the aforementioned sources). There are also some independent hobbyist sites that can be of assistance as well. Like any source on the internet, be wary of relevance, the date of the review or critique, any ratings given by readers, and bias.

Because drone models change frequently, be cognizant of whether that particular make and model of drone is still available in the open marketplace. There are numerous drone manufacturers, and often there will be updates to a product line. Manufacturers will give new model numbers or names without making many improvements other than esthetics. The market is constantly evolving and changing as are products, so when doing research, focus first on what features are available, then decide which features are relevant for your facility, patron use, and potential classes. Next, narrow down the size(s), type (quadcopter etc.), features (camera, GPS) and battery life. Making an informed decision about initial purchases is just the beginning because there is a good chance that almost none of the staff has any previous experience with flying drones. Start with the basics, because most patrons will as well. Before programming plateaus, keep thinking three steps ahead and plan for the next drone purchase as an upgrade from the starting point.

When purchasing your drones, it is a good practice to take a long view of things. Everyone likes to start with the basics, but whether you are planning a curriculum of classes or making drones available for lending, you have to be broad in your approach to purchasing. If your budget allows, have different sizes and features available to patrons. Purchasing is always constrained by budget, but if a number of nano drones can be purchased for training, then a smaller number of small drones with extra features can enhance further development of classes. Remember that flying is only half of what a drone could conceivably do. Features like photography and videography opens the door to more robust programming that patrons will come to time and time again. When coupled with a lending program, a successful program of drone flying can blossom and expand to a level that will attract patrons for years to come.

Space Considerations

Space is often a consideration when introducing a new service, item or collection to a facility. In the case of drones, there are added challenges. Having a controlled environment where patrons, staff and any onlookers can enjoy the experience without the fear of injury is critical to the success of any drone programming. If potentially associated programming is going to take place outdoors, the operation of any device must be in conformity with the FAA rules. Even if the library is not located near an airport, it may be on a flight path that is restricted airspace. If these restrictions are in place, is there a facility, such as a school or town, county, or state park that would allow for library sanctioned drone flying? If the library is adjacent to private homes or businesses, will the operation disturb the neighbors? Drones tend to be loud, and because they are known to have cameras, operating near a property line may draw the ire of neighbors.

If you anticipate operating drones within a building, and the facility is small, has low ceilings, or does not have open space to operate a drone outside effectively (perhaps the library is in a city or within prohibited airspace), purchasing a large quadcopter would not be the best choice. Being aware of the limitations of your facility is essential for any item that is being purchased. Because of the unique nature of what drones do, flying indoors creates its own set of concerns and challenges. Understand that once staff is trained and has some level of proficiency with the drones, patrons will most likely not. For indoor operation, any drone larger than a nano size is not favorable for safe operation because of a larger drone's size and the noise that accompanies it. When operating a drone in an indoor space, the space needs to be secured so that patrons are not in the flying space. Study rooms with windows with some type of guards protecting light fixtures are ideal. If a staff member needs to enter the room to swap a battery or reset a drone that may have crashed, it is advisable that the staff member wear eye protection. Another option is creating a safe space to fly from open space. An indoor option that can be employed is the use of a "drone tent." The space is a 10-foot-by-10-foot pop up canopy tent. The tent is assembled in place, and mosquito netting is hung from the frame of the canopy and is allowed to hang to the ground (see figure 2.1). Small nano drones are flown inside. A staff member wearing eye protection stays inside to correct drones whose batteries need to be changed out or to right a crashed drone. The drone tent is an easy and cost-effective way to bring drone flying to any facility, and it is very easy to bring for outreach.

Another thing to consider, which is often overlooked when making a purchase of any type of item to add to the library's collection of nontraditional materials, is whether there is adequate space to store the item when not in use. A lack of adequate storage space has long been the bane of libraries! So, when making a purchase of a drone or drones, consider storage containers for the devices and where they can be safely stored. Also take into consideration the purchase of and storage of spare parts that may be needed for repairs.

STAFF TRAINING

Planning a robust curriculum of classes can only begin once you have staff who is eager to learn and work with the materials you provide. Having a coalition of the willing will only enhance the success of any training

Figure 2.1 Example of a drone being piloted within a do-it-yourself drone tent. Photo courtesy the Sachem Public Library.

and subsequent programming. This criterion applies to any new service, class or instruction that libraries offer. Without a staff member or group of staff that understands the technology, it cannot be presented for classes effectively. Often with technology and especially with drones, libraries need staff members who can be trained, go on to train the remaining staff, and ultimately be involved in the training of patrons. Having that group of individuals who are motivated, excited, and interested and can devote time to practice and master their skills will be the key to success. This will then translate to the ultimate goal of meaningful patron interactions. Assigning someone who is uncomfortable, ambivalent, or hostile to the tech can be counterproductive and will hinder the success of any technology initiative. Once you identify the individuals on staff who have the interest, it is time to train.

Remember, training to fly drones is only as effective as the muscle memory possessed by the operator. If there are employees outside the department who can assist in programming and training, they should be utilized. Practice is essential. Having a regular training/practice day for staff who are interested is critical to any success with employees who intend on pursuing the safe operation of the drones. Practice for everyone, even if a "lunch and learn," is worth the price of a few pizzas. This process of training will yield staff with varying skill levels. Not everyone will be an expert, but having a level of knowledge and understanding can go a long way toward creating awareness of the general staff and promoting programming. When staff training occurs, identify staff who fit into one of the categories of user outlined below.

Generalist

This employee should be *any* person on staff that has interaction with the public. If this person sits at a service desk or assists patrons in any way, this staff member should know that the item is available at the library, what programming is available, circulation rules, and the contact person who can provide further information. Think of this knowledge level as the same as knowing your loan rules for a book, DVD, or video game. A deep understanding of operation or what the drone does is not required, only general knowledge. An opportunity to experiment and practice with the drones that the library will enhance their knowledge of the device. This training can also gauge whether a particular employee can be a candidate for higher-level training, if interest is expressed.

Specialist

This employee should be the contact person for more specific questions. The specialist should have an operational knowledge of the drones used including size, type, operation, programming, and all pertinent information about the devices possessed in the department. This employee should be the first substantive point of contact for patrons who have very specific knowledge of the drone because they will have had further training than the generalist. This person, after being trained on successful operation (including pairing remotes to the drone, battery life capacity and life and repair), is the employee to whom the generalist refers questions to as the first point of contact. Some of the skills that a specialist should possess include controlling takeoffs, vertical flight, transition to horizontal flight, and landings. Specialists are capable of teaching classes on the basics.

Technician

This is the expert. This person (or group of people) is part of the group who makes the decisions on which drones to purchase, replace or repair and handles all facets of the drones in the library. This person is a "train the trainer" and will give instruction to the specialist-level employee so that person can be the trainer for staff. This person will coordinate programming and make purchases in accordance with the needs of the department. This level of employee will have the same skills as the specialist but also possess additional skills, which include, but are not limited to, agility flight, flying at FAA maximum ceiling of 400 feet, obstacle avoidance, and racing.

As the staff members work with the drones, brainstorm ideas for potential classes and experiences that can be planned into the future. Sometimes the best ideas come from in-house imagination. Considering all of the possibilities that drones can offer the library long term will deepen the types of classes the library can offer and expand the patrons' exposure to the technology. Staff members are the library's greatest asset because they will know the patron base and the community and should have a grasp of their strengths and limitations. Involve and engage staff, tasking them to craft programming that is fun, stress free, interactive, engaging, and hopefully motivating to all involved. Couple that level of involvement with a lending program, and you should have great buy in from the public. Remember, any programming involving new technology may be slow to gain interest. Although libraries publicize their programs in their newsletters and on social media, it is word-of-mouth that eventually brings patrons into programs. This word-of-mouth may take time to build, so be patient if program attendance is not as expected the first few times a class is offered.

Finding outside instructors can be a struggle, especially with a specialized topic such as this. A public library's greatest asset is always the community. There are many drone and other aeronautics enthusiast clubs and associations that can be contacted. Many of these organizations already have programming that can be easily tailored for in house library programs or with meetups in areas where the safe operation and practice of drones can occur. One such group is the Aircraft Owners and Pilots Association (www.aopa.org). This organization has locations in Tennessee, California and Maryland. This group is an aviation enthusiast group that has "Drone Seminars to Go." The seminar and PowerPoint presentation they offer from their site can also be helpful in designing a lecture style class. There is also https://dronetraininghq.com/, which connects people to drone groups. This organization lists colleges and other organizations that have drone flying programs. The site https://www.skyop.com/courses/ also provides course materials and instructors who can be hired to teach classes. These are but a sampling of the many organizations that either connect people to trainers or provide training seminars and resources online.

CIRCULATING DRONES

Libraries have long been adding nontraditional materials to their circulating collections. Within the last decade, the concept of loaning out "realia" has come to the forefront in libraries and circulating these items has become more commonplace. Making large items portable, secure, and trackable (with barcodes or RFID tags) is a challenge for catalogers.

Processing

Many types of drones are rather expensive, and libraries want to have the drones returned free from damage and on time. When creating packaging for the drone, the selection of some type of portable container should take into consideration size, weight, protective properties (such a foam-lined case), and durability. Making an initial investment in protective packaging will only help to preserve the item while it is checked out to patrons. Additionally, having directions somehow affixed to the case with clear and concise instructions on safe operation should be included. There should also be a list of every item that is included in the case, and upon checkout and return, each item contained in the kit should be accounted for by circulation staff.

Loan Rules

Lending out an item requires that you create some loan rules. Like most realia, you'll want to establish the following:

- Accounts must be in good standing or, alternatively, create a threshold for active fines (if your library indeed still collects fines for overdue or lost items).

- If you have multiple items in an equipment collection available, how many items can be loaned from this particular collection?
- Where will these items be housed, and where is the point of contact for pickup (reference desk, circulation department, other area)?
- Where are these materials to be returned?
- What is an appropriate loan period?
- How will the library handle items that are returned in damaged condition?
- What is the time threshold for an overdue item before the individual is billed for the item?
- Will the library allow users to reserve items if they are checked out, or will it be a first-come, first-served basis?

In addition to these standard considerations, lending drones specifically requires that you consider the following:

- Will you require mandatory training prior to checkout?
- What, if any, lending agreement must the user agree to and sign before being able to loan the item?
- Will the agreement have a "Hold Harmless" clause in the event the item borrowed results in injury to the user, operator, or any bystander?

Having a comprehensive lending agreement that is clear and concise will help ensure that a drone is used responsibly and then returned in good condition in a timely manner.

Sample Drone Lending Programs

Today, there are many libraries across the United States and around the world that are lending drones. One early adopter is the University of South Florida (USF). USF received a grant that expanded their Digital Media Commons, and part of the funds from that grant allowed the school to purchase drones equipped with cameras for digital media projects. The scope of lending for South Florida is limited to use for multimedia projects. Students cannot check them out for "joy droning." A person who wishes to check out the drone must explain how the drone will be used, describe precisely where the drone will be operated on campus, and attend a training program. The operation of the drone is supervised by a trained faculty member. The drone may be used off campus with prior written approval. USF rules are very precise and limit the scope of how the user flies the craft (Garber, 2014).

Looking specifically at public libraries, let's examine an active drone lending program taking place at the Longwood Public Library in Middle Island, New York.

The following describes an interview with Alison Mirabella, digital literacy coordinator at the Longwood Public Library, Middle Island, New York, on June 29, 2019.

Ms. Mirabella described how Longwood Public Library circulates three Ryze Tellos as a part of its "Equipment and Gadgets Collection." The collection is a new addition to the library and has become one of its most popular services. This collection includes a variety of nontraditional library items that patrons can take home, such as metal detectors, telescopes, microphones, Cricut vinyl cutters, and more. The gadgets are selected with the goal of facilitating education, creativity, and digital literacy, allowing Longwood to serve its population in new and exciting ways.

Mirabella had wanted to add a drone to the collection since the initial planning phase of the Equipment and Gadgets Collection, but the library had some very specific needs that made finding the right drone a challenge. In order to be added to the collection, the drone needed to be:

- Small. The collection was stored in the Adult Reference closet, which presented severe space limitations.
- Under the FAA size limits. The library wanted a drone in the "toy" category that did not require FAA registration.
- Easy to fly. As patrons may not have previous drone experience, the library wanted a drone that would be accessible for beginners and could be paired with a controller.
- Equipped with a camera. In addition to aviation enthusiasts and families, the library wanted a drone that would also appeal to photographers and videographers.
- Safe. Because the drone might be borrowed by families with children, the library wanted to ensure that the drone could be used safely.

Following some research, Mirabella became convinced the Ryze Tello was a good fit for the Longwood Library. The Tello weighs 0.18 pounds, putting it below the FAA weight limit, and is small enough to easily store in the aforementioned Adult Reference closet. Unlike most drones in the toy category, the Ryze Tello uses flight technology from DJI, an experienced drone manufacturer. Interested in the technology, Mirabella first bought a Tello for herself! Impressed by how quickly it synced with her phone and how well it held a stable hover, she went ahead and purchased three for the library's collection.

The drones are circulated like the rest of the library's gadgets. They circulate for two weeks, and patrons must sign a contract in order to check them out. When a patron arrives to pick up a gadget, the adult reference librarian reviews a checklist on the contract of all the included accessories to make sure everything is there, and a circulation clerk checks that same checklist when it is returned (a copy of this contract appears in the appendix). No special training is required. The case includes the drone, a battery, a micro USB charging cable, a USB wall adapter, a controller, and the instruction manual.

Patrons enjoy the drones, and the library hasn't received any negative reports. According to Mirabella: "One patron told me that her kids enjoyed the drone, but the family cat loved it even more! They flew it around the house while the cat stalked it and once tried to jump on it. Luckily it didn't come back with claw marks!"

PROGRAMS AND CLASSES

Ideally, your drone programs will evolve over time. As one class is developed and implemented, inquiries from attendees can be the impetus for new programs. Classes should be purposeful and fun, with an educational component. Beginning classes can be very similar to the training that is provided to staff. These types of classes can be developed and expanded, addressing the principles of operation and/or piloting, and the sessions can be adaptive, depending on the types of drones the library purchases. Programming should start with basics and build upon those skills. Classes and topics will be partially dependent on basic universal drone features but can be expanded with the use of outside programmers, who may bring in their own, more sophisticated equipment with added peripherals.

Determining the Location of a Drone Program

Before executing a program, you must first settle on a location! This is a critical decision with drone flying because, as was mentioned earlier, libraries must comply with FAA regulations and also be cognizant of safety and privacy concerns. If the library is not within the restricted areas outlined by the FAA, consider an outdoor class. If there are factors prohibiting the safe operation outside on library grounds, consider reaching out to local municipalities that are within unrestricted airspace to ascertain if they can potentially provide you with space. If your library does not have either of these options, then consider an indoor experience. As was discussed earlier in this chapter, utilizing a drone tent or study room with a window can still provide a fun, safe, and educational experience. Indoor experiences are a wonderful opportunity to offer a number of programs because of the flexibility of not being beholden to FAA operating regulations or potential loss of drones by an inexperienced pilot.

General Program Categories

So the drones are purchased, the staff is trained, and your location has been selected. It's time to engage in programming! Generally, your programs will fall into two categories. They are:

- **Lecture:** Instructional in nature. The instructor discusses a topic that can be enhanced with presentations and demonstrative items. Patrons are mainly passive observers and may be able to ask questions during or after the presentation.
- **Active Participation:** Instructor lectures but the participants are able to participate, whether it be a computer class, craft, writing, or any other activity where patrons work alongside the presenter. This type of class involves its participants being active and performing some type of task related to the topic being discussed.

Standalone or Multisession?

It is important to consider whether these types of classes will be standalone programs or a multipart set of classes that function as a series (with or without prerequisites). Both programming types are effective because there are so many types of drones, and the skill set varies from craft to craft. Having multiple types of program structures can be effective to convey, develop, and feature the skills necessary for safe operation.

A standalone class is independent of other classes or can be a prerequisite or gateway for the patron to graduate to more advanced classes, a building block of sorts that prepares the participant for more advanced classes. These classes do not necessarily have to be required as a prerequisite to taking other sessions, and patrons do not have to take this type of class in any particular order. These types of classes can be introductory lectures, or "how to." Having these independent classes allows patrons to experience the technology without expectation and gives the broadest exposure to the experience. Patrons can try these classes out and then determine if they'd like to continue learning in a more in-depth class or series of classes.

As important as standalone classes are for patrons to have exposure to drone technology, having a series of classes can also be effective in building on the skills learned in the previous classes. The series model allows the class instructor to be more focused on individual skills, unlike the single class model, so there can be more concentration on a particular aspect of operation. As flying a drone is a skill that develops over time, having classes that follow a series allow for patrons to have meaningful skills development. If patrons attend advanced classes without first having some level of knowledge with regard to the basics of flying, the inexperience may slow the progress of the class and frustrate other attendees who may have better acumen with operating the drones. The multiple class model may, but does not necessarily, have to require prerequisite classes, but when patrons move to the next class in the series, they can build on the skills they have already learned from previous instruction.

LECTURE CLASSES

With beginning any new hobby or endeavor, it is always important to begin with the basics. This first set of classes will address some of the basic knowledge needed before participants can begin the process of learning to fly. The following description of classes are programs that feature the basics and can be offered as a stand-alone, part of a series, or, in many cases, pop-up style.

Introduction to Drones

Type of Program: Stand-alone, first in a series
Registration: Required for up to 30 attendees
Instructor Type: In-house staff member or qualified expert
Audience: Teens and adults (separate classes by age groups)
Drone Type: Multiple types for display only

Class Duration: 1 hour 30 minutes
Location: Lecture, no hands-on flying
Class Goals: Be able to discuss and expose attendees on FAA regulations, types of drones, and features along with applicable uses and basic operation

This program serves as an introduction. Because this may be a patron's first exposure to drones in person, it is important that this lesson discuss the applicable rules set forth by the FAA, including helpful websites. Although there may be staff members who have knowledge of drones beyond a novice, having an expert who is wholly familiar with FAA guidelines is critical so as to be able to properly articulate the guidelines in a clear and easy to understand manner. Topics in this type of instruction should cover current uses by both civilian and the military and serve as a primer on the types of drones, including size, battery life of the drone and controller, repair, availability of extra parts, and peripherals (such as cameras, GPS controls, and any other potential features). The instructor should also cover the science behind drone flying. Having a basic understanding of lift and steering (for example, with a quadcopter, how some rotors rotate faster than others to affect steering) will be helpful for the novice to understand the basics of flight. Although not required for a course of this type, a short demonstration of a drone by the instructor may be helpful. This presentation should serve as a lecture on what drones are, their potential and purchasing for the hobbyist.

Drone Purchasing

Type of Program: Stand-alone
Registration: Required for up to 30 attendees
Instructor: In-house staff or qualified expert
Audience: Teens and adults (may attend the same class)
Drone Type: Multiple for display
Class Duration: 1 hour 30 minutes
Location: Lecture, no hands-on flying
Class Goals: Give an overview of types of drones and their operation along with available features so the attendees can make an educated decision regarding drone purchases and ownership

This type of program should be designed to instruct attendees on drone types, prices, operation, and features along with supporting materials such as information sheets with resources to investigate. This class should be designed with purchasing as the main focus, although a discussion of drone type and cost range are also important. Discussion should center primarily on the types of drones, their features, ease of operation and associated cost. Having samples of types and sizes of drones should be included along with a short demonstration of the ease of use for each type. A knowledgeable staff member should be more than qualified to teach this program, but having a skilled expert is also an option.

ACTIVE PARTICIPATION

Lecture classes for educating patrons on the uses of drones will only be effective if they are coupled with classes that actually allow for hands-on use. The best way to learn is by doing, and having participatory hands-on classes that allow participants the opportunity to try their hands at flying will only help to develop a robust curriculum. Allowing patrons to try the technology can serve not only as an experience but also as a "try before you buy" opportunity. Having these classes will educate people who are curious about the technology and are considering purchasing a drone for themselves or a family member.

Skills-based classes should be required before patrons endeavor to attend advanced hands on classes. Every library's patron base is different, and the librarians' coordinating classes can be the ultimate determiners of whether a patron should move on to the next level. In order to have effective intermediate to advanced classes, a prerequisite class set should include *Introduction to Drones, Drone Basics and Introduction to Drone Flying Skills.* Depending on the complexity of the next set of classes, consider some type of graduation/authorization to take the next class in the series. Having this layered "graduation" approach will give the patron a feeling of accomplishment and confidence that they can move on to the next set of skill building classes.

Below are class suggestions that can be useful in developing experiential exposure to drone flying.

Introduction to Drone Flying Skills

Type of Program: Stand-alone, first in a series, or pop-up style
Registration: Required for up to 6–10 attendees (consider having multiple stand-alone sessions)

Instructor: In-house staff or qualified expert
Audience: Tweens, teens, and adults (consider different classes for the varying age groups)
Drone Type: Micro quadcopter
Class Duration: 1 hour 30 minutes
Location: Preferably inside, enclosed controlled location or drone tent, or, as an alternative, outdoors in a predefined environment

Setup

Have drones charged and synced to their controllers (see figure 2.2), in the case of quadcopters clearly mark the front and rear of the drone with green and red stickers, map out the area of operation, and reserve and notify staff regarding the program's location (whether in an outdoor location on library property, an area where a drone tent will be set up or a study room with a window which may require pre-reservation). Designate predetermined floor takeoff and landing areas with painter's tape. If the class is being held outdoors, be sure it is not a windy day and lay cardboard or boards with pre-marked takeoff and landing areas. Staff inside a controlled space should wear eye protection.

Figure 2.2 Quadcopter drone and radio controller. Photo courtesy the Sachem Public Library.

Class Goals

After a short introduction and explanation of the safe operation of the drones being featured, patrons will have a hands-on experience with basic flying skills.

This class should begin with basics, which means this class will cover simple concepts. Because this program spans a wide age range, the first half hour should be devoted to introducing patrons to each part of the drone. Explaining the parts of a drone and how they work in unison is very important. Much like a pilot of a large, fixed-wing aircraft, the potential drone pilot should understand what each part of the done does and how to control it. Starting with the scientific concepts of flying, such as which end is considered the nose versus the tail, are important, especially with a quadcopter that is basically a flying square along with why some rotors rotate slower than others to manipulate flight. There should also be a basic understanding of how the remote controller communicates with the drone and how to pair the two together. Instruction should also include realistic expectations of both battery life of both the drone and remote controller. The hands-on experience will begin with controller sensitivity and how the remote responds to the user's manipulation of the vertical and horizontal sticks. Holding this particular program indoors in a controlled area is ideal. If held in an uncontrolled flying environment, with inexperienced operators, drones could fly uncontrolled and fly beyond the property that the class is being held or the drone could be entangled in bushes, trees, power lines, or the roof of a home or building.

Drones: Takeoffs and Landings

Type of Program: Intermediate skill level
Registration: Required for up to 6–10 attendees (consider having multiple stand-alone sessions)
Instructor: One instructor and at least one helper (in-house staff or qualified expert)
Audience: Tweens, teens, and adults (consider different classes for the varying age groups)
Drone Type: Micro quadcopter
Class Duration: 1 hour 30 minutes
Location: Preferably inside, enclosed controlled location or drone tent
Class Goals: Guiding patrons to learn to take off and land on both wide and narrow confined spaces

Setup

Have drones charged and synced to their controllers; in the case of quadcopters, clearly mark the front and rear of the drone with green and red stickers, map out the area of operation, and reserve and notify staff regarding the program's location. Have a table in the space with the tabletop marked out for takeoff and landing areas. Staff inside the controlled space should wear eye protection.

Takeoffs and landings are arguably some of the most important maneuvers to master. Taking off too quickly with too much altitude could cause the drone to fly out of control, and a hard or missed landing can damage the craft. Working in a confined space, such as a drone tent or a study room with windows, will enhance the pilot's ability to learn the subtle manipulations of the drone. Learning to take off and land in a constrained area will help to train the fine motor skills that will also translate in open flight.

Drone Obstacle Course

Type of Program: Intermediate skill level
Registration: Required for up to 6–10 attendees (consider having multiple stand-alone sessions)
Instructor: One instructor and at least one helper (in-house staff or qualified expert)
Audience: Tweens, teens, and adults (consider different classes for the varying age groups)
Drone Type: Micro quadcopter
Class Duration: 1 hour 30 minutes
Location: Where FAA rules allow, outside in an open space; if an open space is not available, a space within the library that is free from foot traffic (preferably with high ceilings)
Class Goals: Focus on both horizontal and vertical controlled flight by navigating through a series of obstacles

Setup

Have drones charged and synced to their controllers (in the case of quadcopters, clearly mark the front and rear of the drone with green and red stickers), map out the area of operation, and reserve and notify staff regarding the program's location. Designate areas for takeoff and landing (preferably in different locations at different heights). Have a series of obstacles, such as small to medium-sized hula hoops hanging from the ceiling with pipe cleaners (if your library has a drop ceiling) along with pool noodles in various configurations hanging from the ceiling or, in the case of outdoor operation, on the ground with coffee cans filled with sand to create a slalom course. Staff inside the controlled space should wear eye protection.

This type of program will be hands-on and have a small class size. Class will begin with a short introduction and explanation of the drones, controllers, and operation. Patrons will have a flying experience while in a controlled and confined environment. They will be able to learn the basics of takeoff and landing, transitioning from vertical to horizontal flight and altitude control. This class should also cover battery life and have a component that discusses purchasing. Holding this particular program indoors in a controlled area is ideal. If held in an uncontrolled flying environment, with inexperienced operators, drones could fly uncontrolled and fly beyond the operational boundaries set out for the class.

Drone Agility Training

Type of Program: Advanced skill level
Registration: Required for up to 6–10 attendees (consider having multiple stand-alone sessions)
Instructor: One instructor and at least one helper (in-house staff or qualified expert)
Audience: Tweens, teens and adults (consider different classes for the varying age groups)
Drone Type: Micro quadcopter
Class Duration: 1 hour 30 minutes
Location: Where FAA rules allow, outside in an open space, and if an open space is not available, a space within the library that is free from foot traffic (preferably with high ceilings)
Class Goals: Build on the skills learned with the previous classes, with more complex maneuvering around obstacles.

Setup

Have drones charged and synced to their controllers (in the case of quadcopters, clearly mark the front and rear of the drone with green and red stickers), map out the area of operation, and reserve and notify staff regarding the program's location. Ideally this flying environment should be outside in an FAA clear area, or in a large area within the library. Have designated takeoff and landing areas (preferably at different heights). Have pool noodles anchored to the ground in coffee cans or small plastic buckets filled with sand to hold the noodles in place. Also add hula hoops to some of the mounted noodles, along with integrating natural barriers if flying outdoors. If flying indoors, create the same types of obstacles and integrate some children's furniture or large play items (toy kitchens or collapsible tents). Staff inside the controlled space should wear eye protection.

Attendees who have learned the basics and intermediate skills involved in vertical and horizontal flight will engage natural obstacles that would be encountered during normal operation in an outdoor environment. This class will discuss obstacle avoidance, including techniques to avoid tree entanglement, landing on surfaces that are in sight distance but not close to the operator, and other maneuvers that cannot be duplicated in a more controlled environment. In circumstances where a library does not have on premises outside space to conduct this class, reserving space at a local park or other open space within FAA guidelines is recommended.

Drone Photography/Videography Training

Type of Program: Advanced skill level
Registration: Required for up to 6–10 attendees (consider having multiple stand-alone sessions)
Instructor: One instructor and at least one helper (in-house staff or qualified expert)
Audience: Tweens, teens, and adults (consider different classes for the varying age groups)
Drone Type: Micro quadcopter or small quadcopter equipped with a camera that can capture photos or video
Class Duration: 1 hour 30 minutes to 2 hours
Location: Preferably inside, enclosed controlled location
Class Goals: Learn basic controlled operation of a drone and capture still photographs or video for playback along with the regulations associated with operating a drone while capturing photos or video

Setup

Have drones charged and synced to their controllers (in the case of quadcopters, clearly mark the front and rear of the drone with green and red stickers), map out the area of operation, and reserve and notify staff regarding the program's location. Have a table in the space with the tabletop marked out for takeoff and landing areas. Have predetermined flight plans with a list of areas to photograph or video. Ideally this program should take place outdoors not under FAA restrictions. Set clearly defined objects that should be the subject of the video or photography. If indoors, section off an area of the library that can accommodate video and photography and mark the areas and the subjects of the video or photographs. Place some objects in areas that are challenging to reach to gauge the participants skills. Think about a grading system as well to measure the patrons flying ability. Staff inside the controlled space should wear eye protection.

With a class of this type, the instructor must be familiar with the FAA regulations regarding the licensing of drone operators for commercial use and be able to articulate to class attendees the requirements for the use of commercial video and photography. Establishing full disclosure of the rules before the class begins is critical to informing the participants of their liability for not following FAA regulations. Although not every library can cover the cost of a drone for each participant, having a drone for each patron in class would be ideal. If that is not the case, then having two to three drones available for the patrons to share would also be effective. The instructor will begin the hands-on portion of the class with the basics of flying a drone and the techniques for capturing basic video and still photography. Other techniques can be demonstrated as time allows. It is recommended that a skilled instructor with experience teach this class.

High Speed Drone Flying

Type of Program: Advanced skill level
Registration: Required for up to 6–10 attendees (consider having multiple stand-alone sessions)
Instructor: One instructor and at least one helper (in-house staff or qualified expert)
Audience: School-age children to adult
Drone Type: Micro quadcopter or small quadcopter
Class Duration: 1 hour 30 minutes to 2 hours
Location: Where FAA rules allow, outside in an open space and if an open space is not available, a space within the library that is free from foot traffic (preferably with high ceilings).

Class Goals: Taking the skill sets developed in earlier classes, participants will learn how to fly drones through a marked course at higher speeds.

Setup

Have drones charged and synced to their controllers (in the case of quadcopters, clearly mark the front and rear of the drone with green and red stickers), map out the area of operation, and reserve and notify staff regarding the program's location. Have a predetermined space for a starting line takeoff and landing finish. Use pool noodles anchored with coffee cans or plastic buckets and mark the noodles with small flags with numbers marking the gate number that they must fly through (hula hoops can also be used for narrow obstacles). Staff inside the controlled space should wear eye protection.

Participants in this program will build on the obstacle course training received earlier to maneuver around a guided course. The goal is to develop controlled flying skills with agility. The concept would be similar to a downhill skiing competition, being able to maneuver between helium balloons being tethered to the ground by string threaded through a pool noodle.

High-Speed Drone Racing

Type of Program: Advanced skill level
Registration: Required for up to 6–10 attendees (consider having multiple stand-alone sessions)
Instructor: One instructor and at least one helper (in-house staff or qualified expert)
Audience: School-age children to adult
Drone Type: Micro quadcopter or small quadcopter equipped with a camera that can capture photos or video
Class Duration: 1 hour 30 minutes to 2 hours
Location: Where FAA rules allow, outside in an open space, and if an open space is not available, a space within the library that is free from foot traffic (preferably with high ceilings)
Class Goals: Taking the skill sets developed in earlier classes, participants will learn how to fly drones through a marked course at higher speeds.

Setup

Have drones charged and synced to their controllers (in the case of quadcopters clearly mark the front and rear of the drone with green and red stickers), map out the area of operation, and reserve and notify staff regarding the program's location. Have a predetermined space for a starting line takeoff and landing finish. Use pool noodles anchored with coffee cans or plastic buckets and mark the noodles with small flags with numbers marking the gate number that they must fly through (hula hoops can also be used for narrow obstacles). Staff inside the controlled space should wear eye protection.

Once they master high-speed flight, participants will maneuver through an obstacle course or a marked course. This class will be a competition to determine who has the fastest and most accurate flying times. The participants will fly one at a time, and race only the clock. The fastest time will be awarded class champion.

Drone Building

Type of Program: Stand-alone or first in a series
Registration: Required for up to 6–10 attendees (consider having multiple stand-alone sessions)
Instructor: One instructor and at least one helper (in-house staff or qualified expert)
Audience: Tweens, teens, and adults (consider different classes for the varying age groups)
Drone Type: Drone kits such as the Airblock, Flybrix, Kitables, Robolink Codrone Pro, DJI Flame Wheel F450 ARF Kit or other simple drone building kits
Class Duration: 1 hour 30 minutes
Location: Preferably inside, enclosed controlled location
Class Goals: Class attendees will have the opportunity to learn about all the parts needed for a drone to fly, build a drone from a kit, and by the end of the program (depending on cost considerations), patrons can take their drone home.

Setup

Workspace with tables for patrons to either stand up or sit. Have all appropriate tools and materials set out for the participants to utilize. Also have a designated flying area for testing. Be prepared for drones that cannot fly by having some type of floor covering or be in a space where finding small parts will not be difficult.

The obvious goal of this class is to build a drone, but building is only the beginning. As the attendees assemble the parts, they will learn what each component's role is with regard to getting the device airborne. Many of the kits that are available are similar to Lego, and other kits have more advanced building options. Choosing the right kit for the appropriate age range will determine the success of the program. Because testing the completed drone is part of the process, and most likely involve participants who will not have experience flying a drone, it is a good idea to have an enclosed space available for testing. Also, if the completed drone is over 0.55 of a pound, remind the participants that they are required under FAA regulations to register the drone after the completion of the program.

LIBRARY-BASED CLUB SESSIONS

Building on the idea of programming, having a "club" that meets on a regular basis will stimulate interested patrons to have even more interaction and use of drones. These clubs can help develop skills. A club environment also allows the library programmer to be more flexible with the topics covered because the patrons attending will have a skill set developed by the classes mentioned above. The flexibility of the club environment gives the members ownership of their skills and allows them to take what they have learned and applied it, especially if the club has a problem or task that they are attempting to solve. Designing a club will depend on the library knowing its particular population and understanding what will work with interested groups.

Junior Aviator Club

Type of Program: Club for children in grades 4–6
Registration: Required for up to 6–10 attendees (consider having multiple stand-alone sessions)
Instructor: One instructor and at least one helper (in-house staff or qualified expert)
Drone Type: Micro quadcopter or small quadcopter
Class Duration: 1 hour 30 minutes to 2 hours (meeting biweekly or monthly)
Location: Preferably inside, enclosed controlled location

Class Goals: This goal-oriented club will have its participants keep up with their flying skills and to perform a specific task at the meeting.

Setup

Have drones charged and synced to their controllers (in the case of quadcopters, clearly mark the front and rear of the drone with green and red stickers), map out the area of operation, and reserve and notify staff regarding the program's location. Have a table in the space with the tabletop marked out for takeoff and landing areas. Staff inside the controlled space should wear eye protection.

The Junior Aviators will begin with warm-ups to acquaint themselves with the basic piloting skills. After warm-up, the instructor will have a task that the participants need to complete. This could be an obstacle course, perform a specific task, or operate a peripheral attached to the drone. These classes give the patron the ability to take what they have learned in basics classes and add a new layer of skill to their drone experience.

Drone Design Club

Type of Program: Club for children, teens, or adults (separate club for each age range)
Registration: Required for up to 6–10 attendees (consider having multiple stand-alone sessions)
Instructor: One instructor and at least one helper (in-house staff or qualified expert)
Audience: School-age children or adults
Drone Type: Micro quadcopter or small quadcopter
Class Duration: 1 hour 30 minutes to 2 hours, meeting weekly, biweekly, or monthly
Location: Preferably inside, enclosed controlled location
Class Goals: Design either a drone with 3D design software or with predesigned design for modification.

Setup

Workspace with tables for patrons to either stand up or sit. Have all appropriate tools and materials set out for the participants to utilize. Also have a designated flying area for testing. Be prepared for circumstances where drones that are not assembled correctly and cannot fly. Have some type of floor covering available and deployed so if parts fall off the drone, finding them will not be difficult.

Participants will be involved in the process of designing a drone, whether from a previous design or from basic shapes. This club will be involved in the process, and when the drone is successfully designed, the club will continue with designing accessories that will function with the design concept and bring the entire project to life.

Teen Pilot Club

Type of Program: Teens from 6th grade to 12th grade
Registration: Required for up to 6–10 attendees (consider having multiple stand-alone sessions)
Instructor: One instructor and at least one helper (in-house staff or qualified expert)
Drone Type: Micro quadcopter or small quadcopter
Class Duration: 1 hour 30 minutes to 2 hours, meeting biweekly or monthly
Location: Preferably inside, enclosed controlled location
Class Goals: Working with teens, this program will teach advanced drone skills with regard to maneuverability, speed and accuracy of landing. The club can also explore design modifications to allow the drones to accomplish tasks or solve problems. The tasks will be assigned for each session that will ultimately lead toward solving the problem. Each task may take multiple sessions to solve.

Setup

Have drones charged and synced to their controllers (in the case of quadcopters, clearly mark the front and rear of the drone with green and red stickers), map out the area of operation, and reserve and notify staff regarding the program's location. Designate areas for takeoff and landing (preferably in different locations at different heights). Have a series of obstacles such as small to medium sized hula hoops hanging from the ceiling with pipe cleaners (if your library has a drop ceiling) along with pool noodles in various configurations hanging from the ceiling or mounted to the floor with coffee cans filled with sand to create a slalom course. Staff inside the controlled space should wear eye protection.

This program will allow for teens to meet on a regular basis and not only learn from the instructor but also have a collaborative experience helping less experienced participants with the "ins and outs" of drone flying. There can be tasks assigned for the club that the participants will need to work together to overcome. This class is more of a collaborative effort to help develop skills through task-based programming. As the club becomes more advanced, consider adding drones that have the ability to lift and move items or take video. Think of combinations of tasks that can solve a problem through drone piloting.

POTENTIAL PARTNERSHIPS FOR LIBRARY PROGRAMMING

Libraries sometimes conduct programming in a vacuum. Library professionals think of a new concept or technology to offer their public but often don't know that there are outside organizations that can be contacted and used as a resource for support. There are organizations in many communities, including hobbyist model aviation organizations. These organizations are made up of people who may actually be patrons. When planning and developing programs regarding aviation, reaching out to these groups can assist in finding knowledgeable experts who can become potential programmers. Additionally, these organizations have locations where model aircraft (including drones) can be operated safely and within FAA guidelines. Members from these organizations may also facilitate programs that may be beyond library staff's acumen, thus broadening the scope of what the library can offer its potential participants.

A national organization in the United States is the Academy of Model Aeronautics https://www.modelaircraft.org. This organization has many facets, including the ability to find affiliated local clubs that can be contacted for programming. There are other organizations that assist with connecting drone enthusiasts with groups and meetups. Exploring and developing those relationships will only help to enhance the programming experience in house.

Exploring partnerships with local colleges or universities that offer aviation programs or have a drone lending program. Many times, college and universities will partner with their library or public libraries. Sharing resources with colleges and universities can be reciprocal and can help to build stronger partnerships that transcend drone operation.

Working with local businesses is something that libraries should be involved with. Developing partnerships with businesses in the community (remember, businesses are entitled to take advantage of the services that many libraries provide) can only enhance connections to the community. Reaching out to the local Chambers of Commerce can deepen the relationship between your organizations. While developing these relationships, libraries can learn which businesses employ the use of drones in their work. Some examples of businesses that employ drones include, but are not limited to, surveyors who employ drones to inspect power lines or areas that are not accessible by foot, real estate agents who use drones to take photos video of properties, construction companies that use the craft for inspecting residential or commercial structures, or companies that assist with digital mapping. Reaching out to these companies to create partnerships can be mutually beneficial. Partnerships with local entrepreneurs, skilled professionals (such as pilots, engineers, attorneys, and tradespeople, to name a few) help to build a network upon which the library can call. Often, members of the community may have skill sets that go beyond their chosen profession and could possibly be an additional source for potential future instructors that can volunteer their time and facilitate robust programming for the library.

STAFF USE OF DRONES

With the investment made in staff training, utilizing those skills to employ drone use within the library can save time and potential injury. Drones can be used for a number of reasons; some are utilitarian and others include marketing. Utilizing drones in many of the same ways as businesses and individuals can enhance how the library maintains the building and can assist in publicity, in webpage development, and in other ways only the imagination can envision.

Drones in Facility Maintenance

Managing a large facility can be a challenge. There will be times when you will need to inspect a part of your building that may be difficult to access. If the ceiling has started leaking during a rainstorm, instead of using extension ladders to gain access to the roof, the use of a drone with a camera that can transmit video to the controller can save time and potential injury! With regard to grounds maintenance, if trees need to be inspected for trimming, the use of drones with camera features to inspect an area can also be effective and time saving. Following inclement weather, you can quickly fly over and inspect your parking lot for damage and any impact to accessibility.

Marketing Opportunities

A flyover by a drone with a video camera can literally offer a new angle to exterior views of your library. In addition to the exterior of your facility, videos can be shot within the building itself, as a sort of walking tour. Creation of video tours via drone can be created, edited, and posted on YouTube for insertion on the library's website or social media to attract attention not only to the library but also to drone-flying programming. Operating within FAA guidelines, flyovers of the exterior of the library can give dramatic effect to social media, website development, or other marketing approaches. Exciting possibilities exist at the crossroads of technology and imagination!

THE FUTURE OF DRONES IN LIBRARIES

What does the future hold for drones in libraries? As the technology becomes more advanced, so shall the uses. As Amazon and other retailers explore the use of drones for the delivery of packages, libraries are following suit. Villanova University has partnered with 3DR, the largest personal drone company in North America, to provide a drone delivery service directly tied to the university's library. Students living on campus can request a drone delivery of a book to their dorm room in 20 minutes. Employees at the university's Falvey Library speculate expanding the service to include interlibrary loan, where a student could request drone-delivered materials from another library (Dierkes, 2017).

One could easily see such a service further refined and applied to public libraries. In this context, libraries could utilize GPS navigation to deliver materials directly to a patron's home. An essential next step would include the ability to schedule the return of materials to the public library via drone. Indeed, drone delivery and return could provide essential, cost-effective service to our homebound patrons!

With the continued rise of AI and GPS technology, rolling drones in the library could take over the tasks of returning materials to the shelf, shelf reading with the use of RFID tagged materials. Taking that same technology another step forward, having AI help to manage and distribute materials that are bookmobile-based could make outreach more efficient. Drones currently assist in construction and inspection of buildings, so could drones help custodians and maintenance professionals in the maintenance of facilities? As USF has done with their lending program, libraries can make drones available for filmmaking, promotional videos and, while acting in conformity with FAA regulations, video large events.

Could the time come where the reference desk could be self-service? Consider a patron searching the digital catalog in the building. One of the biggest obstacles for patrons is understanding the Dewey decimal system versus the organization of the fiction collection. If a patron could ascertain that the book or other material is in the library, it could be imagined that the user clicks a retrieval button, and a drone (whether flying, rolling, or walking) uses RFID technology to locate and retrieve the material. The drone then meets the patron at the electronic catalog, authorizing the delivery with a scan of the patron's library card and delivering it to their hand.

Once viewed as a toy for hobbyists, drones are increasingly emerging as a useful tool for business, government, and individual use. Libraries will play an integral part in their development by providing education, access, and training to our communities, as well as incorporating them into our own business models. We can rest assured that the libraries of the future will embrace this technology, adapting it to best serve our unique communities.

THREE

Augmented Reality

Not quite reality, and not quite virtual reality, augmented reality is a form of technology that straddles both realms. Augmented reality, otherwise known as AR, is a technology that has existed in one form or another for quite some time. AR, generally speaking, is the combined use of a digital camera, a computer, a monitor, and the real world. The merging of these technologies can present the user, or viewer, with digitally created elements that *appear* to exist in our reality.

The best way to explain this, or to visualize it, would be to picture yourself having a nice, quiet walk in the park on a bright, sunny day. You look to your left, and there are children on bicycles, some dogs playing fetch, and a young couple having a picnic. Looking to your right, there is an ice cream truck with music blaring, and a passenger jet can be seen miles up in the sky. Absolutely none of this seems out of the ordinary.

Where things start to seem weird is the space directly in front of you. You think you might be going crazy, but you've spotted something peculiar. Could that be a living, breathing dinosaur? How is that even possible? We are currently in the early 21st century, and the dinosaurs died out millions of years ago!

You suddenly remember that you had actually been looking at our world through the screen of your smartphone. And it also dawns on you that you may have had your child's favorite app running. And then the most important realization of all sinks in—*That is no ordinary dinosaur.* That was actually a giant "Charmander," one of the many cartoony beasts found in the world of Nintendo's "Pokémon Go." That Charmander has been on the run, and it is up to you to capture it. With a quick flip on your finger on your smartphone screen, your Pokémon trainer has tossed a Poké Ball at Charmander and captured him—just a few inches from a tree where you would climb into the branches as a teen.

That giant dinosaur has been captured. Your stable of Pokémon has increased. No one around you in the park that day has witnessed any of this zaniness or that giant orange Charmander.

You've now experienced AR firsthand, and a popular video game has been your first introduction.

A BRIEF HISTORY OF AUGMENTED REALITY

For a sophisticated technology that can appear magical in its applications, AR can trace its conceptual roots back to the earliest parts of the 20th century. Like so many other technologies that have come to fruition and have benefited humankind, such as the submarine (Jules Verne) or the space satellite (Arthur C. Clarke), a primordial seed of AR was planted in the 1901 work of L. Frank Baum, *The Master Key*. In this work, Baum described a technology that can determine the characteristics of a person *simply by looking at them.* A boy in this work is told that a magic pair of spectacles will help him discern the true nature of a person. The example presented is that of "deception"—people often pretend to have good nature when they, in fact, do not. Some people appear to be wise when, in reality, they are foolish. In *The Master Key*, these electrically powered spectacles will show a letter on the forehead of whomever the boy looks at. Good people will have the letter "G" displayed on their forehead, while those who are evil will have the letter "E" displayed on theirs. (Norman, n.d.). It is pretty clear that spectacles such as these would be absolutely helpful for any human being who interacts with others. Wouldn't it be great to know the true nature of someone you are interacting with?

It is easy for a person in the 21st century to visualize how this system would work. Many of us have already seen science fiction movies or even TV advertisements with similar concepts on display. This is because some people in the late 20th century, who had access to highly expensive electronics and computing equipment, began to actually craft objects that could create ARs.

Between the publishing of *The Master Key* in 1901 and the late 20th century, there were additional conceptual designs, writings, mock-ups, and even working machines that seemed close to, but not quite, what we deem AR to be today. It wasn't until the work of Thomas P. Caudell and David W. Mizell that the modern implementation of AR was born.

In 1992, while working for aerospace engineering and plane manufacturer Boeing, Caudell and Mizell drafted a technical paper explaining how a technology coined "Augmented Reality" could aid in aircraft manufacturing. Entitled "Augmented Reality: An Application of Heads-Up Display Technology to Manual Manufacturing Processes," this work detailed exactly how a computerized display affixed to the head of an aircraft engineer could help them to streamline the complex task of assembling a Boeing 747 jet (Caudell & Mizell, 1992). In their own words, Caudell and Mizell hoped they could basically make a wearable computer screen, and all of its important engineering information readily portable and viewable. They worked to "introduce technology to provide this access. The general concept is to provide a 'see-thru' virtual reality goggles to the factory worker, and to use this device to augment the worker's visual field of view with useful and dynamically changing information" (Caudell & Mizell, 1992, p. 660).

An experimental example that they offered in 1992, which is something easily reproduced today, was to have an engineer wear an AR headset and roam inside of an under-construction 747 airplane. The engineer would spot a section of the plane that still needed work completed. An arrow would point to a beam and indicate that a hole needed to be drilled in that exact location. A text box would appear above that arrow and denote exactly what size drill bit should be used and to what depth the hole should go. All of this would only be viewable to the engineer and within their AR headset. And what if the engineer moved their head slightly? The software powering the AR headset would track six degrees of motion to ensure that the drill bit hole never drifted in the engineer's view. The software would constantly correct the view so that it was accurate. The headset would be tethered to a computer in order to power both the headset hardware and software that would make this all possible.

In essence, this was the first time that computer hardware, software, spatial analysis, and human beings were all incorporated into one system to accomplish a task. The fundamentals of Caudell and Mizell's concept were very strong. In fact, the version of AR headset hardware that we see today is *extremely* similar to the setup that was envisioned by Caudell and Mizell. They had basically forged the path that AR continues to navigate.

In the years that followed, many people in various fields began to understand and appreciate the potential applications for AR. Areas such as medicine, archeology, military usage, engineering, and myriad other disciplines started to come up with ways AR could aid a researcher in completing a task far more competently, and in a far quicker manner. However, in almost all of these areas, cost was still a major barrier to implementation.

As costs for computing hardware declined and computing power increased, AR became far more feasible for everyday use. It was when costs had become low enough for everyday consumers to begin to purchase AR equipment, or devices that could perform AR functions, that this technology began to literally appear in the pockets and purses of people all around the world (Flanagan, 2018).

HOW DOES AUGMENTED REALITY WORK?

To best understand and demystify the technology of AR, it is important to explain its underpinnings. The technology has come a long way from its conceptual design by Caudell and Mizell in 1992. While the fundamentals of their concept are still intact, the methods by which these concepts have become "actual reality" are notable and should be dissected. For the purposes of libraries and the introduction of AR to that environment, it is worth stating that in no way should library staff or patrons be expected to know the most minute details of this technology or how it functions in order to best enjoy it. With that being said, it is always important to know the fundamentals of how a device functions so that it can be easily explained and demonstrated to others.

AR is, in a small sense, an umbrella term used to best describe four basic ways computer-generated imagery is presented to a user. Depending on the purpose of the application, one of these four methods will prove to be most effective at achieving the best user experience for the software that is powering the application.

One form of AR is achieved through a system called "marker-based augmented reality." In this method, a unique visual marker is placed on a real-world, physical object. This marker could be something as simple as a sticker. What is important is that the marker itself is complex and unique. This is to ensure that the marker will not be confused by AR software with other objects in the background of the scene. In many cases, these markers may be, or may resemble, QR codes. These codes are similar in concept to barcodes, but far more complex. Like barcodes, they come in a number of varieties and can store differing amounts of data, depending on the form of QR code utilized ("What Is a QR Code?" n.d.). Once this marker is "seen" by a piece of AR hardware, the software powering that application may then place a virtual object onto a display screen to replace the sticker. The user is able to move their AR device around and movement is likely tracked in the AR software via GPS, accelerometers, or solid-state compasses.

A second form of AR is "markerless augmented reality." In this form of AR, a device is able to "look" at a scene and place virtual objects on to the device display ("What Is Augmented Reality?" n.d.). As the user moves the AR device, the virtual objects remain statically placed. In AR uses such as this, the software and hardware powering the device are able to discern unique objects in a scene and use those as spatial foundations for placement of the virtual object. Basically, the device is able to see objects in a scene that can act as QR codes for the AR software. As a user moves the device, accelerometers, gyroscopes, and other pieces of support hardware will work to analyze that motion and maintain the virtual object in static placement on the scene.

Another form of AR has been successfully created that allows a user to interact with their physical environment and cause the AR software to respond accordingly. This method of AR is known as "Projection Based" ("What Is Augmented Reality?" n.d.). For this particular application, a device will project light onto a surface or object. This pattern can be simple or complicated—all that matters is that it can be cleanly and clearly seen by the device that is responsible for running the AR software. A user will then interact with the light being projected, and that interaction is monitored by the AR device.

One of the first, and most striking, examples of this was the creation of a virtual computer keyboard. In this application, a device was able to project an image of a computer keyboard on to a flat surface. The keyboard had exactly the same layout as a standard, QWERTY keyboard. A user could then take their fingers and place them on this virtual keyboard and begin typing. The AR hardware would track where the user was placing their fingers on the virtual keyboard and translate those "keystrokes" into input. The characters on the keyboard that user pressed were then displayed on a computer screen as user input. In short, this device eliminated the need for a physical keyboard—the user could project a virtual keyboard on to any surface, such as a table or wall and begin typing.

The final form of AR is "superimposition based augmented reality" ("What Is Augmented Reality?" n.d.). In this particular instance of AR, a portable device, such as a cell phone screen or tablet, is used to survey an area. The device will use its camera to instantly convey the layout of an area to the user via the device screen. The depiction is 100 percent accurate—it is simply a "video feed" of the area. AR software can then start placing objects or manipulating the scene that is visible to the user on the device screen.

One of the best ways to present this form of AR to a user, in a way in which they will instantly understand the usefulness of AR, is through a specialized app for smartphones and tablets to help consumers shop for residential furniture. The international furniture retailer, IKEA, has created its own AR application based around this exact form of AR. With this app, which is quite astonishing to experience in person, a user can shop for IKEA brand furniture using their mobile device or tablet. What makes this experience truly engaging is the ability to then model furniture in your living or office space using AR. Shoppers are able to activate the app on their device and then begin to survey a room. The app will take some initial measurements and ask the user to move their device around—usually requiring them to point their device's camera at certain locations. This allows the app to properly calibrate itself and determine the size of a room, with a level of precision that is uncanny. From there, the user can import 3D rendered furniture models in to the software and visualize them on the device screen. They can place the objects in the room, virtually. The app ensures that the scale of the object is properly preserved and is a true representation of how the piece of furniture will look in a given space. The effect is as astonishing as it is useful. This particular application will be discussed later, since it is an excellent way to demonstrate AR to those who are unfamiliar with the technology or are skeptical of its potential applications.

USING AUGMENTED REALITY IN THE LIBRARY

Once the basic fundamentals are understood, it does not take much imagination to discover creative ways AR can be introduced to a library setting. Access to AR has, potentially, a very low barrier to entry. On the low end of access requirements—meaning device cost—relatively inexpensive tablets can provide AR functionality. Many patrons may already possess devices, such as smartphones, that allow them to access AR applications. On the higher end of access requirements, devices such as Microsoft's HoloLens can provide library patrons and staff with a window into advanced AR applications.

As we will demonstrate, there are various ways AR can be incorporated into the daily functions of a library. This technology can be used as a tool for patrons to navigate your library. AR programming and events can be used to meet the educational and recreational needs of your community. Even literary materials are now available that implement AR as a way to enrich a reader's experience and make content, whether fictional or nonfictional, be engaging on a level that has not been available in the past.

The next few segments of this chapter will detail ways your library can provide these AR experiences by explaining which equipment, media, software, and other materials are recommended for use.

Technology Items You Will Need to Support AR in Your Library

In order to provide an AR experience for community members, some simple pieces of electronics and computing hardware will be required. With a relatively small budget, hardware can be acquired that will allow users to experience basic AR functionality. As an alternative, many of the devices that support AR may already be owned by members of your community and can reduce the financial overhead required to support AR initiatives by your library. Often, this is referred to as "bring your own device," or "BYOD" for short. As an added bonus for libraries with limited budgets, many of the software applications (apps) that are available to showcase AR are free or extremely low-cost. This combination of factors can make the introduction of AR in your library quite appealing.

In order to support AR in your library, computing hardware of some sort will be required to power the software that runs AR applications. For the purposes of this guidebook, these tiers will be divided into two levels—low and high.

The "Low Tier" of Augmented Reality Devices

Google Android

The introductory, or low tier, of AR-supporting hardware can be centered around the use of Google Android operating system tablets and Apple iOS iPads. For libraries that wish to purchase their own devices so that they can be used for event programming, they will have to secure devices that run a specific version of an Android or iOS operating system or higher.

For example, Google has released a software development kit that allows computer programmers to make software that can incorporate basic AR functions. In order for this software to work properly, devices must be running Google Android operating system version 8.0 or higher. It is important to note—and this may seem a little bit confusing—not all devices that are running that version of Android may be fully able to support AR software. To aid consumers, Google has posted a chart detailing which devices fully support AR and the version of Android that must be installed for the software to work. That chart is available at: https://developers.google.com/ar/discover/supported-devices. Generally speaking, Android tablets that have enough computing (or CPU) power and have the required operating system installed to run AR applications may cost several hundred dollars.

The Google Android operating system is fairly widespread, especially as it is used to power many popular smartphones. It is for this reason that many libraries may think about promoting AR events and services by relying on the fact that community members may own these devices already. With that being said, it is extremely critical to note that community members in your area may still be utilizing devices that are several years old. If your library decides to host a library event that focuses on AR, it will be absolutely essential to note the operating system version requirement. As many of our community members are not always "tech savvy," which is one of the primary reasons libraries host technology events (as a means to educate), be sure to mention this requirement in event promotional materials. It will also be critical to inform library staff of this limitation. Perhaps the most helpful thing that can be done to alleviate problems and library patron frustration is to train staff and patrons on how to determine which version of the Android OS they are currently running.

Apple iOS Smartphones and Tablets

Another perfect example of a "low tier" cost device is those created by Apple Computer, such as the Apple iPad tablet. With regard to cost, Apple iPad devices that support AR apps start at a little over $300 (at the time of this writing). These new devices have full support for AR applications right out of the box. The operating system that powers these devices, as well as the main CPU that drives the hardware, are all rated to support AR.

Like Google, Apple has worked hard to embrace AR and to provide resources for app developers. These resources ensure that the AR apps created for iOS devices are polished and run well on supported Apple hardware. If your library has older Apple iPads in possession, of if your library plans on using BYOD as a means for support AR initiatives, it will be important to note the hardware and software requirements that you must meet. According to Apple, AR is supported on devices that are running iOS version 11 or higher. Apple devices must also have an A9 processor or later ("isSupported," n.d.).

Be aware that individual AR apps may require higher versions of iOS than version 11. Apple has been known to limit the installation of iOS upgrades to newer hardware only. For instance, an older iPad may only be able to upgrade to iOS 11, while brand new iPads can update to iOS 12 and beyond. At some point, apps may no longer be supported on this older version of iOS, and you will be forced to purchase new hardware in order to run those apps.

For those looking for the lowest cost Apple device offering to support AR, look no further than their recently refreshed iPod touch line. These devices are extremely similar to their iPhone line of products but have lower-speed CPUs and lack cell phone capability, in an effort to keep costs low. As of this writing, devices are available from apple.com for as low as $199. These devices may be popular among tweens and teens. Parents often buy these devices because they do not allow cell phone access, but they can still run popular apps and have functional cameras.

The "High Tier" of Augmented Reality Devices

For libraries that have larger technology and programming budgets, there are some forms of AR hardware available that can certainly be considered "high tier." These are AR devices that are specialized and may require an entire desktop computer in order to properly power them. These devices support higher-resolution AR graphics and 3D model presentation. They may be able to provide users with much more precise camera tracking and environment analysis. In some sense, consumer-level devices that fall under this category can be considered the "cutting edge" of AR devices.

Microsoft HoloLens

When it comes to showcasing AR and its potential real-world applications, few devices are as stunning as the recent offerings from Microsoft. Several years ago, Microsoft made a splash when they revealed their "mixed-reality" HoloLens project. They had coined a new term to describe this experience, but it certainly falls under the umbrella of AR experiences.

In its effort to utilize AR, this device functions a bit differently from offerings from companies such as Google and Apple. For Microsoft's HoloLens hardware, users are asked to put on a set of glasses. These glasses are highly specialized, however. For Microsoft's latest iteration of their product, HoloLens 2, all of the necessary computing hardware is located in the glasses/headset. The unit is entirely self-contained. The headset has all the necessary computing power to drive the software for AR and perform renderings of any 3D objects. The glasses themselves are a bit unique. They are composed of glass that does not obstruct the user's view of the environment. Amazingly, computer-generated imagery can then be projected onto the glasses. For this arrangement, only the user wearing the headset can see any of the AR aspects.

The HoloLens 2 hardware is able to provide a level of immersion that is not currently available or easily possible with the "low tier" forms of AR. The HoloLens headset is completely untethered, so the user does not need to connect to any personal computer in order to power the graphics that are displayed. The headset has integrated headphones so that audio can be clearly heard by the user. There is a built-in microphone that can recognize voice commands. The unit has cameras that can monitor the user's eye movement to facilitate something known as "eye tracking." Eye tracking can help the software determine where the user is looking and "highlight" objects, or make them easier to interact with.

Finally, Microsoft has improved upon one of the biggest complaints about the previous HoloLens hardware: user hand interaction. After listening to feedback, Microsoft has worked hard to make the interaction between users and virtual objects displayed on HoloLens more intuitive. The software can now spot normal human gestures and determine what the user is trying to do. For instance, HoloLens can now easily see users reaching for objects and attempting to spin, resize, or relocate them. The software will make rendering adjustments accordingly.

And the reason this device is considered "high tier"? The price. Microsoft has been slow to roll out this hardware, and purchasing equipment has to be done directly through Microsoft sales staff. According to the latest information, as of this writing, HoloLens 2 hardware is expected to cost $3,500 when it is finally released (Weinberger & Shontell, 2019).

Magic Leap One

Another vendor has recently released hardware that is geared entirely toward supporting AR apps: Magic Leap. The company's first product had been in development for some time. In fact, the development process took so long that many had feared that the product was "vaporware"—essentially something that would never be released (Meyer, 2017). After several rounds of funding from Google, the Chinese funding group and technology conglomerate Alibaba, communications company AT&T, and a strategic partnership with Disney's Lucasfilm, the company has basically turned a corner (Kharpal, 2018).

Magic Leap has also hired a number of individuals to give the organization some "star power." The ranks of the company include famed science fiction author Neal Stephenson as the "Chief Futurist" (Mlot, 2014). Richard Taylor, from the famed motion picture special effects studio WETA, praised for its work on the film version of *The Lord of the Rings*, has joined the company. Rounding out this list of intriguing staff members is Graeme Devine, a significant figure in the video game development community (Hollister, 2014).

Recently, Magic Leap unveiled its AR headset, known as the Magic Leap One Creator Edition. Selling for $2,295, this version of the product includes the headset and a few vital accessories. Reviews of this product have been mixed, and a visit to the main product page reveals that there is only a limited amount of software available to showcase this piece of hardware. With that being said, this particular product is promising and may improve with time. It is surely something that those interested in AR should keep track of.

Google Glass Enterprise Edition 2

Not to be outdone, Google has announced a successor to its first and second forays into the AR product space. Its first product, Google Glass, was a bit of a curiosity. It was the company's first attempt at creating an AR headset, and the device could occasionally be seen on commuters on subways and buses and on pedestrians walking down the street. However, it was a bit of a rarity. The combination of cost and lack of software doomed this initial product to commercial failure.

Interestingly (and very surprisingly), Google has announced another follow-up in its AR product line and has called it "Google Glass Enterprise

Edition 2." This product features a number of refinements, including a new processor to run more robust software, better camera quality for tracking, a USB-C connector for faster charging, and increased battery life, and the frame of the headset allows for replacement of the glass lenses with prescription lenses or safety lenses. The software powering this device is Android OS-based, with the hopes that this will allow for easier software development (Fingas, 2019). All indications are that these glasses will, as the name implies, specifically target enterprise clients, with usage in places such as warehouses, factories, and shop floors. With that being said, the hardware is a notable improvement from its predecessors, and fans of AR should also stay alert to any news items surrounding this device.

STAFF TRAINING

For any of the technology items mentioned in this work, staff training will always be the key to organization-wide adoption of that specific tech item and to the successful launch of AR programming and events. In the case of AR, the technology can be a bit bewildering, and the key to having staff embrace this technology will be through simple exposure.

Effective staff training will likely require multiple phases to fully introduce AR. After that, staff should observe and participate in library events and programming. Repeat trainings may be needed and, if possible, should be actively pursued. An ideal end goal for staff training should be the creation of an environment in which all staff are comfortable explaining a certain technology in layman's terms to library visitors. Even better, staff should be presenting new ideas or software that utilizes AR to other staff.

Layers of Training

In order to reach a positive outcome with staff training, libraries should first have one or two key staff members that are basically the early adopters of a certain technology. These staff will become evangelists who, once comfortable with a technology, can begin to explain and demonstrate that technology to others.

In order to empower your "tech evangelists," you need a few key ingredients. First, libraries should absolutely be willing to provide staff with time off of service desks so they can simply experiment with new technologies for a few hours. Giving staff the "head space" to explore a new technology and understand its underpinnings, without having to focus on customer service tasks at service areas, will allow them to better understand and absorb the intricacies of the new technology they are experimenting with. Libraries may consider buying one piece of hardware, such as a tablet, to give staff the physical resources they need to install AR applications. If budget is an issue, libraries should encourage staff to bring their own devices to work to experiment with.

Once your "tech evangelists" have become familiar with AR and have selected some applications that may best showcase the technology, they should prepare to give brief demonstrations to other staff members. During this brief demo, tech evangelists should describe the underpinnings of the technology in layman's terms to their colleagues. From there, they should simply demonstrate one or two applications, and those applications should be simple.

In the realm of AR, two applications that work especially well in showcasing the technology include the IKEA furniture application and the Pokémon Go game. Those particular applications will be explained in further detail later in this chapter. What is particularly ideal about one of those applications is that it is fun, popular, engaging, and game-based. Many staff may easily identify and understand how AR is enhancing the experience. The other app is extremely utilitarian but readily apparent in its usefulness. The ability to instantly place furniture in a room and to immediately see if it will fit or not, and if the color choices are correct, is something that should wow staff.

Be sure to invite library administration to training events like this. Once they see and understand the true impact of AR, it will be far easier to get buy-in from them when it comes time to ask for newer, more expensive equipment, expand technology budgets, or secure more staffing hours to facilitate programs based around AR.

Once you've completed some staff-wide training in a fun, low-pressure learning environment, you should see positive results. Any staff members who were at that meeting will now have a very basic understanding of AR, how it works, what it looks like, and the types of devices it can run on. This is going to be critical—these are likely the staff members who are working at service desks or your main circulation desks. After you've taken the plunge and started to run some library workshops based around AR, these are the staff members whom library patrons will approach and bluntly ask, "What the heck is that AR program about?" Instead of staff responding, "I have no clue," they will be able to explain the technology in simple terms and talk about the fun they had shopping at IKEA or catching Pokémon. In a way, your frontline staff may find this knowledge empowering. Your tech evangelists will still be the ones who can explain these technologies more in-depth or showcase more advanced apps.

There is a middle layer of staff who are, perhaps, going to be the most important. These are the staff members who will be genuinely excited about this new technology. These are the staff members who sometimes surprise you by being the very last whom you would expect to embrace something new. For the most part, these will be the key staff in helping a library to introduce a new technology to the community.

It is vital that this middle layer of staff be given tools, resources, and direction in your library's pursuit of AR programming and other initiatives. These are the staff members who will be leading seminars, workshops, and researching changes and improvements in AR. They will be the ones who will come running, excitedly in to your office to tell you about the latest AR tech that was showcased at the consumer electronics show or about a cool new AR app that was just released. Be sure to support these staff members. Allow them to run workshops that best suit their own personal styles. Do they like standing up, talking, and giving seminars? Great! Are they nervous about public speaking and prefer to sit with half a dozen patrons, huddled around devices? Great! Again, these will be the staff who are vital in best explaining technology to members of your community. With perseverance, these staff will also start to build a following among library patrons, and you can expect these patrons to return to future workshops, whether they are focused on AR or other exciting technology areas.

Using Fun, Quirky, and Utilitarian Augmented Reality Apps to Train Staff

As previously explained, in order for your library staff to fully embrace AR as a technology to share with the community, it will be vital to showcase many of AR's "killer apps." These are going to be simple, straightforward apps that are easy to understand and have an immediate effect on the staff member. In practice, a healthy combination of gaming, quirky, utilitarian, and just downright cool apps should be demonstrated for staff, as one of those particular apps will be sure to "click" with a certain staff member's personal interest.

For basic staff training and demonstration of AR, some of the apps discussed below may prove to be most effective.

Pokémon Go

Pokémon Go is an AR-based game that incorporates characters from the much-loved Nintendo Pokémon gaming franchise. While almost all previous video games with Pokémon characters have sold extremely well, the popularity of this game skyrocketed after its release. It was available at launch for free on Apple iOS and, later, Google Android.

In some ways, this game was the first "killer app" for AR. By making AR the key way to interact and participate in the game, it forced Pokémon fans to quickly embrace this technology. Since the game was both fun and addicting, people who had no awareness of the Pokémon craze soon became fans.

The basis of this game is simple—collect Pokémon. These cute creatures often take the shape of dinosaurs, fish, turtles, and all sorts of fun animals, but with a fantastical and whimsical twist. In order to catch Pokémon, users have to take out their smartphones, launch the Pokémon Go app and then look at their screen. They will see their actual environment. As the user walks around, their phone may vibrate, indicating that a Pokémon is close by. The user then sweeps their phone either left or right and they may "discover" a Pokémon immediately next to them—standing on a sidewalk, on a lawn, in the water, pretty much anywhere! The user will then swipe up with their finger on the phone screen to toss a Poké Ball at the Pokémon and attempt to capture it. There is more depth to this addictive game—it involves training Pokémon and growing them in to larger creatures—but the basics are enough to hook people (Dayus, 2016).

In a smart marketing move, Niantic (the game's developer and publisher) declared this game a fantastic way for people to get exercise. They encouraged users to get outside and walk around their neighborhoods looking for Pokémon. For a short period of time, it was not unusual to see kids, tweens, teens, adults, and even seniors walking around their neighborhoods and squealing excitedly when a Pokémon was captured. The ease of playing this game, its colorful graphics, and the high range of smartphone hardware it will work on ensures that this game can be easily demonstrated for library staff.

Google Translate

When contemplating the perfect app for use in demonstrating the power of AR and how it can be used in real-world applications, look no further than Google's Translate app. When properly showcased for library staff, this software application will appear to be like a science fiction tool straight out of *Star Trek*.

The premise for the Google Translate App is relatively simple—Google provides access to dozens and dozens of spoken languages to users, for free (Zibreg, 2017). This app allows users to access these language dictionaries through the internet, or to even download the dictionaries on to their smartphone or tablet device for later use. The ability to download these dictionaries makes the app perfect for traveling. In execution, the app is extremely simple to use, as well. It will allow users to type in text and it will translate it to another language. Fans of this application were excited when Google added the ability to speak a language in to a device microphone and have the app translate it on the fly. This was also extremely useful for travelers—you could hold your smartphone up in the air with the microphone on and instantly translate what a waiter may be saying in a restaurant, or understand what a taxi driver had indicated, or find someone to help with travel directions.

Google took this app even one step further, and the results have been absolutely amazing. Several years ago, Google added a "camera" icon to the app, just below where a user would type in text to be translated. When this feature is activated, the app will suddenly open up the smartphone or tablet camera feature and prompt the user to point their device at a sign, menu, book, or other printed text. Seemingly like magic, the app will then translate that text into the desired language. Simply put, if you are in a foreign country's railroad station, and you are looking for the restroom, you can point your Google Translate app at the various signage in the building, and it will quickly change all the text into your native language (and much to your relief!).

It goes without saying that this particular use of AR will immediately demonstrate its real-world importance to staff.

Google Image Search

At this point in time, it is clear that Google has been working hard to integrate AR technology in to many of its other services. Part of the reasoning behind this is to showcase the technology offerings of Google's

Android operating system and supported hardware, as well as to stay one step ahead of Apple, Microsoft, and other competing technology. The latest step in this showcasing of AR technology has been the introduction of "View in 3D" to their Google Search functionality (Liptak, 2019b).

The implementation, so far, is pretty basic. If users search for certain, specific animals, such as "wolf," Google will return with its normal results listing. You may see some wolf photos, links to the Wikipedia page on "wolves," and even pages talking about wolf studies or news items. In addition to that is now a 3D model of a wolf and a button saying "View in 3D." Clicking that button will present the user with a 3D model of a generic wolf. The user can zoom in, zoom out, and rotate the model to see if from multiple angles. On devices that support AR, an "AR" button is now present at the top of the device screen. Clicking on that icon opens up the device's camera, and the 3D model of the animal then appears in your room or outdoor area. You can reposition the animal in the real world, and it should maintain the proper scaling (see figure 3.1). You can "wow" library staff by showing them just how big a wolf is compared to your library's reference desk!

Although, again, this is a new functionality and pretty basic, it is extremely accessible and doesn't require the installation of any additional apps. This particular functionality could be a fun and educational way to introduce kids in a children's library to various animals and also to AR technology.

IKEA Place App

As was previously teased earlier in this work, a fantastic AR app for smartphones and tablets, which wonderfully showcases the utilitarian usefulness of AR for staff, is the IKEA Place app ("IKEA Place Augmented Reality App," n.d.). Make no mistake about it, this app was solely created by IKEA to help sell furniture—but IKEA's use of AR to help consumers make smart purchasing decisions is certainly cutting edge.

The fact that this app will work on any newer Apple iOS or Google Android device ensures that many of your staff may already have the hardware necessary to give this piece a software a test drive on their own. Compounding that with the app's extremely streamlined and intuitive interface (again, this app was made for making the process of purchasing furniture as simple as possible) means that library staff will be able to start using this app very quickly. Most importantly, they will likely run home

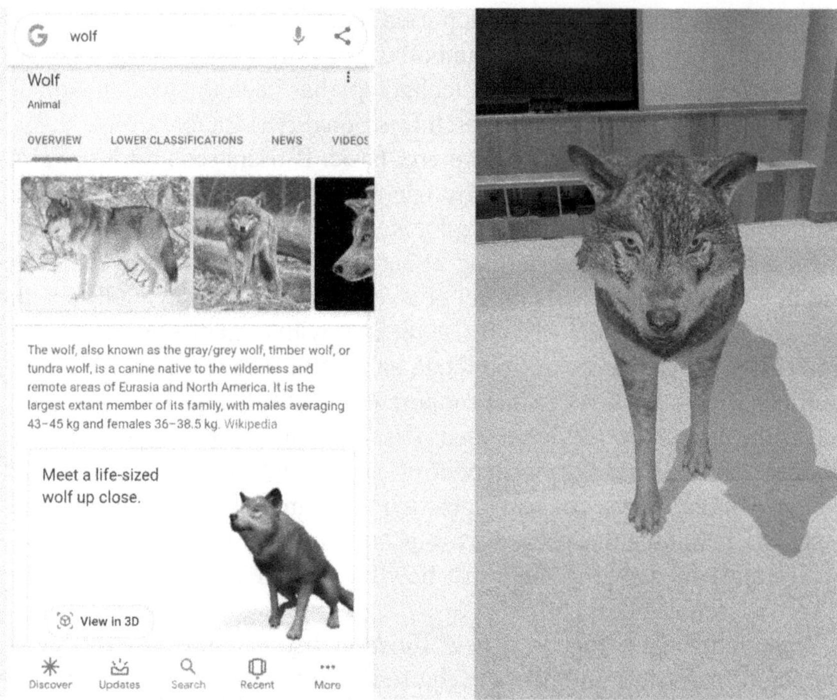

Figure 3.1 A Google search for "wolf" gives the option to place an augmented reality wolf within a library space. Google and the Google logo are registered trademarks of Google LLC, used with permission.

and want to demonstrate it for their families. That aspect alone makes this a perfect training tool.

The app works very simply. After installing the application, the user is prompted by a quick greeting, and then their device's camera screen should open up. Depending on the flooring in your room and the lighting, the app may prompt you to move your device around and scan sections of the floor. That will aid the application in understanding the layout of your space. It's a very quick process and it is amazing the amount of "AR software voodoo" that is happening behind the scenes to make this aspect of configuring the app so quick. At that point, the IKEA catalog should open up on your device screen, and you can begin to select different pieces of furniture to showcase.

As you select various pieces of furniture and colors of items, you can instantly start placing them into your room, virtually speaking. Items are placed on the phone screen, and, using your finger, you can move them to different areas of your room and move them closer or farther away from you. You can also rotate the items. The best way to summarize or to demonstrate this would be to start with a completely empty room and place objects such as a kitchen table, kitchen chairs, a new lamp and other items in to the space. In a few quick seconds, you will have created a fully decorated area. You can walk around the room with your smartphone or tablet in front of you, and the furniture objects will stay put. This allows you to examine your own space from multiple angles and see furniture layouts from multiple perspectives. It is truly remarkable to experience this app in person.

MERGE Cube and the Dig! App

Often, AR applications may require unique pieces of hardware to accompany them. This is exactly the case with the MERGE cube. At first, the cube can be a bit puzzling in appearance. It is clear that it is cleverly designed to serve some sort of function. Once the software component is launched and utilized with the MERGE cube, some extremely astonishing AR magic becomes quickly apparent.

What is unique about the MERGE Cube is how mysteriously conspicuous it appears. It is a black cube covered in strange markings and, to the casual observer, it would be hard to tell that it has any sort of technology implications ("AR/VR Learning & Creation," n.d.). In reality, the markings on the cube almost serve as QR codes (otherwise known as Quick Response Codes), which are unique identifiers that camera-based software on smartphones and tablets can recognize. These QR codes are highly specific, can be easily user generated, and typically take smartphone users to informational websites. In the case of the MERGE Cube, all six sides of the cube are covered in these unique markings. Any apps written to use the MERGE Cube platform can recognize these proprietary codes and tell what side of the cube is facing the smartphone camera. As a person holds this cube in the air and moves it in their hands, the MERGE Cube software recognizes the cube codes and knows to manipulate a rendered object on the screen accordingly.

A fun way to demonstrate the MERGE Cube for staff can be through the use of their free "Dig!" app ("Dig! for Merge Cube," n.d.). It is hard to deny that this game carries a passing resemblance to the insanely popular game Minecraft. The Dig! App uses a very similar art style. In this particular game, the MERGE Cube acts as a tiny world—almost like a

Figure 3.2 An in-progress building session featuring the MERGE Cube and Dig! app. Copyright of Merge Labs, Inc. All rights reserved.

miniature planet—that rests in your hands. As the user, you are able to modify the terrain of the planet using small pixelated blocks. These blocks represent a variety of art styles and characteristics. Some of the blocks look like stone, some look like grass, some like tree bark, and others like tree leaves (see figure 3.2). Overall, the aesthetic is very "Minecraft-like," with users creating castles and homes on their tiny worlds, built out of even smaller cubes.

What should hopefully resonate with staff when they play with this app is how they can move the cube around in front of a tablet or smartphone screen and see their creation from every possible angle. Some portions of the world are even animated—objects like water will flow across the surface. This game should be easy for anyone to pick up and play with and should generate some instant smiles from staff experimenting with it.

Instagram and Snapchat Face Filters

One final way to showcase AR is through a means so popular that there is an excellent chance that many of your staff have already experienced it—social media selfie photo filters. In recent years, the popularity of social media photo sharing sites, such as Instagram and Snapchat have absolutely exploded. These sites allow users to "follow" or "friend" each other and share photos taken on their smartphones or tablets. While many use this service to share everything from vacation pictures to photos of their adored pets, other users share images of themselves taken through the front-facing camera on their device. This is otherwise known as a "selfie."

Selfies are indeed one of the most utilized features of these social media apps, and it is very common to see selfies that celebrities have taken on news or gossip websites. As a way to innovate in this area, social media platforms have begun implementing AR as a way to add stylistic, artistic, creative, or simply silly flair to selfie images. As these apps are free to use and download, and many staff members may already have them, demonstrating that the AR-enhanced selfie mode can be extremely entertaining.

The basic implementation of AR selfies is pretty straightforward. A user will pick up their device, launch a social media platform such as Instagram or Snapchat, and then put the app in to selfie mode for the purposes of taking a photo. From there, the user can select effects that will be immediately rendered in 3D, on the device screen, through the use of the front-facing camera. As of this writing, Instagram has added some interesting filters. Some of these filters darken the scene in real-time, but add a rainbow across the face of the person taking a selfie. One selfie converts the user's face in to a bunny rabbit, with ears that flop and other flourishes that happen in real-time. Another will convert the camera's view to black and white and then add lipstick and a beret with veil over the subject's head—whether they are male or female! In a similar vein, Snapchat has added a selfie filter that will gender-swap subjects. It can attempt to make males look more feminine in appearance or vice-versa. In some ways, that particular selfie mode had created interesting topics regarding gender and gender representation on social media. All of these AR-based selfie filters are fun to use and extremely accessible.

AUGMENTED REALITY PROGRAMS AND EVENTS

The introduction of a seemingly "magical" technology, such as AR, can provide a perfect opportunity for your library to provide information, instruction, and demonstration of something new and exciting. Thankfully, there are many simple ways to demonstrate AR to your library patrons, and that can be accomplished with some easy-to-use tools.

"What Is Augmented Reality?" Performing a Lecture-Style Presentation for Patrons

Through use of an Apple iOS or Google Android device, such as a smartphone or tablet, library staff can demonstrate the uses of AR firsthand. In order to best showcase this technology, it would be ideal to have your device be fully loaded with apps, and talking to a "casting" device, which is attached to a TV or Projector via an HDMI connection. If your library has Apple products, such as iPads or iPhones / iPods, you will need an Apple TV (as low as $149, as of this writing). If your library is using Google Android devices, you will likely need a Google Chromecast (as low as $35, as of this writing) to display the content from your device screen on a larger TV or Projector. Basically, you want to be able to have AR apps running on your device, with everything you are doing being fully viewable to your audience, through the use of a large TV or projector. These casting devices are the critical piece that can make that happen.

For the purposes of teaching library patrons, it is recommended to rely on easily findable tech, such as smartphones and tablets. You would not want to run a workshop that would require technology that is unique, rare, or fragile—for instance, a Google Glass device. Again, it would be wise to stick to the more common devices that support AR, just so patrons can likely return home and start playing with the apps that you have just demonstrated.

In addition, the use of readily available tech, such as an Apple or Android smartphone means that there is likely a wealth of software already available for download. Much of it is free, further reducing the cost barriers to experience this technology.

In terms of actually laying out a space for doing a presentation, demonstration, or a "hands-on playground" (where users bring their own devices), you have a number of options to consider.

The first option is pretty standard—audience-style seating (see figure 3.3). With this layout, a room is set up with audience-style seating, consisting of rows and rows of chairs in the rear of the room. In the front of the room, a presenter will stand with a device. Ideally, that device will also be linked up to a TV or projector, either through a physical connection or by "casting" the device screen onto that display. This layout is best suited for libraries that may be wishing to pack as many attendees as possible in to an event. It should be noted that this layout will not leave much room for attendees to test out these apps with our own devices, should they decide to bring them to the lecture or discussion.

A slightly modified option will allow library staff to perform a lecture or demonstration for attendees, but it will also give patrons a space to try out their own devices (see figure 3.4). In this arrangement, chairs are laid around the periphery of a space. The presenter will be at the front of the room and will be linked up to a TV or projector, either through the use of

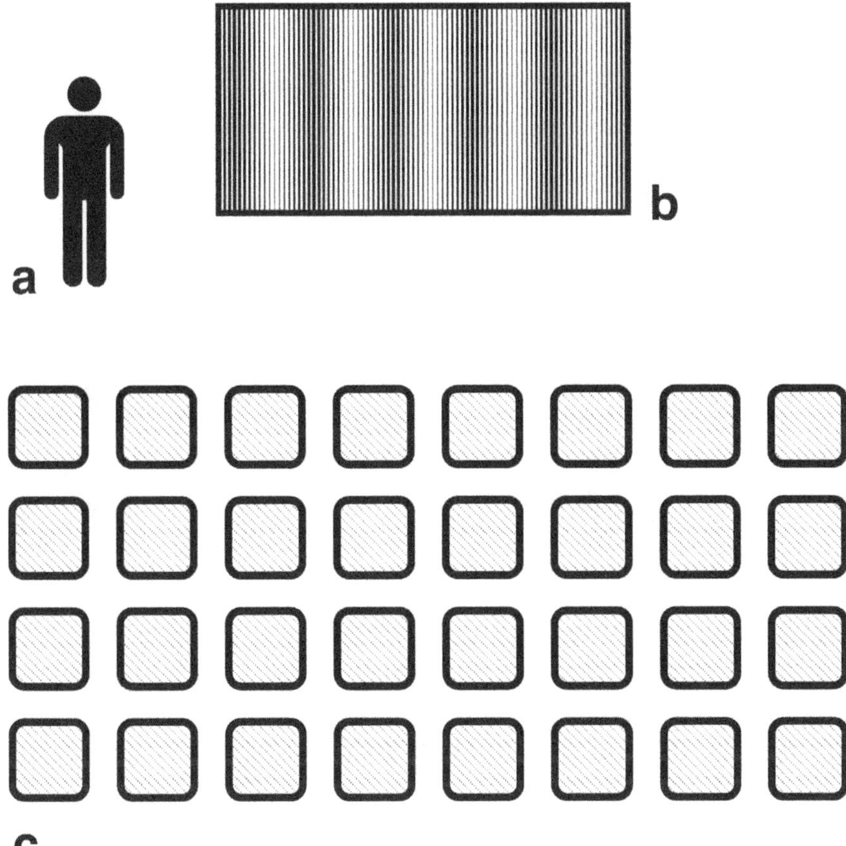

Figure 3.3 AR Lecture Class Setup. a - Presenter with smartphone/tablet AR device. Presenter may be showing content on screen via PowerPoint. b - TV or projected screen to display AR content or PowerPoint content. c - Audience members, seated and facing screen.

a cable or by casting the device. The center of the room is largely open. This gives the presenter some space to showcase apps that may require quite a bit of movement and walking around. This layout also gives attendees their own physical space to test drive an AR app right in front of them. The only downside to this layout is that much of your space is intentionally left open and this limits how many people can attend or participate in your program.

One additional option, which can be quite a bit of fun, is to host an AR demonstration outside. The advantage to this setting is that many AR apps

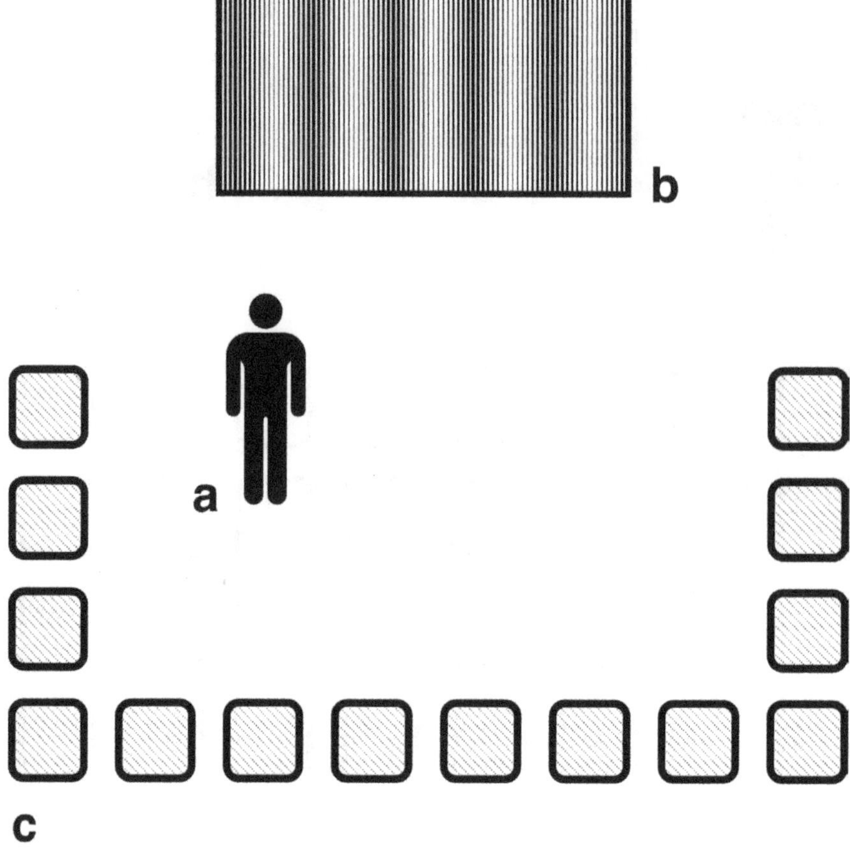

Figure 3.4 AR Class with Audience Participation. a - Presenter with smartphone/tablet AR device. Note: there is ample space for presenter to move and generate AR content. b - TV or projected screen to simultaneously display AR content. c - Audience members with AR devices, positioned around perimeter of room to provide space for Presenter.

are created for the purpose of being used outdoors. Though it has been mentioned before, Pokémon Go immediately comes to mind as an AR app that is absolutely meant to be used outside, with the intention that users will walk around a large area in order to capture Pokémon. Hosting an event outside will also give users the space to walk around with their own devices and test out various AR apps, without fighting for space in an enclosed room.

There are some notable downsides to hosting events outdoors. The biggest downside is that you will likely not have a TV or other large display to use to show off what an app is doing. Users will have to be close to the presenter or have their own devices in order to follow along with the instruction. The other obvious downside is that events are limited by weather. You will likely be unable to perform lectures or instruction outside if it is raining or if there is snow on the ground.

The "Measure" and "IKEA Place" Apps—Starting Simple with AR

As is the case with any library classes that may attempt to introduce complex technology to the public, it is vital to start simple. As of this writing, Apple has upgraded its iOS operating system for portable devices (smartphones and tablets) to include an AR-based app. This app is entitled "Measure." The purpose of this app is rather straightforward—it is used for measuring distance or the size of objects through the use of AR.

The app takes a few quick seconds to calibrate in your environment. First, the app will instruct the user to wave their device around. This helps the software to use the camera and the phone's built in gyroscope to determine the orientation of the device. Typically, it will then ask you to point your device at a smooth surface (often, one that has texture and color). From there, you can add a starting "point" to an object by pointing at a beginning spot on an object. After tapping the screen, you can then move your device around and begin to measure length.

You can have users measure an object, such as a pencil on a desk. Many will disbelieve the measurement discerned through AR, so be sure to have an actual ruler handy! Your event attendees will quickly become astonished by how accurate the measuring app can be. Moving on from simpler objects, such as a pencil, you can measure the lengths or heights of tables, walls, and bits of furniture. The Measure App will also allow users to measure the volume of an object, such as a rectangle. This can be completed quickly through the use of the app's additional features.

As of this writing, the popular furniture manufacturer IKEA has created its own product catalog app. AR is a key component of this app, as use of this technology allows potential IKEA customers to see exactly how a piece of furniture will fit in to their home. This is another excellent way to convince library users of the legitimacy of AR, as they will quickly be wowed as they use it.

For the best experience, make sure to showcase this app in a room that has enough space to fit a physical bed, dresser, kitchen table, or couch. As you use the app, you can select nearly any piece of furniture from IKEA's catalog and "place" it in your room. After you drop the certain piece of furniture, you can walk around the room, smartphone in hand, and see how the furniture will look from multiple angles. The accuracy is startling—it really does give the user a sense of how a new piece of furniture will fit in to a room and remove some of the uncertainty that often comes with furniture shopping.

AR Apps and Materials for Kids

For public libraries that hope to introduce AR to their youngest demographic, there are several ways this can be accomplished—through both event programming and materials offering. As with some of the other technologies listed in this work, it is important to be mindful of age limitations and restrictions when working with this particular demographic. In some cases, devices themselves may not be recommended for use with children of a young age. In other cases, be sure to screen the content that is presented in an AR app to ensure that it is age appropriate. With both the Apple iOS App Store and Google's Android Play Store, all software comes with a specific age rating. Absolutely screen all content before using it in a library environment.

One of the simplest ways to introduce AR in a place such as a children's library is through loanable tablet devices that have a carefully curated selection of AR apps. These devices could be either Apple iOS-based, such as iPads, or they could be Google Android-based tablets. For protecting these devices, there are excellent kid-friendly cases that are colorful and put up with quite a bit of abuse. As stated before, be sure to playtest all of these AR applications to ensure that the content is appropriate for your audience. In addition, it is generally recommended that the camera feature on these devices be turned off for privacy and safety reasons. With that being said, modern versions of Apple iOS and Google Android allow you to toggle this setting on an "app by app" basis. So while the camera feature is turned off device-wide, it can be allowed for the handful of apps that you grant permission to.

Once you are ready to start constructing a list of apps to offer your younger audience, the best place to start is website ARcritic.com. This website will periodically release a review of the best AR apps and games available for the iOS (iPhone/iPad) operating system, and is an excellent and timely source of information ("10 Best iPhone iPad AR Apps," 2017).

As kids that attend activities and utilize services in a children's library will tend to range in age from several months old to 12 years old or so, be sure to offer a variety of apps that have content that is engaging enough for various ages.

ARrrrrgh—A Treasure-Hunting AR App

For younger audiences, and library staff hoping to roll-out their first AR app that requires very little training, "ARrrrrgh" is an excellent choice. In addition, it is one of the few AR apps that is two-player, which allows two people to share in the fun ("ARrrrrgh," n.d.). This app can be played with two kids participating, or the app can be played between parent and child. The app is free and rated for ages four and up. It will work on both smartphone and tablet devices.

ARrrrrgh is very straightforward game and, as the name funnily suggests, it has a pirate theme. The objective of the game is pretty straightforward—bury your treasure in the ground and then have your friend try to find it. Once you launch the game, you are greeted by a very simple menu screen. There's no real options and no complexity, which is absolutely ideal for a younger audience. When you start your first round, the camera on the device will open up and you can view your surroundings. In our test drive of this game, we walked through several rooms and then "buried my treasure" under a small rug. The animation was very cute—a 3D rendered shovel started digging through my floor and then buried my treasure. The animations definitely brought a smile to our faces, as well.

Once your treasure is buried, you are asked to walk quite a distance away from your treasure and then hand your device to another player. They will then be forced to wander an area, using the device screen as a guide to determine how close they are getting to the treasure. Once they think they are on top of the treasure chest, they stake their virtual shovel in the ground and start digging. If they are lucky, they have discovered the buried treasure!

That's all there really is to this game, but one could easily imagine kids have a ton of fun with this AR app as they "bury" treasure throughout your library!

QuiverVision—An AR App That Brings Coloring Books to Life

Imagine if you could color in a penguin, a car, a house, a person—pretty much anything—on paper, and it would suddenly jump off the page in front of you. Your creation would come to life, be fully animated, and have all of the wonderful colors and other personalization you had given it. This is now possible through the use of AR and the unique QuiverVision app.

The concept behind this application is pretty simple. After users download this app to their smartphone or tablet (QuiverVision supports Apple iOS and Google Android), they can visit the QuiverVision website and download "coloring packs." It should be noted the app itself is free, as are many of the packs. As of this writing, some coloring packs range in price from free to $4.99. Users must also print out paper copies of the images they wish to color. All of the images for printing are free, but they cannot be animated and "brought to life" in AR without first unlocking them via payment.

The results are stunning. Children (and adults!) can quickly color in objects with any color they choose. Once you are done coloring, the QuiverVision app will scan the QR code located on the bottom of the worksheet, look at the colors used, and then render an object on your smartphone or tablet screen with those same color choices. This app could easily allow children's libraries to create events with small groups of kids that are coloring in worksheets and then surprising each other with their colorful creations.

It is easy to see how this particular app can promote artistic creativity in children. It is currently recommended for ages four and up.

Children's Books with Augmented Reality Features

As AR has become more accessible, in the sense that many more devices now natively support this functionality, some very interesting applications have begun to appear in areas like childhood learning. As a way to make learning more interactive, AR has now been incorporated into children's books. With this particular use, books are often sold that have special QR codes embedded on pages that will trigger an AR image or 3D model to appear on a smartphone or tablet screen. Many of these books will work with an AR platform, such as FarSight XR, to help bring "life" to these printed works ("About FarSight XR," 2019).

It should be noted that this area of publishing has become quite popular and new titles are being created and sold all the time. If your library is considering creating a "Books with Augmented Reality" collection, be sure to include a simple handout or instructions indicating that the books in that collection may work with Apple iOS and Google Android devices. It will also be critical to demonstrate those books and how they integrate with AR with your library staff. They will almost certainly be asked questions from the public on how these books work with AR, and it is vital that they have a basic understanding of how that functions.

As a simple example of an AR book, one particular work looked interesting for its method of making science fun and interactive. *Tide Pools: An Augmented Reality Book* by Ernest King is a spiral-bound work that helps children to learn about tide pools, how they are formed, and the creatures that live in them. As of this writing, this work costs $20 and is available at a major online retailer.

What seems especially fun about this work are the elements that are recreated in AR. Children may turn to one page and see a starfish jump out of the book's page and onto the screen of their AR device. Other pages demonstrated the various water levels of pools, based upon what time of day and what tide it currently was. The app incorporates sound, video, and narration to hold the reader's attention.

Be sure to type "Augmented Reality Children's Books" into any search engine in order to see a more current listing of titles that are available. Librarians should, like any other published works, be sure to read reviews for these items and see if there are any technical concerns that may limit borrowers from fully enjoying this experience.

AR Apps for Tweens and Teens

When it comes to AR apps that can be used to entice tweens and teens into the local library, there are quite a few to choose from. Luckily, it seems the largest amount of AR apps that exist are already marketed towards that particular demographic and the apps that stand out most are extremely well polished. They showcase AR technology in a way that is often jaw-dropping and engaging to the point of addiction!

In order to facilitate the use of some of the following recommended apps and programming ideas, there are two possible solutions. The first solution would be to encourage tweens and teens to bring their own devices in order to participate. This solution is low-cost, but it can introduce a few issues. Will all the teens have compatible hardware? Will they know their Apple store and Google Play store passwords so that they can install an app on the day of the event? If you choose this route, be sure to have many of these details figured out ahead of time, either by helping teens install apps or sending them clear instructions ahead of the day of an event.

Harry Potter: Wizards Unite—An AR Walking App

Working off the immense success of Pokémon Go, Niantic Games decided to create another AR game based on another extremely popular franchise: Harry Potter. Entitled "Harry Potter: Wizards Unite," the gameplay mechanics of this particular app are very similar to those of Pokémon Go, so teens and tweens that have played that version of the game should be able to jump right in ("Harry Potter," 2019).

The basis of the game is pretty straightforward. After you install this app on your Apple iOS or Android device, you create a character. Character codes, or identities, can be shared with friends in order to create a basic multiplayer experience. Whereas Pokémon Go was based around capturing Pokémon and then leveling them up in order to do battle, the way to win in this game is to free "Foundables" and return them to where they belong. Players will use their fingers to quickly cast spells, as they wander the real world looking at an interactive map on their device screen. Very much like Pokémon Go, players should expect to walk many miles in order to fully enjoy this game.

As of this writing, the game is very new, but early reviews have been both positive and supportive. Niantic Games recognizes there are some small fixes that need to be made. They are also aware of some of the issues that plagued the launch of Pokémon Go (such as dreadful network issues), and those annoyances seem to be minimal this time around. In addition, Niantic Games is hoping to maintain a multiyear storyline to keep players engaged (Andriessen, 2019).

If Pokémon Go is any indication of success, public libraries should keep an eye on this game and be ready to jump on the bandwagon, should the popularity explode. Libraries became "PokéStops" for Pokémon Go and that generated considerable amounts of foot traffic from teens and tweens in to libraries. Be ready to embrace this phenomena! Harry Potter: Wizards Unite is currently free, but has in-app purchases which are not necessary to enjoy the game. It is rated for ages nine and up.

Minecraft Earth

Several years ago, you would have been hard-pressed to find a teen or tween who did not know about or play the sandbox game, Minecraft. Microsoft purchased the franchise in 2014 and, in an effort to boost the waning popularity of the franchise, has cooked up something extremely imaginative: Minecraft Earth. Microsoft, as we have seen with its HoloLens AR headset, has an affinity for AR these days and they believe that blending Minecraft and AR will be the key to success and increased revenue for this beloved franchise.

For those who are unaware, Minecraft takes place in a giant world that, for this type of gameplay, is often compared metaphorically to a "sandbox." Players wander a gigantic planet and are able to place small cubes (or "blocks") of varying materials on the ground. Users can dig down, way below the surface, in order to discover caves and find rare resources. They can then use the materials they harvest to build upward and outward, often creating homes, castles, giant buildings, towns—just about anything that can be imagined. These structures are made out of blocks, and these blocks have different properties, similar to their real-world counterparts—dirt, lumber, stone, glass, diamond, water, lava, and others. While there is a gameplay element at work here that sort of guides players, the beauty of Minecraft is the openness of the game and the fact that it is such a powerful creative outlet for kids, tweens, teens, and adults. Coupled with the fact that this game is multiplayer and people often band together in order to build huge structures, Minecraft is a force to be reckoned with.

So, how does Microsoft hope to introduce a new generation to Minecraft? Through the launch of Minecraft Earth. This AR-enhanced app will be supported on both the Apple iOS and the Google Android platforms. Though details may change upon release, Microsoft has stated that the game will be free and will be for audiences 10 and older ("Minecraft Earth FAQ," 2019). Microsoft and their developers have taken everything that was fun, cute, endearing, and addicting about roaming the Minecraft world and has done something that is rather incredible—imported it to our own realm. Through the use of AR, players will be able to use Minecraft blocks to create structures in our own reality. Players will be able to see their creations through their device screens. In Microsoft's launch trailer, it is teased that building blocks will be "life-sized." What this means for players is that the giant castles they create will easily tower over the actual homes and buildings in their own neighborhoods, when viewed through the device screen. Imagine deciding that you never really were a fan of the look of your local library. Whelp, go ahead and change it! Create giant spires on the roof! Have lava flows coming out of the second-story windows. Give your library a moat, and add some enemy characters to protect the library's books! All of this sounds like it could be in the realm of possibility with this title, and it should lead to hours of enjoyment. It's unclear if this game will support multiplayer participation so that Minecraft fans can team up to build giant, complex structures. What is clear is that this game could lead to hours of fun for teens in your library, if it is preloaded on iOS or Android devices that could be borrowed inside a teen area.

ARia's Legacy—AR Escape Room

In the world of public libraries, one phenomenon has completely taken off—the introduction of "escape room" programming for tweens, teens, and adults. Escape rooms, for those who are unfamiliar, are gigantic puzzles that people must solve in order to win. The goal is to work together to look for clues, solve puzzles, and eventually free yourself and your team from a locked room with no immediately easy way to escape. This game usually takes place in a meeting space—and no, the doors are not chained shut, with patrons forced to find a way out or face starvation. Instead, the players are asked to imagine themselves in a dark dungeon cell or a strange room in an odd house, longing to find a way out. Basic rules are set, the game is almost always timed, and players who are "stuck" and unable to progress can ask for clues (usually with a penalty). The teamwork aspect makes this an excellent social exercise, and physical ability is nowhere near as important as mental capability and puzzle-solving skills. While all of that seems fun, escape rooms can be limited by the quality of the props used. Also, escape rooms in libraries can lose some of the fun aesthetic that commercial escape rooms with dedicated spaces can offer. How can libraries bridge that gap a bit and engage patrons in a manner that will have them leaving this experience with a higher level of fun experienced? The answer is to incorporate AR.

While there are a number of AR escape room apps available on both the Apple iOS and Google Android platforms, one particular app seemed to have garnered the best overall ratings: ARia's Legacy—AR Escape Room ("ARia's Legacy," 2018). The purpose of this app is to make the escape room experience as immersive as possible. Many library escape rooms take place in rather simple, if not drab, meeting spaces and rooms. It may be hard for library staff to decorate a space and make it more of an ideal setting for a fanciful escape room. This app, which is only available on Apple iOS, works to overcome those limitations. As users launch the app and start their escape room experience, they can move their device around a room to scan the location. AR technology will place important objects and props in the space, all of which are only visible on the device screen. Many of these props may be animated or have sound effects that act as cues or clues. In some cases, moving a device around a room may reveal a secret code or clue in a funny location, adding a bit of whimsy to this activity.

It should be important to note that escape rooms usually consist of teams participating, and, in the case of ARia's Legacy, a team would likely have to share one device in order for this app to work effectively. ARia's Legacy is a free download, but it has an additional "add-on pack" for $2.99, which enhances the experience. This game is recommended for ages four and up.

AR Apps for Adults

Presenting AR programming for adults is sure to be a fun and exciting experience. Many adults may already have access to devices that support AR and have no idea that they can access this technology at the tip of their fingers. Many adults have grown up familiar with *Star Trek* and other science fiction tales, so AR will definitely be somewhat familiar to them, yet surely still astonish.

However, there is also another reality that library staff must be able to anticipate and address: technophobia and digital literacy deficiency. When crafting ideas to support AR lectures, programming and events at your library, be sure to keep in mind that adults may not always be on par with each other when it comes to ease of technology use and familiarity. Be sure to keep initial lectures and programs simple and streamlined. If you plan to run a BYOD event, make sure the promotional literature details exactly what devices will be supported and what operating systems must be installed. Will you be demoing certain apps? Be sure to list those ahead of time. Encourage adults to seek out staff before a presentation or event takes place so that they can be sure that their devices are compatible. If your library is able to secure the funding, it would be ideal to have a number of Apple iOS and Google Android devices on hand (preferably tablets) that can be passed around to participants. Those devices will already be prepared by staff and ready for use. If you are doing a hands-on event, make sure you keep the ratio of staff to participants as close to 1:1 as possible. If you run a hands-on event for 50 people and there is only one staff member present, it will make for a very frustrating experience for patrons as they wait for assistance.

With all of that being said, and some pitfalls explained, these programs can be the most rewarding. We've used the term "magical" several times already, but there is certainly a very fun moment that occurs when an adult discovers this technology for the first time and understands just how powerful a tool it can be. So let's look at some potential event, demo, and lecture ideas.

The Apple iOS Measure App and IKEA Place App

When looking to showcase AR and to explain some of the basic principles, it would be best to keep the initial part of any lecture or presentation as simple as possible. Again, for reasons described above, an adult audience may have varying degrees of technology awareness, and, if they are attending a lecture, they may be exposing themselves to AR for the very first time. With that in mind, it would be highly recommended to give a quick overview of the technical underpinnings of AR and how it works (and be sure to avoid using industry jargon or extremely technical terms) and start with presenting two simple apps: Apple iOS "Measure" and the "IKEA Place" app.

Using these two simple apps, both of which have real-world applications, should hopefully make it easier for audiences to understand exactly why AR is exciting and has huge potential. The Measure app is easy to both explain and showcase. It is also easy to hand off to patrons and have them measure simple objects in a room. Start with a pencil. Then measure the size of a table. From there, try to use the app to determine how tall a wall is. Finally, you can attempt to get the size of an entire room. Although the app isn't 100 percent accurate, it is pretty darned close, and the results should wow people in the audience.

It is very likely that you will see the same effect when you start to demonstrate the IKEA Place app. You can easily use one of the room layouts as described earlier, although a room layout with all of the chairs around the periphery of the space would work best. You can launch the app and start to demonstrate how to select a certain piece of furniture, rotate it, and position it in the space. The fun part of the demonstration may occur when you ask a member of the audience to come up and try to create a simple dining area layout with a kitchen table and chairs. This will force them to pick product models that they enjoy, position furniture in a certain way, and start to personally experience how to utilize this app to imagine a space. To be sure, this particular exercise should be pretty fun, and many jokes will likely be made at either the presenter or participant's expense.

An Instagram and Snapchat Face Filter Demo with AR

It has been pretty exciting to see AR start to creep its way into social media platforms and the mobile apps that are used for posting content. One of the ways social media platforms, such as Instagram and Snapchat, have been able to implement AR is through the use of "selfie filters."

As explained earlier, selfie filters are a fun, quirky, and downright silly way for social media users to enhance the photographs that they take of themselves or their loved ones. Typically, a social media user may point the front-facing camera at themselves to take a portrait for sharing on social media sites. In an effort to make this more interesting, these platforms have created "on-the-fly" filters that can appear on your image as you are lining up your shot for that perfect photo. Through the use of AR, these filters will allow you to see yourself with make-up on, silly glasses, lipstick, a beret, dog ears and tongue, and all sorts of other nonsensical additions. Social media platforms seem to rotate new selfie filters in to their offerings pretty frequently and will often remove filters that have become a bit "stale." It would be fine to expect the selfie filter offerings on either Instagram or Snapchat to be completely different from the specific ones listed here. However, due to their overwhelming popularity, there will surely be some sort of offering on these platforms for the foreseeable future.

It should be noted that these applications of AR, while fun, will only take a few moments to demonstrate and would not likely be able to take up an hour of a presentation or lecture. We would be reluctant to recommend this as a stand-alone AR workshop. Instead, it would be perfect to add this to a standard lecture, perhaps after demonstrating the Measure App or IKEA Place, in order to show some of the whimsical ways AR has started appearing on devices.

Google Translate for Travel

One "killer app" to showcase AR is almost certainly the Google Translate app, which is available free on both Apple iOS and Google Android Devices. Even though it was mentioned before as a great way to train staff and introduce them to AR, this particular app is sure to make a splash with patrons. Like some of our other previous examples, this app might be best demonstrated as part of a general lecture on AR, or it should be part of a "How to Travel like a Pro" informational program. After talking about ways to find the cheapest airfare, hotels, and best restaurants in an area, your library could then show potential travelers the power of Google Translate.

The power of this particular app, when it comes to understanding foreign languages and easing communication, cannot be overstated. This is another instance of an AR app that, when demonstrated, will have people completely awed.

When showcasing this app, it would be advisable to show the basic functions that it provides. Yes, it will translate text from one language to another. In our experience, the translation is actually very good and is greatly improved from the translate functionality that online dictionaries or translation services have provided in the past. One example of this app's advanced features is its ability to translate the spoken word. It will work with your device's microphone to record a snippet of a conversation and then translate it to another language. This is helpful for understanding what a person is saying or for communicating to a person who may not speak the same language as yourself.

This app really shines when the camera feature is enabled. As described earlier, this will allow a user to pick up their device and point it at a sign that is written in another language. Are you at a restaurant and unable to read the menu? Use the camera feature, point your device at the menu, and prepare to prevent your jaw from dropping as you watch it instantly translate the menu in to your native tongue and present the results on your device screen, through the use of AR. Are you at an airport, train station, or museum and unsure how to navigate around the facility? This app can be a lifesaver as you furiously attempt to find the nearest restroom. Simply lift up your device, launch the Translate app and camera function, and point it at the signage that you are unable to comprehend.

One critical piece of advice when demonstrating this particular app: be sure to show attendees how to download "language packs." This will be absolutely important for travelers, especially since they may not be able to have data plans on their smartphones or find Wi-Fi easily. Instruct participants to download any language packs that will cover the regions they plan to travel to while they are home and have access to bandwidth. This will alleviate any potential letdowns as library patrons travel to a country for the first time, only to realize that this app will not function properly without them scrambling to find the nearest Wi-Fi hotspot for Internet access.

Night Sky App

One of the coolest applications of AR, and one in which education and fun are so intelligently intertwined, is the Night Sky app for Apple iOS devices. Before we even discuss the many aspects of this app, we should point out that the basic app is free, but there are add-on packs, subscriptions for added content, and even the ability to make a onetime purchase of the full app, as ways to support the developer. As of this writing, much of the basic functionality of this app is still entirely free. The app is rated for ages four and up.

Previously, as potential room layouts were detailed for demonstrating AR apps, it was suggested that some demonstrations can and should take place outdoors. This is exactly the perfect location for showcasing this app. In addition, this app may best be experienced at night, although it can absolutely be used in the daylight hours.

The best way to frame or explain this app might be the following: "Have you ever been in absolute awe of the night sky? But are you like many of us and have no idea where many of the popular constellations may reside? Do you ponder where the International Space Station is at any given moment and wonder if it is visible to the naked eye?" There is no doubt that many of the individuals in your audience have had those thoughts and questions. If you decide to showcase this particular app, you will be able to answer all of those questions for your attendees and also empower them to become amateur astronomers.

Through the power of AR, global positioning systems (GPS), and your device's accelerometer (a tool that helps the device track if it is being moved left or right, up, or down), your smartphone or tablet can become an instant guide to the stars with the Night Sky app. After launching this app and taking a quick tutorial, users will be able to point their devices to the sky and start seeing exactly where certain constellations reside above their heads. As users start to move their devices left or right, up or down, other constellations will begin to come in to view. The experience is absolutely amazing. Thankfully, the developer has taken this app several steps further and has added many other features, many of which rely on AR in order to work properly.

Besides standard "sky tracking" of constellations, this app will allow users to pinpoint planets in our solar system and where they current sit in the sky. By touching a planet on your device screen, the planet will suddenly increase in size and the user can rotate the planet to see its physical characteristics. If a user decides they would prefer to know more about a specific constellation, especially to learn more about the stars that make up that constellation and where they reside, they can touch the constellation, and it will go in to "glass mode." The constellation's mythological representation will remain on the screen, but the user can rotate it to see exactly where the stars that make up its appearance reside in our universe.

One new feature of Night Sky that seemed especially cool is the ability to open up "planetary portals." Using your device, you can "step through" a portal to another planet's surface. For instance, you could step through a portal and suddenly be on the surface of Mars. Looking up at the sky, you would see the constellations as they would be viewable from that planet. Looking up at the night sky would also show you that planet's moons and their current location, as well as their surface features. This is something that is pretty cool to see, and it is also mind-bending in a way. It is a great way to take the idea of night sky viewing and put an interesting twist on it.

After you have shown your library patrons this particular app, you can be sure they will leave your AR demonstration program and look to the sky with confidence as they begin naming and tracking its various features.

An Augmented Reality Programming Spotlight: *The Mukwonago Community Library's MetaSpace 511*

An Interview with Angela Zimmermann, Library Director

This chapter has covered some of the basic AR apps that exist and provided a few ideas for library programming and events. But let's take a moment to look at the work that Angela Zimmermann, director of the Mukwonago Community Library, has undertaken in order to introduce AR to her community.

Angela and her team at Mukwonago thought that it would be exciting to find a way to merge difficult scientific concepts with AR, in the hopes of making these concepts easier for her library patrons to grasp. To be fair, earth science, geography, watersheds, and computer science can be painfully detailed and hard to digest. "With that, the goal of this project was to build a hands-on sandbox exhibit combined with 3D visualization applications. While the primary purpose was to be a hands-on exhibit and educational tool to teach earth science concepts, geography, watershed and computer science, we have discovered that participants have one of three general experiences, based on their age," explains Angela.

Mukwonago also decided that the best way forward for this project would be to try to hit all age demographics and allow them to participate in the experience. "The younger children, pre-teen, tend to enjoy the sand because it changes color as they change patterns in the sand. When a group is around the sandbox, they usually become a collaborative, often building 'a big mountain in the middle,'" states Angela.

The next age group to interact with the AR sandbox are teens, and it is clear that they have different objectives in mind and embrace the sandbox differently than do younger kids. "The second group, teens, mostly, start to get the idea of the sandbox and often will form ideas on their own to make geographic forms and features. Again it becomes a collaborative effort. This group seems to really like to "make it rain" and fill the rivers, lakes and ponds they make," according to Angela. Teens are starting to grasp some of the scientific concepts presented and are working on how to present the science with the most notable effect.

Exactly how do adults respond when they encounter the AR sandbox? "Adults, generally, are most interested in the sandbox because it is 'relaxing.' They tend to be more solitary when working with the sandbox, but also leave with the 'I need one of these' comments," Angela shares. It is definitely an unexpected outcome, but it seems that the AR sandbox is helping to meet a need.

Perhaps the best takeaway from speaking with Angela and measuring success is revealed when she discloses that the library has now hosted many classes on physical geography, map reading, and watersheds. It seems clear that the AR sandbox has created an excellent starting point for members of her community to become aware of some interesting scientific concepts, and then the library was able to draw those patrons in to programming and events that provided "deeper dives" into the topics.

So, now that we've discussed some successful applications of the Mukwonago AR sandbox, let's look at the nitty-gritty of how they created it. Angela Zimmermann was able to provide some extremely important details. "Obviously, there is a wooden box filled with sand. Our box is about five and one-half inches high filled with about four inches of white sand. We also have a Microsoft Kinect 3D camera and a BenQ short throw projector. We have a Linux powered computer (outside the sandbox) to run the sandbox software," says Angela. It should be noted that the Microsoft Kinect 3D is an "off-the-shelf" piece of equipment that is used by the popular Microsoft Xbox 360 (and later versions) video game console to do movement tracking of gamers. Linux is a free computer operating system that can be loaded on to either brand-new or older computing hardware, in order to run free, open-source software.

When it comes to additional costs and items, Angela shares the following: "We built the sandbox ourselves and thus kept the [labor to] build cost down. The cost of materials, the computer, projector, camera, sand and materials to build the box came to about $1,600. We have purchased two boxes, at twenty pounds each, of sand. Sand was $10 per box." It should be noted that some of these items could be repurposed library equipment. Did your library just purchase a new projector to show movies? Why not hold on to the old one to create a sandbox? Did one of your staff recently upgrade their Xbox 360 to an Xbox One? Perhaps they could donate their old Kinect hardware piece.

Anytime a new service or technology is introduced in the library, it is critical to have staff "buy-in" and acceptance of these changes. Admittedly, that can be a very difficult process. For Mukwonago, the AR sandbox was an element of a larger project, the MetaSpace 511 (their version of a MakerSpace). "Once a conceptual plan was presented and staff saw how excited the community was about offering such a room to the community, the buy-in for more and more innovative things like the Augmented Reality sandbox has been remarkable. Staff are excited to share with patrons the many things we offer," remarks Angela. To retain staff enthusiasm and keep them engaged in MetaSpace activities, it has been important for them to do ongoing training sessions. "In regards to training, we dedicate some time during each in-service training day to learn about new equipment added to MetaSpace 511, such as the Augmented Reality sandbox," explains Angela. It seems that having repeat training sessions is vital.

After money has been spent on materials, and time has been spent on staff training, one metric for success will be how well a community receives a new library service or technology. Thankfully, it seems that Mukwonago has a hit on their hands! "Anytime we turn the AR sandbox on, it steals the show and nothing else in the room seems to matter. This also held true at the Milwaukee Maker Faire. Last year, we were the only public library in attendance at the Milwaukee Maker Faire and we can confidently say we were by far one of the most popular because of the sandbox," states Angela.

Expanding on their experience at a recent Milwaukee Maker Faire, Director Zimmermann explains, "It was Sunday. The weather was poor. The Green Bay Packers were playing and, frankly, we thought attendance would be down at the Maker Faire. Much to our surprise, multiple times that afternoon, even with two sides of the box obstructed by tables and barriers, we had ten or twelve kids crowded around the sandbox at the same time. We truly cannot turn the sandbox on without it being the center of attention."

While all of this sounds pretty straight forward, the devil can be in the details. We were sure to ask Angela Zimmermann if she had any library policy considerations to point out to other libraries that may want to introduce their own AR sandboxes. "Right now, the sandbox is only used when staff are present in MetaSpace 511. We currently do not have a specific policy for it nor do I see the immediate need to have one. The only issue, if anything, is we must monitor for some sand being thrown in excitement across the room," shares Zimmermann.

After reading about the exciting things Mukwonago Community Library has accomplished with the AR sandbox, you can attempt to create your own AR sandbox for your library. Feel free to visit the University of California–Davis website to find instructions on how to create your own implementation (https://arsandbox.ucdavis.edu/instructions/).

LENDING AUGMENTED REALITY BOOKS AND EQUIPMENT

As we explore all of the fun ways in which that AR can be presented to our library patrons, through events, programming, lectures and other methods, it is easy to forget about what libraries are most known for—material lending. There are many different ways in which members of our community can take AR home with them, and libraries have a few different options for providing that experience.

MERGE Cube & MERGE Headset Combo

Earlier in this chapter, we discussed the MERGE cube as a wonderful item for demonstrating AR. For our purposes, we had talked about the Dig! app and how, due to its roots in gaming, it could be a great way to showcase AR for children. Due to its low cost—approximately $15—this device could easily be lent out to library members. Along with this device, a suggested list of MERGE apps could be distributed, explaining to patrons that many of those apps are free. Age restrictions and content would be assessed, and those recommendations could be passed along to our library users.

But why not take things a step further? MERGE Labs, the company responsible for creating the MERGE cube has a device that partners extremely well with the cube. Known as the MERGE headset, this is a very low-cost AR/virtual reality (VR) solution. As of this writing, headsets can be found at major online retailers for approximately $30. This durable, yet flexible, headset appears to be comfortable and includes a head strap. Popular smartphone brands should have models that will fit in the "cradle" on this headset, thus allowing users to see a device screen in landscape format, right in front of their eyes. This frees up both of their hands to hold the MERGE cube and manipulate it. It also allows for a far more immersive experience. While this headset has VR applications, it allows for an AR mode. In this setting, users will not be whisked away to some strange virtual world. Instead, they will still be able to see the actual world around them as they manipulate MERGE objects and try various types of MERGE AR software.

When looking to create a lending program for a MERGE cube and MERGE headset, be sure to note that the headset is recommended for people age eight and up ("MERGE Headset," 2019). If you are hoping to make a curated list of recommended MERGE apps, you may want to start by browsing their app marketplace, located at https://miniverse.io/home. As you browse the marketplace, be mindful of a few details. The apps do have recommended age groups for use. In addition, not all of the apps are free. The apps do have ratings to determine how enjoyable they are, but it would certainly be a good idea for staff to playtest many of these free apps to check content before recommending them for download. If you are not lending an electronic device to go with this cube/headset combo (and, admittedly, that may be difficult to do in this circumstance), be sure to look at the device compatibility listing and include a list of which devices patrons can fit in to the headset.

AR Books for Children

This topic was touched upon earlier in this chapter, but there is a fair number of AR-enabled books that are currently available from publishers. While libraries should absolutely consider adding these works to their collections, librarians may want to consider making book bundles that families can borrow.

In addition to creating book bundles, staff may want to look for AR-based apps that cover a certain topic. For instance, if a library is able to find an AR-enabled children's book that talks about space exploration, why not put in a bookmark that recommends AR-based apps that are space-themed, such as Night Sky for amateur astronomers? Fun games could also be recommended for download. This may take some curation on the part of staff, as staff will have to ensure that content is appropriate and that the apps are free. However, this might be an excellent way to give a library user a very well-rounded AR experience at home.

An Augmented Reality App List, Like a "Book List"

An even simpler way to help families bring AR home is through something similar to a "book list" or a "recommended reads" list. Why not create an up-to-date listing of fun AR apps? This listing could be the size of a bookmark or pamphlet and has a few key elements. The "AR apps list" should start with a simple explanation of AR and how it works. Likely, this would only be a small blurb. From there, staff could list a few of their favorite apps. These could be educational and recreational apps. They should probably cover a wide variety of topics. On this information bookmark or pamphlet, be sure to indicate the recommended age for the user of the app. In addition, be sure to denote which devices, whether Apple iOS or Google Android, the app is supported on. It is probably best to only list apps that are free; however, there may be a handful of apps that only cost a small amount of money and those may be listed, with pricing clearly identified (or marked as "Paid App").

Preloaded Devices

Within this chapter, many examples of AR apps have been presented and recommended, all with the notion that members of your community already own Apple iOS or Google Android devices, whether they are smartphones or tablets. The truth is that not every member of your community may own one of these devices or have easy access to one. If they do own one of these devices, it may not be set up properly or be up-to-date, or they may be unsure of how to install apps on it. In order to still bring an AR experience to your patrons, you may want to consider lending tablets.

When it comes to lending electronic devices, some of which may cost several hundred dollars, some libraries may hesitate. There are valid concerns about policy, in regards to damage, theft, installation of apps, use of a web browser on the device, and other issues. However, as devices are steadily lowering in price and becoming more ubiquitous, some of these concerns should be lessening. In addition, many libraries currently lend tablets and other electronic devices. They may have solid lending policies in place that can act as a template for your own library, as you look to provide this service.

If your library decides to lend tablets for the purposes of providing an AR experience, there are a few key items you should consider. Will your tablet be an Apple or Android tablet? Will you remove *all* other apps installed on the device, in order to have less clutter?

From there, your staff should come up with a curated list of AR applications that will be installed on the device. Each lendable AR device should come with a simple instruction sheet that gives a one-sentence explanation of each installed app and the app's age recommendation. This will prove extremely helpful to parents. Critically, library staff should be given an overview of the device so that they can give patrons who wish to borrow the device a quick tutorial on how to turn on the device, charge it, launch apps, and do basic troubleshooting. The goal is to help patrons have the least frustrating experience possible, yet have tons of fun exploring the world of AR.

AUGMENTED REALITY SIGNAGE: HELPING YOUR PATRONS NAVIGATE YOUR SPACE

There have been some very interesting developments in the world of digital signage and public relations, all of which rely upon AR to create a connection with library patrons.

One of the many ongoing struggles taking place in libraries is finding the proper balance of appropriate signage in a library and lack of clutter. As many library directors will tell you, staff can often become "overzealous" when creating or posting directional signage in a public library. One way to carefully control the overt use of signage in a library space might be to utilize AR-based directions. It is now possible to create digital maps of library collections. These detailed maps indicate on what floor and in what specific location an item may be located.

Imagine a patron enters your library and walks up to a self-service online public access catalog (OPAC). They were searching for a copy of Shakespeare's *Hamlet* and, to their enjoyment, discovered that a copy is available at your library, in your building. Here's the issue: it's the weekend, your building is lightly staffed, and the information desk has a line four patrons deep. It looks like that staff member may be tied up for a while. Here's the second issue—and this one is significant—your library has multiple floors and can be a bit maze-like in some sections. A simple "turn left at the fiction book display" will not be adequate instructions for our patron attempting to locate *Hamlet.* The actual directions would be more like turn around 180 degrees, proceed to the water fountain, turn left, go around that tight corner, get in to the elevator, proceed to the fourth floor, exit the elevator, bypass the Young Adult service desk, immediately turn left, and walk past five sections of shelves until you find yourself about 10 feet into the Dewey 800s. AR is a potential tool to alleviate any confusion that this patron may experience. It can serve as a way to enhance customer service and prevent a library user from walking away from your building empty handed.

Now, picture a situation in which a patron can be guided to exactly where that copy of *Hamlet* is located, all without staff assistance. In our new scenario, a patron has seen that *Hamlet* is currently available at the library. They see a small button on the OPAC results listing labeled "Help Me Find It." Clicking that button generates a unique QR code for the item and location. Our patron scans that QR code with their smartphone camera, and an app on their device is launched. Their phone screen and backside camera now combine to serve as a digital guide, able to steer our patron exactly to the location of *Hamlet*. The app asks the user to quickly scan the ground (which helps the AR software to calibrate distance) and then to scan a nearby "marker" on the end of some library shelving (which tells the software the exact location of the user). From there, using the smartphone's built-in compass, the app is able to steer our patron to that tricky-to-locate elevator bank. They are instructed to proceed to the fourth floor. Once there, they are greeted by another "marker," which tells the app that our patron has arrived on the correct floor. Following some more visual cues on the smartphone screen leads our user precisely to the location of *Hamlet*. The user tells the app that they have located their item. The app asks if they need help locating anything else—another item, the restroom, the check-out desk. Our user indicates they no longer need assistance, and this task is complete.

This may all sound like a fantastical science-fiction idea, and that is partially true. Unlike some other sections of this chapter, this concept is somewhat speculative. Outside the world of libraries, there has been a push to implement AR-based signage for customers of shopping malls, large stores, and public transit areas. Google has been instrumental in helping to roll out this form of AR application, and it teased its development status at the 2018 Google I/O Conference. There have been a few updates here and there from Google staff, indicating that, while they hope to integrate this technology in to their Google Maps platform, it just isn't ready for prime time yet (Liptak, 2019a).

With that being said, the technology is promising, and early reports from test users indicate that it works quite well. As some public locations have now mapped their interior layouts and allowed Google Maps, via "Indoor Maps," to integrate that into their software, it is certainly reasonable to estimate that Google may extend AR features to that functionality, or open up with Google Maps API to other developers to play in this area. Keep looking for news on this specific topic!

LIBRARY POLICY AND BEST PRACTICES

Dealing with Patron Privacy—Camera Usage in AR Apps

As with all new technologies that you may be introducing in to your library, it is vital to have smart policies in place to manage this technology properly. Ideally, you will want to work with your organization's administration to craft policies that allow this technology to be safely implemented. You will also want to keep the needs and concerns of patrons in mind when crafting policy language. Many of your policy concerns surrounding AR will likely deal with the use of device cameras, software content appropriateness, and, potentially, device lending.

For internal library usage, such as promotional or directional signage, organizations will want to make it clear to patrons how that signage is used, where it is placed, and how its implementation may affect them. For instance, libraries may want to utilize language, such as:

> In our ongoing efforts to aid patrons in the finding of materials, AR-based electronic maps may be made available throughout the building for patrons to utilize with devices that support AR.
>
> - AR-based maps will be established in easy-to-spot locations.
> - Efforts will be made to place these maps out of high traffic walking areas.
> - AR markers for maps will be placed at an appropriate height to facilitate providing information for all of our library users.

It is not uncommon for public libraries to have behavior policies that forbid the use of video and photo cameras in the library. In an age when so many people have camera-capable devices in their pockets, purses, or on their person, this policy will likely have to be updated to better reflect the times we live in. Banning the use of cameras outright may be difficult to enforce and may run counter to the goals of a library looking to embrace AR. Softer policy language, such as a general statement like "No one may take photographs of patrons without their consent," may work best.

As most public library antiphotography and antivideo-recording policy language is to preserve patron privacy, it would be ideal to place things such as AR map tokens in locations (such as on a wall, pillar, or shelving end cap) where patrons will likely not be standing in the capture area of the camera.

For patron events and programming where AR may be a key component of the event, it would make sense to put disclaimer language on any promotional materials:

> **Note:** This event requires the use of cameras. Your image and voice may be recorded by others during this event, although solely for the purpose of having our AR devices function properly. Ask a staff member for more details.

Ideally, the disclaimer should be informative, but not written in a way that will discourage patrons from participating in the event. As the event begins, staff should explain the purpose of the disclaimer, which may function as a good lead-in to a description of how the actual technology works.

As is the best idea with the creation of any library policy language, work with library administration and library attorneys to ensure that policies offer the best balance of protection for both your institution and your patrons, while allowing some leeway for libraries to experiment with these new technologies.

Appropriate Content for AR App Events and Programs

As has been stated previously in this chapter, it is critical that library staff carefully examine AR apps for age- and content-appropriateness.

When searching for AR apps to preload on to devices for programs or events, or when creating an "AR App List" to recommend to patrons, be sure to check the "Age Rating" (Apple iOS) or "Content Rating" (Google Android) suggestions all major app marketplaces. Large marketplaces, such as the Apple App Store and the Google Play Store, will make age recommendations very easy to spot on app product pages. Library staff should be somewhat wary of introducing AR apps to patrons who may be below the suggested age range.

As we have discovered, there are many AR apps now in existence that may be somewhat text or "story heavy." These might be apps that help facilitate an "escape room" experience or may be an adventure game with a plot and character dialogue. Again, it is vital for staff to fully explore these games before recommending them to patrons or using them in library events. Some of these games may use colorful language or ask users to pretend they are in violent situations. Always think about what is most appropriate for your audience, and make it clear to them what sort of content may be expected and experienced.

Lending Devices with AR Apps to the Public

When hosting AR events and programming at your library, it can be quite tempting to run these workshops with preloaded devices that will be used solely for that particular experience. In this case, you would likely have few policy concerns to consider, aside from potential intentional or accidental damage of a device. Many libraries already have policies in place to deal with patrons that may damage library materials, and you should make it clear that your devices are covered under that policy language.

Where things may get a bit more complex is if your library decides to lend these devices out to patrons for use outside the building. The lending of electronic devices by libraries is not exactly a new phenomenon, and policies have been laid out by libraries for a number of years. The key things to consider when lending these devices to the public should be the following:

- **What is a comfortable lending period?** You will surely want to give your patrons a few days to play with various AR apps and discover their favorites.
- **What is the replacement cost?** Unfortunately, library materials do get damaged. Is your organization comfortable with confronting patrons to repay the entire cost of a device? Can replacement costs be prorated to reflect the age of a device being lent? Will your organization be flexible and forgiving?
- **What AR apps will you load on there, and will you note "age restrictions?"** Surely, you will want to create an app list for patrons that are borrowing a device. Patrons may be bringing these devices home to their families for use, and they will appreciate knowing which apps are appropriate for each member of their families.

This is an area that, after doing research, it is revealed that public libraries have a wide variety of answers to these particular questions. With that being said, do not let a few policy questions or snags prevent your library from lending devices. It almost all cases, the lending of electronic devices is a fun and worthwhile leap for libraries to make!

CONCLUSION: WHAT DOES THE FUTURE HOLD?

What does the future hold for the world of AR? It is quite hard to share specifics, but, as with all technology, there are certainly some predictable trends. We can absolutely expect companies such as Apple and Google to continue to refine their AR offerings and the underpinnings to their iOS and Android operating systems. There is still much room for growth in that area, and it seems that both companies are devoting money, staff, and other resources toward further focus, development, and refinement. We can expect third-party developers that are creating AR software to continue to improve their content. Expect unique and ingenious ways for users to have fun playing AR-based games and educational software in the future. Apps like Pokémon Go and Minecraft Earth are surely just scratching the surface. We can expect "quality of life" improvements in AR, with things like better graphics, devices that are more responsive to our movements, and better immersion. Prices for devices will surely continue to drop. It might be fair to say we may see more "free" apps in the future that will have optional, paid "download packs" or plugins to further beef up the app experience.

With all of that being said, there will surely be some unexpected developments. It may not be too long before AR devices are as small as a contact lens. Or AR devices may soon be small attachments for our reading or sunglasses. From there, can we expect to start experiencing AR-based billboards and signage on city streets? That scenario has already been envisioned by science fiction authors, and, as we have seen in previous parts of this book chapter, many of the elements to make that vision a "reality" are already here!

FOUR

Virtual Reality

When it comes to exciting technologies in the world of libraries, we have to admit that we were particularly excited to share our knowledge and experience regarding virtual reality (VR). There are many definitions of VR, some highly technical. At its most basic, VR is "a three-dimensional, computer generated environment which can be explored and interacted with by a person" (Virtual Reality Society, 2017). And while there are several *types* of VR, it is immersive, first-person VR that we most commonly encounter in our day-to-day lives. This is the familiar form that we often see in films or read about in science fiction. Immersive experience VR involves a head-mounted display (HMD), some type of physical controller, and a dedicated sound source (Bardi, 2019).

VR can be so immersive and illusionary that the brain is tricked into thinking the experience is *real*. It is for that reason that the experience can be transformative for all of those who participate. Combining this with the fact that VR can be relatively inexpensive and can enrich the lives of those that utilize it, we have become confident that libraries should strongly consider adding this technology to their stable of offerings.

HOW VR WORKS

So if VR is essentially a form of illusion, how is this trickery performed? In his book *Experience on Demand*, Jeremy Bailenson describes how VR induces "psychological presence," which is the sense of "being there" (Bailenson, 2019, p. 19). It achieves this using three components:

- *Tracking* is the process of precisely measuring body movements. For instance, as a user moves their head, the headset sends that data to a computer or device, for interpretation, which is then rendered in the VR environment. Basically, if you look up in a VR office space, the system knows to display the ceiling.
- *Rendering* is the process of taking a 3D model and then placing it exactly in the right location in a virtual environment. For example, if I walk away from an object in a VR environment, it should grow smaller. If it emits sound, that sound should grow fainter as my distance from it increases.
- *Display* is the manner in which digital information is used to replace what we would normally experience with our physical senses. Simply put, it is what we see, hear and in some cases, feel (Bailenson, 2019, pp. 20–21).

While still an emerging technology, VR is steadily entering the consumer market. Current market predictions expect to see 168 million VR systems sold by 2023, an astounding number (Rogers, 2019). With clear and growing interest from our public, now is the time for libraries to begin investing in their own equipment.

WHAT ARE THE TYPES OF VR SYSTEMS?

As we will soon discover, VR hardware can come in many forms. Running on those hardware platforms are unique software solutions to assist with tracking, rendering, and display. For the purposes of our work, we are going to zero in on four main types of VR hardware that are accessible to public libraries. Even more importantly, these four types of hardware are easy to explain and model. Public libraries looking to introduce VR to their communities will likely be considering one of the following options:

- Computer-tethered VR systems
- Game console VR systems
- All-in-one VR headsets
- Smartphone-powered VR solutions

Computer-Tethered Virtual Reality Systems

VR, as we have hopefully described, is a complex technological achievement that, for best results, requires cutting-edge computing hardware and software. While we will be giving an overview of the many VR solutions that exist, all of which are at different tiers of capability, we should start with the very top tier first. If your library is hoping to provide the most photo-realistic and immersive experience to your community, you will likely be looking for a "computer-tethered" VR solution.

For this particular setup, the hardware components have been split apart in a way that ensures that each piece of the VR solution is providing maximum performance. With a computer-tethered solution, you will likely be providing the user with a top-tier VR headset and a set of controllers, all while utilizing a powerful PC or Mac computer to do all of the display, audio, and haptic feedback rendering. Let's take a deeper dive into this VR solution and explore some of its key characteristics.

Key Features and Defining Aspects

When exploring the computer-tethered VR solution, libraries must understand that this will likely be the "bulkiest" of VR technology offerings. For the purposes of VR hardware development, companies have historically used this format of technology setup in order to maintain the "bleeding edge" of VR experiences. Companies working in this space know that they can compartmentalize their offerings, and work to tweak individual components in order to gain the best performance and experience for the user. Libraries looking to provide a computer-tethered solution must absolutely understand that there will be a unique dichotomy of impressive experiences, as well as impressive computing performance required to exceed user expectations. When giving this solution a holistic overview, be prepared to purchase, maintain, or interchange the components of headset, controller / feedback device, and main computer as months and years go by and new pieces are released to the hardware marketplace.

Pros and Cons of This Solution

As we have alluded to, this form of VR solution will require staff with some pretty decent technical know-how. Staff will also need to be keen to changes in the VR hardware marketplace in order to ensure they are providing the best technology to their communities. Basically, although this solution can absolutely be the most impressive, it will likely require the most oversight and upkeep.

As this is considered the high tier of VR offerings, it should be noted that this approach will likely be the most costly. The core component of this solution with be the PC or Mac computer that is used to drive the VR software and the displays for the user-worn headsets. For the purposes of this work, we will be focusing solely on the PC solution for powering VR experiences. In our opinion, while there are Mac solutions that are available, there are certain notable drawbacks to an Apple-powered approach. The first drawback is the overall cost of Mac computing hardware. It is typically much more expensive that its PC counterpart. In addition, we cannot say with confidence that you will find the same breadth of VR software titles available for use on the Mac platform. So, with that being established, we will be keeping things "PC-centric" for the purposes of this chapter.

When examining current computer-tethered VR solutions, we decided to use the HTC VIVE's recommended PC hardware requirements as a target for libraries looking to roll out this form of VR. We have hands-on experience with the particular headset and find it to be the most accessible option, cost-wise, for libraries to consider. As of this writing, HTC has formulated this specifications list:

- CPU: Intel Core i5-4590 or AMD FX 8350
- GPU: NVIDIA GeForce GTX 1060 or AMD Radeon RX 480
- RAM: 4GB or more
- Video output: HDMI 1.4 port or DisplayPort 1.2
- USB port: One USB 2.0 port
- Operating system: Windows 7 SP1, Windows 8.1, or Windows 10 ("What Are the System Requirements," n.d.).

We do have something extremely important to note for our readers regarding this vendor-supplied recommended hardware list—it may still be too low. For us, the CPU, RAM, video card, and operating system requirements all seem to be inadequate. If you are looking to offer this form of VR solution to your community, we would strongly recommend going above and beyond these listed specifications. Please consider the listing of hardware below this paragraph as somewhat more "future-proofed," ensuring that your VR setup will stay relevant and maintain performance for a longer period of time. However, understand that purchasing these components will likely mean your computing hardware will cost $1,000 or more.

- CPU: Intel Core i7 class processor
- GPU: NVIDIA GeForce RTX 20 series
- RAM: 16GB or more
- Video output: HDMI 1.4 port or DisplayPort 1.2, with multiple outputs preferred
- USB port: One USB 3.0 port, or possibly two
- Operating system: Windows 10

With all of that explained—and hopefully rationalized—we can make it clear that this will certainly provide the most robust and cutting-edge VR experience to your library patrons. The combination of strong VR hardware, computing power, and the ability to access a wide software collection will undoubtedly provide the most immersive experience possible.

Current Computer-Tethered Virtual Reality Solutions

HTC VIVE. The HTC VIVE line of VR provides a robust and immersive experience for its users. As of this writing, HTC has two VR solutions that it is offering to the public: the HTC VIVE and the HTC VIVE Pro. As of this writing, the basic VIVE costs $499, and the VIVE Pro "starter kit" costs $1,098 ("Product Comparison," n.d.). The VIVE is near the top of the line when it comes to a virtual experience. The newest VIVE unit, the VIVE Pro HMD has superior resolution to the original VIVE HMD, but either will provide an incredible experience. Not every system has the ability to allow the participant to physically move within a defined space, but the VIVE does.

When purchased, both of these VR systems come with an HMD, a face cushion for the HMD, the link box and power adaptor, two hand controllers with power adaptors, lanyards (to keep the controllers from accidentally falling from a user's hands), and two micro USB cables. Additionally, the units have two base stations, which will define the space the participant will interact in.

If your library is going to keep the VIVE somewhat portable, then it is definitely recommended to get tripods that can mount the base stations. The VIVE is one of the few VR systems that will allow the participant to have the ability to move within a defined area or be set up for a stationary experience. Setting up the defined area is simple, with on-screen tutorials which can guide library staff through this process.

Again, be aware that these units are tethered VR solutions, and they will require a PC or Mac to operate. The VIVE system, along with any PC based VR setup, does not include a computer. Because of the intense graphics that the VIVE creates, it requires a powerful PC with a high-end video/graphics card. Although HTC has a minimum system requirement, the VIVE may not function properly without the recommended system requirements. Many libraries or library systems opt to, instead of purchasing an "out-of-the-box" computer, build a computer that is powerful enough to not only handle the volumes of data that the VIVE generates but also anticipate updates and further hardware developments going into the future. When considering building a computer that will have the power for the VIVE, start with the graphics card (GPU) and build the machine around that component. Even if you purchase a powerful processor, without a very powerful GPU, your video output will be lackluster and will not satisfy the senses. If you believe that you have a computer onsite that can power a device like the HTC VIVE, but you aren't entirely sure, HTC's website has an online diagnostic tool to test computers to determine if they have the correct specifications to run the VIVE and VIVE Pro HMD. That online tool is available here: https://www.vive.com/us/ready/.

As of this writing, it is important to note that HTC has announced a new entry into their VIVE product line—the VIVE COSMOS. Like previous models, this unit will also require being tethered to a PC or Mac in order to function properly. Details are extremely light as of now—information such as specifications, PC requirements, and pricing almost non-existent. Be sure to keep an eye on news items regarding this piece of hardware.

Valve Index. Not one to miss a chance to "disrupt" an industry and throw its hat in the ring, Valve Software has recently unveiled the foray into the VR space—the "Valve Index." This particular VR solution also requires a PC (note: no Mac support) that is running either Windows 10, Linux, or Steam OS in order to work properly ("Valve Index," n.d.). The specifications recommended seem on par with the minimum requirements listed by HTC—and we would remain cautious about that. Again, the more powerful computer you are tethering this device to, the more likely you will have a better VR experience and be able to support new software in years to come.

This device is being sold to customers and shipped as stock becomes available. Currently, the product website has a package VR kit, and piecemeal offerings of the Valve Index's components for "reservation." An entire Valve Index VR Kit, with headset, two controllers, and two base stations, is being sold for $999. The components themselves sell separately for $499 (headset), $279 (two controllers), and $149 per base station, with two stations being a recommended quantity ("Valve Index," n.d.).

As of this writing, this headset is still very new and has only been on the market for a few weeks. What makes this system so enticing is the fact that Valve software manages one of the largest—if not *the* largest—software marketplaces for PC and Mac gaming in the industry. This means that owners of this device will have access to thousands of pieces of VR software to play with. Likely, most of these VR experiences will be game-oriented and require quick reflexes in order to play. Currently, the Valve software store does put a "Valve Index" logo on software items that have been confirmed to work with that specific hardware.

While keeping in mind that this device is extremely new and rather "bleeding-edge," in terms of VR headsets, the reviews have been mixed. As we were researching this exciting piece of hardware, we were somewhat disappointed to hear from Polygon.com that the device had garnered a mixed review. To summarize, they felt that when the device was working perfectly, it was amazing. It was absolutely the best offering out there. However, the review team was constantly plagued by technical glitches, snags, and crashes, all of which frustrated the user / reviewer (Kuchera, 2019). We would caution readers about these issues, but, because this is Valve software, we remain optimistic that many of these kinks may be worked out in the coming weeks and months. Be sure to read current reviews before purchasing!

Oculus Rift S. It is absolutely impossible to discuss current VR experiences without mentioning Oculus and its offerings. This company was basically the first on the scene. Exciting technology and VR enthusiasts around the world with its attempt to use Kickstarter.com to fully fund its first set of head-mounted displays, Oculus smashed its public financing goals and successfully released products to consumers. Oculus and its attempts to make consumer-accessible VR a reality caught the attention of Mark Zuckerberg (CEO of Facebook), who purchased Oculus in 2014 and brought many of its key engineering staff onboard.

Oculus's latest iteration of its tethered VR solution is known as the Oculus Rift S. Retailing for $399, this kit includes a head-mounted display, two touch controllers, and necessary cables ("Oculus Rift S," n.d.). In regards to tethering this device to a PC, the recommended specifications do not stray too far from requirements stated by both HTC and Valve. This device is not Mac compatible, and it appears to only work with the Windows 10 operating system. Again, we personally feel that utilizing this device with a PC means that you will want to tether it to a computer that has much higher specifications than those listed by Oculus.

Compared to other devices, how does the Oculus Rift S fare? Sadly, reviews have not been too positive. It seems that the price may be right for many libraries that are budget conscious. However, according to a recent article by The Verge, reviewers found the device to be disappointing in that it was only a minor improvement over its predecessor (Robertson, 2019). In their experience with this particular product, The Verge seemed most upset that the resolution of the screens in the head mounted display were only slightly sharper than the last version of the product. In addition, they reported some issues with the "refresh rate" of the displays inside the head mounted display. In this case, the refresh rate is a bit slower than the competition, and that can lend itself to motion sickness.

All in all, it is not a bad piece of hardware for the price. It should be noted that this headset does not require "base stations" for head tracking. The head mounted display has built in cameras to serve this purpose. For that reason, this may still be a viable option for some libraries, despite some notable limitations.

Where to Acquire VR Software for This Hardware Option

We sincerely hope that the way in which we discussed tethered-solution VR and its reliance upon being connected to a computer does not dissuade libraries from considering using this as a VR center piece in their library. While there may be increased cost, there is one substantial benefit to using this particular form of VR—the plethora of software you can use to showcase your device and VR technology.

With every vendor solution we have listed thus far, each of them presents hardware owners with its own "marketplace" of VR software. These options range from free demonstration pieces, which are usually extremely simple and showcase one aspect or "gimmick" of VR, to $50 or more, for professionally produced gaming titles.

If libraries are willing to venture beyond vendor marketplaces, and we strongly encourage that they do, they should visit Valve software's VR marketplace, located at https://store.steampowered.com/vr. Valve software requires that users create an account on their platform and install a small client on their PC to purchase games, download titles, and manage the user's software library. In our experience, this client is extremely simple to set up and takes up very little computing overhead on the VR workstation.

Once libraries begin shopping this marketplace, they will find that all titles are presented in an easy-to-browse fashion. Besides listing software titles, compatibility with various VR solutions is clearly noted on product pages. Age ratings are visible, and there are even user reviews for specific bits of software. This is an easy way to pick through and quickly find quality titles that can show off your VR setup. Additionally, there are seasonal sales in this marketplace and the price cuts can be enormous. Libraries may want to wait for these seasonal sales to stock up on a number of titles, and slowly roll out these experiences to their patrons throughout the year. A credit card can be linked to a Steam account to facilitate purchasing. For libraries that may be reluctant to do this, one option can be for the library to purchase a Steam Gift Card via a credit card and then load that gift card balance on to the Steam account. Without linking a credit card, staff and patrons will be unable to make accidental purchases. Absolutely visit this marketplace and browse the title selection!

Game Console-Based Virtual Reality Systems

In the world of VR, it's not a big secret that video games have been a big driver of the technology and have helped to push it forward. VR device engineers and programmers have surely wished their own creations could whisk them to virtual gaming worlds where they could compete with others, go on adventurous quests, or simply have a quirky, unique experience. Paradoxically, while video games have been a big driver of VR improvements, video game consoles have lagged behind. Game consoles are typically sold at prices far below powerful gaming PCs. For that reason, they simply have not had the "horsepower" to provide truly immersive VR experiences.

That paradox has rectified itself, fortunately. In recent years, video game consoles have become absolute powerhouses. Console makers like Microsoft and Sony have been trying to provide 4K graphics, huge amounts of storage, lightning quick framerates, and other cutting-edge features. These improvements have finally put enough processing power into these consoles to allow them to support true VR experiences.

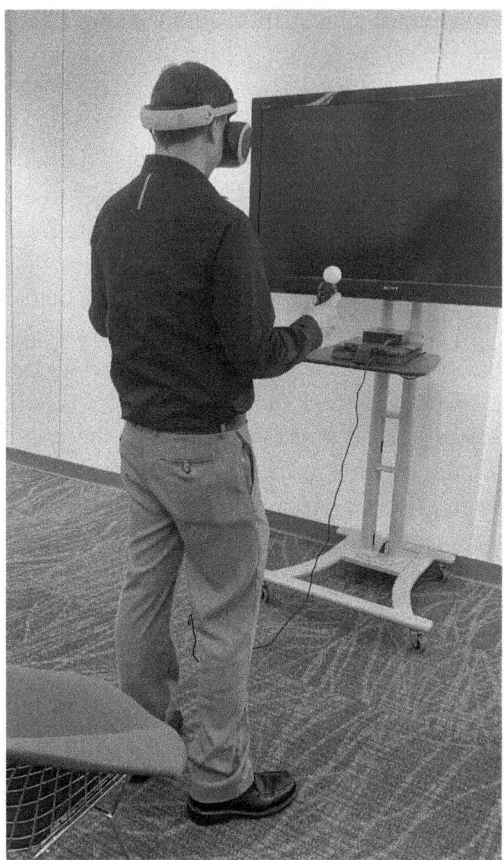

Figure 4.1 A Playstation 4 VR with participant, connected TV, and safety chair.

Key Features and Defining Aspects

Historically speaking, the allure of video games consoles has been their ease-of-use. Throughout the years, while PC and Mac gaming solutions have been able to create amazing experiences—either with or without VR—they have required their users to have a certain level of technical know-how. For many, this was a pretty significant barrier to access and it prevented people from experiencing gaming on those platforms.

What has made game consoles so insanely successful over the years is their simplicity. Contemporary game consoles are typically sold as one box, which houses an optical drive for loading games, a hard drive for downloading games and keeping save files, an integrated graphics card and CPU, and plug-and-play controllers. In a sense, every Microsoft Xbox One console is going to be identical, as will every Sony PlayStation 4 Pro. Software is made to run on these machines, and because there is no variation of hardware, there is little chance of software glitching out or crashing. Contrast this to PC gaming, which often consists of enthusiasts creating machines out of randomly salvaged parts.

Game consoles are relatively inexpensive, easy to acquire, hook up to any modern TV in a matter of minutes, and are extremely reliable. They are a robust piece of computing hardware and make a worthwhile choice for libraries looking to provide a VR experience to their communities (see figure 4.1 for an example of a typical game console VR setup).

Pros and Cons of This Solution

It is hard to describe a game console without mentioning its immediate positive aspects. Game consoles are mass-produced machines that were created with the sole purpose of providing entertainment. They are made with a level of hardware consistency that is not generally seen in the PC world. This consistency means that games created for this console are guaranteed to operate without glitches and crashes, and all add-on devices will be compatible.

In today's world, game consoles pack quite a bit of horsepower under the hood. In many cases, the latest game console offerings from Microsoft and Sony rival their powerful PC gaming counterparts. These devices have the strength to provide VR gaming experiences at a quality level that will grant users full immersion. In addition, for the amount of power they provide, gaming consoles are relatively inexpensive. As they are mass produced and identical, manufacturers are able to keep pricing extremely competitive. Game consoles are so widespread and popular, there is a very good chance that many people in your community may already own them. Thus, their experience at a console-based VR event could potentially be reproduced by them at home. This also makes the prospects of finding and training volunteers to assist in running VR programs much easier.

The only notable downside to gaming consoles as a VR solution is the lack of upgradability. Once you own a console, there won't be any way to open it up to upgrade a CPU or video card. Because the development costs of complex game console accessories is so high, don't expect to see more than one iteration of a VR headset for a game console's generational lifetime. This is counter to the PC world, where outdated and underpowered components can be easily replaced without having to replace an entire system.

Current Game Console-based Virtual Reality Solutions

PlayStation VR. Arguably, the first console-based VR solution is Sony's PlayStation 4 VR—and it is impressive. The PlayStation gaming console has been a popular platform since its release in 1994, and that success has helped it to grow into subsequent hardware updates. The most current version of this popular console has a fully functioning VR component, known as the PlayStation VR. Coupled with PlayStation 4's powerful CPU and graphics card, this machine is able to drive VR simulation with ease.

As of this writing, there are a number of elements that will be have to be acquired to have a VR experience as immersive as the tethered-VR solutions mentioned previously. The main component required will be a PlayStation 4 console. This comes in two variations, with the basic console costing $300 and the PlayStation 4 Pro costing $375 at a major online retailer. The important difference between these two versions is that the Pro model will allow 4K video output to a television. That may not be that important for our VR programming, but might be a nice bonus if you plan to use this gaming console for video game tournaments or other uses. The PlayStation VR basic headset costs $215 at a major online retailer and comes with a demo disc with a few VR experiences. With that being said, *we would highly recommend that libraries purchase a PlayStation VR bundle that includes two PlayStation VR Move controllers.* These devices will absolutely make the experience more immersive and are worth the extra cost. As of this writing, a VR bundle with two controllers also includes two VR games and the demo disc for $350. Additional details about Sony PlayStation VR and components can be found here: https://www.playstation.com/en-us/explore/playstation-vr/.

Altogether, you could have a pretty compact, easily portable VR gaming solution at your library for a total cost of $650.

Nintendo Switch—Labo VR. We were a bit reluctant to mention the following VR solution in this chapter; however, we have received some positive feedback from people that have used the Nintendo Labo VR device. Our only trepidation is due to the fact that this implementation is very basic, and there have been legitimate complaints regarding the level of immersion. With that being said, let's take a look at this particularly quirky instance of gaming console-based VR.

So, what exactly is the Nintendo Labo VR? After Nintendo launched its enormously successful Nintendo Switch console in 2017, the company began to secretly work on fun console accessories made out of cardboard and other materials. The purpose of these add-ons was to offer families fun projects that they could work on together, in the sense that the accessories could sometimes take a bit of effort to piece together and test. After many of these "Labo" projects were released, Nintendo revealed their fourth Labo project, the Nintendo Labo VR—which surprised the entire industry.

In order to work correctly, this $80 Nintendo Switch accessory will require the $300 Nintendo Switch base console. The kit is made out of cardboard and some other basic components. It is a bit clunky—there is no head strap. Users will have to always hold the device up to their heads in order to get the proper VR effect. Headphones can be used for a better audio experience, but they are not incorporated in to the actual Labo design itself. The Nintendo Switch Joy Con remote controllers do work in tandem with the device, thus giving an elevated sense of immersion. Included with this Labo kit is a "60 bite-sized games," which ensures there will be some basic content to enjoy ("Nintendo Labo," 2019). In addition to that, Nintendo has enabled some VR functionality on their insanely popular Super Mario Odyssey, The Legend of Zelda: Breath of the Wild, and Super Smash Bros. Ultimate games.

Reviews of the device have not been stellar, but for the price, this Labo accessory may be a great way to affordably introduce VR to your community. Engadget declared the device to be "cute . . . and kinda boring," so the experience may be fun in small doses (Naudus, 2019). For libraries that have especially tight budgets, there is a strong chance that a member of your staff may or someone in your community may already own a Nintendo Switch console that the library could borrow for event use. Beyond that, your library would have to make an $80 commitment in Labo to offer a basic VR experience. Nintendo promises to continue adding VR content to future games that the Labo can access, so stay tuned for news on that front.

Where to Acquire VR Software for This Hardware Option

When it comes to the use of console-based VR experiences, one of the notable benefits is how easy it can be to acquire software for use, and often at a discount. For libraries that are planning to use this hardware option, modern game consoles have software marketplaces that can be accessed online, through the console itself. These marketplaces allow credit card purchases, or for libraries that are wary of using credit cards, gift card balances can be loaded on to an account.

Just like we had previously explained with the Steam software marketplace for PC, game consoles often have seasonal sales in which games can be purchased at steep discounts through their respective marketplaces. In addition to that, software intended for these gaming consoles may be able to be purchased used. Online retailers such as Amazon and GameStop allow customers to buy used copies of physical game software discs at a discount. For budget-conscious libraries, this is another way VR can be implemented in a cost-effective manner. Be sure to read reviews on gaming software before purchasing. Even in the gaming console world, there are occasionally games and other bits of software that are lackluster.

We will touch on this aspect later in the chapter, but be aware that the popular PlayStation 4 console does have free access to the YouTube app and that it will allow playback of VR-enabled video content. There is a possibility that you can offer VR experiences without purchasing any software at all. While that isn't an ideal solution, it might be a way to build interest in your VR events before committing money towards software purchases.

All-in-One VR Headsets

Up until this point, we have spoken at length about VR solutions that require the user to remain somewhat close to whatever machine was powering the VR simulation. If you were using VR, you were never more than a few feet away from a personal computer or a gaming console. But now, imagine the ability to experience high-quality, fully immersive VR without the need to be tethered. With the latest VR technologies, you can! The improvements in VR technology and components, as well as cost reductions and hardware speed increases, means that many of the tech that was required to power a VR experience can now fit into the headset.

In short, VR technology has finally hit a point where speed, size, and cost have intersected, and companies are offering hardware that looks similar to what many of us have witnessed in science-fiction movies. Being untethered means freedom, and it also means impressive immersion.

Key Features and Defining Aspects

When it comes to VR, and when our past selves consider what we envisioned VR devices to look like, the all-in-one VR headset was very much on the mark. Ten years ago, as it became apparent that accurate, high-resolution VR was just on the horizon, many in the technology field imagined users wandering about with very basic headsets, waving their arms around and interacting with virtual elements. The actual reality was that VR, for many years, required immense amounts of computing power to be possible, and head mounts would simply have to be tethered to bulky computers in order to work properly and believably.

We are now far closer to our initial vision of what VR head mounts and other hardware pieces would look like—comfortable, cutting-edge entertainment technology that allows the user to have significant freedom of movement. All-in-one VR solutions consist of a head mount that is packed with high-resolution displays, in-ear audio, head tracking, and the ability to wirelessly talk to haptic feedback controllers. There are no tethers that prevent the user from moving freely, feeling the snag or pull of a cable reaching its limit, suddenly jarring the user out of the experience.

All-in-one VR headsets are the experience that many companies, such as HTC and Oculus, have been striving to provide. And from indications we have received, all-in-one devices are where many of these companies will be focusing the majority of their research and development funds as we move forward.

Pros and Cons of This Solution

While it is easy to think that the all-in-one VR solution is the most impressive and the one that libraries should gravitate towards, there are some very important aspects to point out. This solution tends to have the smallest footprint for the level of realism that it provides. There are few cables to worry about, as it is an untethered piece of hardware. It is extremely portable and can be easily brought to locations "off-site" from libraries, such as local community centers, schools, churches, fairs, and other events.

However, keep in mind that VR technology is still advancing pretty rapidly. In addition, these strides in hardware mean that software is increasing in complexity and presentation. Just like the major issue that plagues game console-based VR solutions, all-in-one systems cannot be upgraded easily—or at all. Unlike the PC-tethered solution, where a CPU or video card upgrade may boost VR performance, once you have an all in-one VR piece, you will not be able to squeeze faster performance or higher resolutions out of it.

All-in-one solutions appear to be the general direction that VR hardware manufacturers are headed in. However, that does not ensure that software for these all-in-one hardware pieces will be backward compatible with older models. Basically, manufacturers may force you to purchase new software to run on new devices. As of this writing, something very troubling to note is that software for the all-in-one devices we are showcasing is only available from the Oculus website. It seems this device resides in a "walled garden" where only Oculus-approved software will run on the device (Computer Hope, 2019). This may severely limit the abundance and quality of software that can be experienced. It greatly limits consumer choice. That may change in the future, but we are unsure.

Current All-in-One VR Solutions

Oculus Go and Oculus Quest Headsets. In the realm of all-in-one VR headsets, there are quite a few options available. However, the only brand that is creating any sort of substantial footprint in the marketplace is Oculus. At this time, Oculus has two versions of an all-in-one headset currently for sale—the Oculus Go and the Oculus Quest.

As stated before, both of these headset solutions are all-in-one and completely untethered. The Oculus Go was the company's first foray into this space, and this device currently retails for $250 for the 64GB edition. The hardware comes with one basic controller and essential components, such as a charging cable and a frame spacer for users with eyeglasses. The headset is very simple in appearance and borders on the "bulky" side of things. There is integrated audio, so there is no need for earbuds or headphones ("Oculus Go," n.d.). It should be noted that the head tracking on this device is rather basic. It shouldn't be expected to be as smooth as the follow-up piece of hardware, the Oculus Quest.

The Oculus Quest is the second iteration of Oculus's all-in-one VR solution, and it is marketed toward gaming. The 64GB version of this headset retails for $400, but as it will be for gaming purposes, and the internal storage space may fill quickly, we would recommend the 128 GB version for $500. Like the Oculus Go, this solution is packaged with a charging cable and a frame spacer. However, this unit is bundled with two controllers instead of one ("Oculus Quest," 2019). That is sure to make gaming experiences far more interactive. Further improving upon the Oculus Go, this unit has head-tracking cameras mounted on the exterior of the device, which make head movement in a VR experience much smoother. In addition, the display is of a slightly higher resolution than the Oculus Go.

As of this writing, it is important to note that Oculus has announced that their Quest VR solution will eventually be able to run software designed for the Rift headset via a tethered configuration (Horwitz, 2019). This is a big development for this specific piece of hardware. With release details still somewhat vague, those libraries looking to add VR to their offerings should be aware of this update to the Oculus Quest hardware and know that, if implemented, the software library will be greatly increased.

Where to Acquire VR Software for This Hardware Option

We should admit, we are a bit disheartened to see how Oculus has decided to implement software access for their range of all-in-one VR devices. For both of these units, software must be purchased directly from Oculus. While there are some free games available for these systems, we cannot vouch for the quality of the titles. Other games with some level of name recognition, such as Beat Saber and SUPERHOT VR, were available in the Oculus marketplace. Either of these titles are sure to impress, though they can rely on fast reflexes in order to play adequately. There are free YouTube VR apps for both systems, which means that YouTube 360-degree videos should be playable. We are unsure if Oculus will ever open up these devices so that users can download the software from a rival marketplace like Steam. Be aware that if you do choose to employ this VR solution at your library, you may be limited in the amount of quality software that you can showcase.

Again, as of this writing, there is the strong possibility that the Oculus Quest will have access to an expanded software library, through use of tethering the device to a PC (https://venturebeat.com/2019/09/25/oculus-quest-will-get-hand-tracking-oculus-link-to-play-rift-pc-games/). Libraries should check product details to see if this promised update has become active before purchasing this device.

Smartphone-Powered VR solutions

Although top-tier, high resolution VR experiences are amazing, not every institution has the financial means to afford such sophisticated systems. But the good news is that there are other experiences that are lower in cost and can provide a VR experience without breaking the bank. Even better news: many of the patrons walking in to libraries may already be capable of experiencing VR on the smartphones in their pockets.

Smartphones have come a long way in the last 10 years. Although they have always been impressive, with their ability to surf the Internet, install applications, take photographs, and do a myriad of other tasks, they have generally only provided a small fraction of the processing power of a standard computer workstation. That is hardly the case anymore. Today's smartphones rival basic computer workstations in many ways. They have substantial processing power, high resolution screens, the ability to run complex applications, and 3D rendering capabilities due to powerful graphics hardware. All of this packed into a slim, sleek device.

Seeing the potential to provide a VR experience, some companies, such as Google, have come up with innovative ways to demonstrate VR for their device owners. Smartphone-powered VR solutions are a significantly important option for libraries looking to introduce VR to their communities.

Key Features and Defining Aspects

Smartphone-based VR devices are amazing for one simple reason: they basically fit in your pocket. As the processing power of smartphones has dramatically increased in recent years, due to the usefulness and versatility of smartphone operating systems and apps, they have started to replace computer workstations for many critical functions. One positive side effect of that increase in processing power and screen resolution is now the ability to power VR software. Coupled with devices like Google Cardboard or Gear VR, people are now able to have a VR solution that is light, portable, and potentially head-mountable. As software for smartphone app markets tends to be lower-priced, this means that there are many VR applications that are both impressive and inexpensive. Finally, we can't help but point out that smartphone operating systems are designed with ease of use in mind, so these devices and software solutions tend to be very easy to navigate.

Pros and Cons of This Solution

We've lightly touched on some of the positives and negatives of smartphone-based VR, but we should be frank: there are some notable limitations here. To be fair, the smartphone-based VR solution might be very enticing to libraries for the simple fact that so many people in our communities already own a smartphone, and the odds of its being able to support VR apps is very high. That means that hands-on demonstrations and workshops, where patrons are handed Google Cardboards and can test-drive different VR apps on their own phones, is certainly a possibility. There are some free VR apps available for smartphones already and also YouTube "cardboard VR" videos (note: these are not the same as YouTube 360-degree videos) are freely streamable. For apps that do cost money to purchase, users can expect them to be relatively inexpensive.

On the negative side of things, we should point out that these VR experiences are very basic and essentially "no frills." Smartphone VR is usually presented in a split-screen format. Basically, your smartphone screen is divided into two sections, with one side acting as a display for your left eye and the other side acting as a display for your right eye. The accessories required to separate these images and provide magnification are very basic. The experience is nothing close to what a dedicated VR headset can provide. The software engines powering the VR experience on the smartphone usually have bland graphics and refresh rates are poor. If your smartphone VR head mount includes a strap, that is ideal. Otherwise, you have to hold your device with your hands, and your arms will get tired . . . quickly. Finally, even if the device includes a head strap, don't expect the weight to be balanced evenly. This can make for an awkward experience. Overall, this is a great way to take your first dip into VR, but do not expect a fully immersive experience.

Current Smartphone-Powered VR Solutions

Google Cardboard. Regarding inexpensive ways to provide a VR experience, few options come close to Google Cardboard. And why is it called "Google Cardboard?" The viewing device is literally made of cardboard. Costing only a few dollars—it was even included free of charge with the Sunday *New York Times* several years ago (Robertson, 2016). Google Cardboard is basically two independent eye-pieces that can be used to view a split-screen smartphone display. When using Google Cardboard–approved apps, this device does trick the brain into thinking it is in a virtual environment. However, the effect is extremely basic, and users will have none of the "quality of life" features that make other devices far superior. The level of immersion with this device is absolutely minimal. It should also be noted that this device, in cardboard form, does not have a head strap, so users must hold the device with their hands. That experience gets tiring very quickly, so only short VR sessions are possible. It may not be the perfect solution for high-end VR experiences, but Google Cardboard does fit a niche for simple, cheap, and potentially lendable VR for libraries. It works with both Apple iOS and, obviously, Google Android smartphone devices. Also, out of our devices listed, it seems to have the lowest age requirement, with Google stating "Cardboard is not for use by children without adult supervision" ("Product Safety," n.d.).

Samsung Gear VR. If you are looking for a smartphone VR device that offers a much better experience, look no further than the Samsung Gear VR. This VR solution sells for about $40 on major online retail websites. There are a few notable details that make this device considerably better than Google Cardboard. The Samsung Gear VR is a head-mount unit with head strap and smartphone cradle. That means it is a hands-free experience, and that is sure to be far more comfortable to users than the Cardboard alternative. In addition, this device ships with its own controller, allowing better movement and immersion in VR experiences. With this being probably the lowest-tier of decent VR experiences, some reviews of the device are rather positive. Tom's Guide (www.tomsguide.com) gave it a very favorable rating several years ago, when the device was first released (Smith, 2017). The only drawback to this particular device is that it works on Samsung smartphone devices only. That may limit its practicality for library lending and BYOD VR workshops.

Where to Acquire Smartphone-Powered VR Software for This Hardware Option

When it comes to finding VR apps for use on either Google Android or Apple iOS smartphone devices, libraries will almost exclusively be acquiring content from these respective app stores. When looking at either the Apple App Store or Google Play Store, be sure to look at app reviews, age restrictions, content warnings, and definitely price. As is the case with many apps on smartphones, "free" does not always mean "good." "Free" also does not mean "free." Many apps will have "in-app purchases" that will require you to pay to unlock additional content. If you plan to do a workshop with a free app that has additional paid components, there is a very strong chance that your participants will hit a part of a game or experience that will suddenly turn into an advertisement. Be sure to playtest all apps before using them during an event or recommending them to patrons. With that being said, there are certainly some gems out there!

POLICY CONSIDERATIONS FOR VIRTUAL REALITY

The ability to be immersed in VR allows libraries to expand their roles in many different areas. Just as the physical collection of books and other tangible materials allows library patrons to transport themselves through the "mind's eye," the addition of VR allows that eye to expand to an actual visual and audio experience. Before a library can make the technology available to the public, a careful evaluation should take place asking the following questions:

- Why does the library need VR?
- What are the goals of VR in the library?
- What are the potential limitations (e.g., age, medical conditions)?
- What experiences are appropriate for a library setting?
- Where will the equipment be set up?
- What types of programming will take place?

These are all relevant questions that need careful consideration when purchasing, designing, and deploying any new technology for public use. Fulfilling the "why" is a question that is as old as libraries themselves. Why does a library need VR? VR in many respects is similar to reading a book, or listening to music, or listening to an audiobook. When people read, it engages their minds, ignites imagination, or causes insightful thought. When someone listens to music, views a movie or television program, or listens to a podcast, they are somehow transported to another place that only their mind can take them. These are all experiences that occur in the mind of the participant. VR takes that experience and, in some ways, transitions that "mind's eye" into a visual and audio experience. It pulls the idea out through the eyes into a fully immersive experience. VR's goal in libraries is to inform, educate, and to inspire all that attempt the experience.

Selection Criteria of Content

There are many games and experiences that are available from VR programmers and developers, but, as librarians do with all types of collections, the experiences need to be carefully curated to conform with the mission of both the library and the goals of the use of VR. There are games and experiences that may not be suitable for a library setting, so a good first step is to reach out to other libraries that have VR technology and ask what software and experiences they have recently utilized for patron engagement and programming. Knowing what experiences are available and have already been tested and approved by other libraries will only be helpful in developing a catalog of age- and library-appropriate games and experiences. It will also drive future programming.

As there are with many home electronics - whether they are gaming consoles, tablets, smartphones, and even smart refrigerators - there are video games and other forms of entertainment. But with VR there are also experiences. An *experience* is defined as ". . . something personally encountered, undergone, or lived through" (Merriam-Webster, n.d.). This definition certainly applies to the types of games and experiences in VR. There are many traditional games that are similar to video games of the past but have now become immersive, such as saving the world from alien invaders, but other types of VR software do not involve competitions or games. They are engaging experiences that trick the brain into thinking the user is inside another world. This illusion of sight and sound transcends playing a game and becomes an experience. The user is transported to another place, whether walking down the Champs-Elysees in Paris, exploring inside a Picasso painting, or visiting the International Space Station. That is when the potential of VR is unlocked.

So, with the plethora of games and experiences that are available in SteamVR alone, it is important to make these patron interactions entertaining and educational. Research is always a starting point. Visit sites that review VR software, especially sites that review VR games and experiences. SteamVR will have user ratings, but it is also important to see reviews that are not generated by the sites that also sell the content. Some good resources include, but are not limited to, the following websites:

- http://www.digitaltrends.com
- http://www.pcmag.com
- http://virtualrealityreviewer.com
- http://vrgamecritic.com
- http://tomsguide.com

Unlike standard PC or console games, a rating system does not currently exist for VR games and experiences. When evaluating VR software, whether it be on SteamVR, through Google Expeditions, or any other hardware, consider the American Library Association's list of criteria for selecting non digital content (ALA Office for Intellectual Freedom, 2018). The criteria outlined by ALA do not include this type of digital content in its criteria, but taking the spirit of the selection process will be helpful in making sound decisions regarding VR game/experience purchases. Here is a list of content criteria for VR gaming that is born of ALA's "Selection Criteria":

- Is the material compatible with the systems owned by the library?
- Is the material educational or entertainment based?
- For what age group is this content appropriate (Child/Teen/Adult)?
- Is there violence/graphic content?
- Are there sounds or experiences that may alert, startle or frighten?
- Does the material require the participant to be stationary or mobile?
- Does the material adhere to the mission of the library?

Every library will evaluate these criteria differently and make determinations regarding appropriateness for libraries and the age groups they are curating for, but having a general set of guidelines will help the library professional make educated decisions regarding the best content.

Age Concerns, Health Concerns

Safety is a concern with VR, especially with HMDs obscuring the users' sight. Oculus Rift and Gear VR headsets are recommended for ages 13 and older. PlayStation VR limits age to 12 and older, and the HTC VIVE is not designed for children. Google states that Google Cardboard is safe for children with adult supervision (Gent, 2016). There are health concerns for children under the age of 13 who utilize VR, particularly since very young children may not be able to properly verbalize discomfort to a parent or adult. Additionally, they may not be aware of pre-existing conditions that could be triggered by a VR experience (LaMotte, 2017). With that being said, there are many simple VR experiences designed for children. Without any real research data on the long-term effects of VR on the eyes and brain of someone under the age of 13, having a prohibition against children's use or a waiver in place may help to insulate the library from any potential liability in the long term. Additionally, all of the major manufacturers recommend no more than 30 minutes of time in the virtual world and to take 10- to 15-minute breaks between sessions (Fagan, 2018). People prone to seizures because of rapidly blinking lights are also not advised to wear VR HMDs (Fagan, 2018). People who are prone to motion sickness may also experience nausea. Prolonged use of VR HMDs can also cause eye soreness or trouble focusing. If the library is concerned about these potential risks, then policy needs to be crafted along with waivers if the library is going to allow these at-risk groups to experience VR.

Waivers

Please note: *The following section is not legal advice. The information provided in this section is meant to inform the reader of potential VR risks. It is highly recommended that any policy or waiver created from the information in this section, for the purposes of protecting patrons from harm and libraries from liability, be vetted by library administration and library legal counsel.*

As is the case with many modern forms of library event programming, there are some potential risks involved with VR experiences. With that being said, the potential for harm is slight. We'll work to detail some of the more prominent risk factors, but do not let these factors prevent your library from experimenting with VR programming. In order to limit library liability, we strongly recommend that libraries craft a waiver that must be signed by participants before any event and that library staff are made aware of and trained to deal with potential VR side-effects.

First off, libraries must be prepared to give VR participants space to maneuver in. For example, as a player is engaged with an active game like "Beat Saber," there is absolutely the chance they will be flailing around—perhaps even with force. With the headset attached to their face, they will be unable to see their actual surroundings. While the library presenter will be on hand to keep a player's movements in check, there is always the chance they could make contact with another patron, despite the presenter's best efforts to clear a space. Any waiver that is crafted should detail this risk and explain to participants that physical contact may occur. It should also be stated that some VR experiences are tethered to a computer or console. There is always the chance that a participant may get tangled in or trip over a connecting wire. Library staff should be mindful of wire placement and be quick to halt a VR experience if a patron is in immediate danger.

Similarly, if a patron is flailing around or is about to lose their balance, a library staff member may have to grab them—forcefully and quickly. This should be mentioned in a waiver or, at the very least, verbally explained to participants by staff before the experience begins.

Another serious concern for libraries should be the fact that a small portion of the human population may have epilepsy and be at risk for conditions that can trigger the symptoms. This can be an issue in VR, since many of our experiences that will be offered to patrons will be video game content that may contain repetitive flashing lights, in complex patterns. To be fair, this risk is not necessarily new to library programming. Many libraries have offered video-gaming events and tournaments in recent years. All of those gaming events and tournaments events would have carried a small risk of triggering epilepsy as well. There is a concern among device manufacturers that the VR experience may trigger that effect on those that are susceptible (https://www.cnn.com/2017/12/13/health/virtual-reality-vr-dangers-safety/index.html). Since many adults may have had Epilepsy and have not been exposed to triggers, there is a slight chance that a VR experience may be the first time they experience symptoms. An epilepsy warning should absolutely be added to any VR event waiver that a library creates.

When talking about VR and negative experiences, the one that is most likely is motion sickness. VR is still in a state in which the displays, head tracking, resolution, and fresh rates are not exactly "perfect." They are still far from what the human eye and other senses feel when interacting with a true environment. For that reason, some people may experience a level of motion sickness when using a VR headset. This may cause dizziness or nausea. Patrons must be aware of this risk before starting a VR session, and library staff must be able to respond to this situation quickly. Patrons may lose their balance and need to sit down or be assisted. Other patrons may become physically ill and get sick to their stomach. It isn't pretty, but some VR events at libraries have a garbage pail in close proximity to participants. These effects are usually remedied very quickly by removing the headset and sitting down. The act of getting physically ill can be hugely embarrassing for a library patron, so, again, it is critical to have them understand the risks of participating.

Finally, some VR participants may experience blurry vision when utilizing VR. This could be due to a variety of factors, and it should be explained to patrons that this may occur. Again, have staff close by to assist with patrons who may be uneasy with movement while experiencing vision issues.

For a terrific overview of potential VR risks, we highly recommend reading "A Super Quick Safety Guide to Letting Your Kids use VR Headsets" on Wareable.com: https://www.wareable.com/vr/guide-vr-headsets-children.

With all of that being said, these effects are rare and will likely only afflict an extremely small number of VR participants. Surely, the positive experiences that your program attendees will have will quickly show that anxiety regarding VR sicknesses are largely unwarranted. As with any library event that requires a waiver, be sure to have all waiver and policy language vetted by library administration and library legal counsel.

STAFF TRAINING AND RESPONSIBILITIES: THREE LEVELS OF STAFF ENGAGEMENT

A well-trained staff is essential for the successful adoption of VR technology at your library. To this end, we have identified three categories of staff interactions with the technology and the requisite knowledge needed to do so. It is important to note that these categories do not address job titles, merely responsibilities. In the absence of formal requirements, such as civil service regulations, contracts, or other restrictions, you may wish to assign responsibilities based on staff enthusiasm. One need only think about one's favorite teachers growing up. Likely, these educators loved the subject matter and conveyed their enthusiasm when showing it to others. As you train, seek out those employees expressing excitement and determine if they can be offered a greater role in the development of programs and services.

Empowering All Staff with Basic VR Knowledge

While every single employee of the library is unlikely to utilize VR in their day-to-day job responsibilities, this does not exempt them from staff training! This first level of training is more akin to an orientation to the technology, and more specifically, how you intend to use it at the library. Structure this training as a show and tell. Explain to staff what VR is and what specific equipment you've invested in. Demonstrate how it works. With transparency in mind, describe the potential side effects of using a VR headset. Whether or not staff members wish to try the equipment themselves, attempt to give them some insight on what it looks like to a user. In the case of a PC-connected headset, you can display the experience on a monitor or through a projector. For an all-in-one, more will be left to the imagination, although you could show a trailer that conveys the general idea.

Depending on how many staff members you will be training, you may wish to split the instruction between the orientation and demonstration portions. Though all staff can usually sit through a lecture, providing individuals with a VR experience can be time-intensive. A good option is to simply have people sign up for 10-minute slots during which they can use the equipment for themselves. In terms of the content of their VR experience, consider using something that is low-intensity and doesn't require a lot of explanation. Watching a 360 video is a good entry point, as a user can simply put a headset on and observe, gaining an idea of how immersive VR can be. If you instead decide to provide access to a game or more active experience, you may need to first have the user go through a VR orientation experience offered by many manufacturers.

VR Event Programmers and Facilitators

Programmers are those staff members who will be using the technology with your public, and may include enthusiastic staff members that you've identified in your general VR orientation. These individuals will need to be shown how to operate the equipment in depth. This training should include how to turn on and calibrate your equipment, and how to adjust the sizing on the headset. They will also need to know how to open and use the experiences you intend to offer, and some basic troubleshooting will be useful in case you encounter an issue requiring immediate attention during a program.

In addition to managing the equipment, your programmers must be shown library procedure. Ensure that they understand age restrictions and your library's policies regarding content. If you are using a waiver, these staff members should be familiar with it. While some individuals may know how to use VR personally, they must be comfortable instructing others. Can they relay instructions effectively and courteously? Do not ignore the customer service component of training!

VR Technicians

The technician has the highest level of staff training, and subsequently, technicians are the smallest group to contend with. This employee(s) are the lead staff trainer for your VR equipment. Paradoxically, as your library's first user, they will often lack any formal training themselves. In absence of formal training, your first technician will need to be self-taught.

As a first step, they should devour the owner's manual cover to cover. They may then need to rely on product forums and web tutorials to first find their way.

Once familiar with the equipment, your technicians will become responsible for the long-term operation of the library's VR equipment, including advanced troubleshooting. They should immediately register and file away any warranties that came with the equipment to protect against potential equipment failure. Following this, they must work with library administration to develop a cleaning/maintenance cycle for the equipment that complies with the manufacturer's instructions.

In addition to managing the equipment itself, employees in this category are responsible for purchasing and downloading content for your VR equipment. This requires them to be familiar with your library's collection development policy, particularly if you have one specific to VR. They will need to manage storage space and keep an eye on the budget associated with your VR equipment.

While the above represents a suggested assignment of responsibilities, you should feel free to develop a process that works for your own organization. Roles can, of course, be combined. Ultimately, you should choose an approach that allows you to effectively operate your equipment without creating a complex workflow that burdens staff unnecessarily.

HOSTING VR PROGRAMS: EVENT IDEAS AND PROPER PLANNING

When it finally comes time for your library to introduce VR to your community, you have a few options at your disposal. Read on for a few different ways VR can be presented to your community.

When introducing a new technology to your library's community, whether it is 3D printing, drones, AR, or, in this case, VR, a simple lecture format may prove to be quite functional. However, just be aware that when showcasing VR for the public, you will encounter some limitations.

If your library staff members wish to do an explanation of VR technology, explaining the fundamentals, demonstrating some VR tech, sharing a buying guide, and speculating where this technology may be headed in the future, a classic "lecture-style" presentation may perfectly suit your needs. Typically, the layout for this type of presentation is an audience-style room configuration, with a large section of space left free of objects and clutter in the front of the room (see figure 4.2). Presenters will likely want to utilize either a large TV or projector for the purposes of showing PowerPoint content. This content may be some brief history, web content of device manufacturers, or YouTube videos of various VR news tidbits.

If possible, during a lecture-style presentation, an actual VR headset or solution should be present for a live demonstration of the technology. The TV and projector should, ideally, be a way for audience members to see the content that is being displayed on a VR solution that the participant is experiencing. This will allow the audience to understand why the participant is moving and reacting in the manner in which they are.

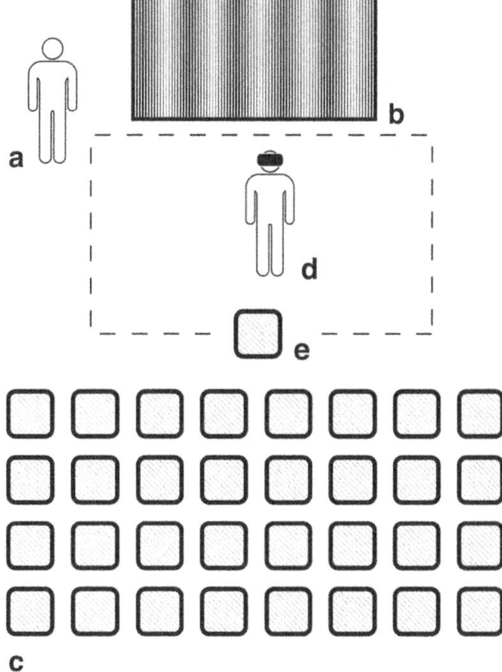

Figure 4.2 VR Lecture. a - Presenter, in close proximity to VR Participant (d), is able to intervene if there is a problem. Note: Presenter is outside of marked "safety area" on floor. b - TV or projected screen to simultaneously display VR content. c - Audience members, seated and safely outside VR "safety area" marked on floor. d - VR Participant. Note: Participant is wearing headset, is in "safety area" marked on floor, and is in close proximity to a safety chair (e). e - Safety chair. This chair is to allow the participant to sit, should they become tired, or experience motion sickness or dizziness.

The actual VR demonstration should probably be short—perhaps only twenty minutes or so. It should showcase a few different forms of VR content, such as gaming and a 360-degree video experience. The demonstration piece of the lecture presentation format is the only notable handicap for this event type. Honestly speaking, if you are doing a VR lecture for an audience of 30 people, and then you start showing off the VR hardware in action, there is a very strong chance that all 30 people will want to try VR. This means that, with each person getting approximately five minutes to

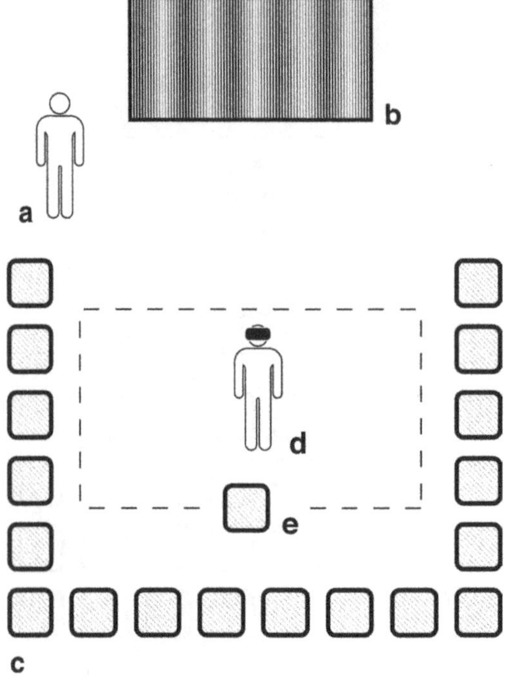

Figure 4.3 VR Experience Class. a - Presenter, in close proximity to VR Participant (d), is able to intervene if there is a problem. Note: Presenter is outside of marked "safety area" on the floor. b - TV or projected screen to simultaneously display VR content. c - Audience members, seated and safely outside VR "safety area" marked on the floor. d - VR Participant. Note: Participant is wearing headset, is in "safety area" marked on the floor, and is in close proximity to a safety chair (e). e - Safety chair. This chair is to allow the participant to sit, should they become tired, or experience motion sickness or dizziness.

try VR, you will be hosting sessions for two and a half hours. The likelihood that attendees will get bored and frustrated with waiting is extremely high, and they may leave disappointed.

With that being said, there is another form of VR presentation that may garner a better reaction from patrons, and that is the "VR Experience" program.

The wonderful problem to have with any VR event at your library is that every person who sees the technology being demonstrated will want to experience it for themselves. Thankfully, there is an easy way to facilitate that and ensure that participants in your program will have a memorable and enjoyable time. For our purposes, we are simply calling this event format the "VR Experience" program.

For starters, libraries must understand the time commitment needed to ensure that all participants that partake in a VR experience will require in order to be fully satisfied. For most attendees, their experience should likely last between 10 and 15 minutes. That amount of time should also include a buffer of a few moments, allowing a library staff member to assist in placing and removing the VR headset or resetting the VR smartphone solution. Each mini-session will also require the staff member to give a very quick tutorial on how the participant can properly navigate the virtual world. Give strong consideration of limiting attendance to only 8 to 10 people.

The layout of this program experience will differ from the VR lecture-style presentation format in that this session will accommodate far fewer attendees—and that is by design (see figure 4.3). For this event setting, you will likely have a TV or projector in front of the room. You will have the presenter or staff member at the front of the room and then a chair close to the center of the space. This chair will be utilized to assist a patron to sit down if they get motion sickness or dizziness. Be sure to have ample space around that chair so that no other patrons in attendance can be hit by the person experiencing VR, as they might be flailing their arms around or possibly losing their balance. Around the perimeter of the room should be seating for a small number of people. It is vital to have the TV or projector at the front of the room and showing the same content that the VR participant will be experiencing. This is a great way to keep others in attendance entertained while they await their turn to try the "VR Experience." If you feel that some people in attendance are getting a bit bored, it would absolutely be an option to hand out a few Google Cardboards and devices for them to play with while they are awaiting their turn. This will also be a fantastic way for them to compare and contrast the experiences that can be offered by different tiers of VR devices.

Fully Immersive Experiences—Some Recommendations

Regardless of your library deciding to expose your community to VR through either a lecture or "experience" format, you are going to want to find content that will have the most impact. It should be made clear that new VR content is being released all the time. The content selection and vetting tips we provided previously will certainly be helpful in determining which type of content will be appropriate in a library setting.

With that in mind, we do feel comfortable making a few recommendations of software we feel could have a fantastic impact on your library patrons and leave them with a positive impression of VR. While all of these titles are not available on all VR hardware solutions, there are often variants or "knock-offs / clones" of these titles that will be extremely similar. Will they be as polished as the top-tier titles? Not exactly. But, they will still convey the same concepts and experiences, perhaps with a bit less immersion.

For your VR events, you may want to create a "VR Menu"—sort of like a dinner menu at a restaurant—that will allow patrons to gravitate toward experiences they feel they may enjoy. Do all of us like riding on roller coasters? Nope! So it is smart to also offer a simple walking experience so that those among us who are not thrill-seekers can have a comfortable experience.

Beat Saber

Rated "E" for Everyone—available on tethered-VR, all-in-one (Oculus Quest), PlayStation 4 VR

Well, we may as well dive right in and discuss one of the most popular VR games to be released thus far. Beat Saber is an insanely addictive VR game that forces players to duck, dodge, and slice their way through challenging stages as they use their laser swords to chop blocks flying at them. There is a catch, though: often blocks can only be sliced in a specific direction. And there are often blocks that fly at you that can't be sliced, and you must dodge them or be penalized. The gameplay is very simple, and the soundtrack is amazing. The game is coordinated to the music, so be sure to play this game loud! This game takes a bit of coordination, so it isn't for everyone. However, it is very fun for the audience to watch VR participants slice their way to a high score.

Job Simulator

Rated "E 10+" for 10 and older—available on tethered-VR, all-in-one (Oculus Quest), PlayStation 4 VR

Who says VR games have to make sense? And who says you can't pretend to have a job while you are having fun? Try a few rounds of Job Simulator, and you will be absolutely cracking up. We have to admit, we've played a few rounds of this, and we can't even tell what the goal of the game is. Participants have so much fun pretending to be sitting in an office and hurling their staplers across the room, making photocopies, and checking emails. It's wild, ridiculous, and so much fun. The controller and head tracking (not to mention the in-game humor) always ensure the game is immersive and hysterical.

Ocean Descent—PlayStation VR Worlds Demo Disc

Rated "M" for Mature 17+—PlayStation VR

Don't let the rating dissuade you from considering the use of this game for a VR session. This software comes as a free pack-in for the PlayStation VR kit. Along with Ocean Descent are a number of other games that can be a bit more violent and may not be suitable for a library experience. Ocean Descent, on the other hand, is an extremely immersive jaunt through the depths of the ocean. Here, participants will sink lower and lower as they enter the darkest parts of our ocean planet and evade sharks and other native creatures. The tension is thick in this game, and we've elicited a few scares from some of our patrons as we've used this title. Be sure to ask patrons if they are up for it before throwing them in to this experience. This is also a great title for audiences to watch VR participants.

Proton Pulse

Rated "E" for Everyone—available on tethered-VR, PlayStation 4 VR, Google Cardboard (Android & iOS), Samsung Gear VR

Here is a fun game that may give some of your old-school gamers in attendance a bit of a flashback. One part Pong, one part Breakout, all parts VR, this game takes the best parts of those decades-old video game classics and puts a modern spin on them. For this experience, you are basically in a computer-generated gameplay area, and you are controlling a wall that can bounce balls around that arena. The goal is to smash bricks, far down the gameplay field. If the ball bounces back and makes it past your defense, you lose. It's very simple, and it takes some moderate reflexes to play. It has a fantastic soundtrack and, like some of our other mentions, should keep audiences entertained as well. What is especially nice about this particular game is that it will run rather well on a wide variety of VR platforms. Give it a shot (pun intended!).

Google Cardboard App—Various Experiences

Rated "E" for Everyone—available on Google Cardboard (Android & iOS)

We have to be honest, the experiences included with the Google Cardboard app are a bit of a novelty, and they are certainly not as impressive as software such as Beat Saber. However, the price is right—it's free—and it works on a wide range of devices. As long as you have a smartphone that is compatible with Google Cardboard, and that includes Apple iOS or Google Android, you should be able to download this app and start exploring. There are a few experiences included, although we had the most fun with the very relaxing Arctic Journey, where players simply view the night sky or take a fun flight with Arctic terns. If you are looking for some low-budget solutions for doing basic VR demonstrations at your library, don't overlook this app.

YouTube VR—Custom Playlists

Content Rating Varies—works on any devices that will launch YouTube

We should be very clear about this. Not every successful VR event at libraries should be based around video gaming. In fact, many of us have had more success with low-key events than with music-pumping, fast-action, quick-reflex video games. As we are trying to give our communities a unique VR experience, perhaps we should turn toward content that is simple, unique, requires little engagement, and is more about "wonder" than anything else. YouTube now hosts VR, or "360-degree videos," and they can allow libraries to make these unique experiences possible.

With the advent of inexpensive 360-degree cameras, many people have started taking video footage of real-life experiences and then uploading them to YouTube. Through use of this 360-degree footage, viewers are able to move their viewpoint left, right, up, and down in order to see footage as if they were personally there. The effect, especially with high-definition content, is as immersive as it is impressive. Many VR devices now have native YouTube VR apps, or allow users to view YouTube content via a tethered PC. The head tracking on the VR device will allow the VR user to move their head in any direction and view the video content as if there were actually there. The best way to describe this: 360-degree video will allow you to feel as if you are sitting in the front seat of a roller coaster at your favorite amusement park. As the coaster starts to move, you mind will be tricked into thinking you have some forward movement. You can tilt your head, spin it around, look up and down—you will be able to see objects whizzing by and the experience will quickly become very immersive. Since it is a video, you will not be able to freely walk around. Your experience will be "on rails," literally and figuratively.

Just like with video game experiences, libraries can create YouTube Playlists of these 360-degree videos and offer them to patrons in a menu format. Like video games, be sure to fully screen all videos for content before allowing patrons to view them. Here are some potential ideas for YouTube content, which cover a wide variety of topics, including:

- July 4th—Take a tour of the nation's capital
- Veterans Day—Walk in a Veterans Day Parade
- Travel to exotic places like Fiji, Iceland, Antarctica
- Venture inside an active volcano
- Walk through the Amazon rainforest
- Jump off a waterfall
- Skydive out of an airplane
- Sit in the pilot's seat of a jet fighter
- Go for a rollercoaster ride
- Swim with great white sharks
- Go spelunking in the world's deepest caves
- Stand on stage during a rock concert
- Visit the surface of Pluto
- . . . and so many more. The possibilities are endless.

Be sure to check YouTube frequently for new content, even if the purpose is to swap out content in your playlist for newer versions of these experiences. Always be sure to add the highest resolution versions of these videos to your playlist, which will help maintain a significant amount of immersion for your participants.

Setup

Like most things in libraries, the ultimate commonality that vexes any planning is the concept of space. Libraries are always under some sort of space constraint. In recent years, with the advent of digital reference materials replacing the hardbound materials, physical reference collections are being scaled back or in some cases eliminated. This is one example of space repurposing that is happening now across libraryland. Having a place for the VR experience is a challenge, but many of the systems can be portable. Some of the systems, like the VIVE require base stations that define the space in which the participant is going to interact. Having a dedicated space for that type of device to be mounted is optimal but not required. There are solutions available that allow for peripherals to be mounted on tripods or stands. Many of the systems can be housed on carts and connect to the Internet via Wi-Fi networks in the building. Even if the systems are kept mobile, a space is still needed for the user to enjoy the experience, and finding that space is always a challenge.

Community/programming rooms are not always available, and depending on the system that the library invests in, a large space may be required. When making the decision to purchase a particular brand or type of VR system, always be mindful of the type of experiences you will make available. Google Cardboard is certainly a different experience than the HTC VIVE, not only because of the technology involved, but because of the level, type, and space needed for the experience. So, when making a decision about the type of system the library is considering purchasing, be mindful of space constraints.

Staffing

One of the keys to success for any library program is to have the right amount of staff and ensuring they know how to effectively run the program. For most VR programs, your library will likely only need one or two staff members on hand in order to facilitate the event. These staff members should be able to give a quick overview of the technology before the event starts, be capable of using any VR equipment, and troubleshoot any basic technical issues. Staff should be aware of the content so they can make appropriate recommendations, and staff should be able to spot signs of motion sickness or dizziness. They need to be able to react quickly to those situations, for instance, by carefully sitting a patron down and removing the headset. You will want staff that can also look around the room and ensure that participants are not waiting too long for their turn at an experience.

Running an Event—Example Procedure

Libraries should have a pretty clear-cut game plan for how they are going to run an event. Is it a VR lecture? You may want to do 30 minutes of VR history, vendor comparisons, simple content explanation. Then be ready to do 30 minutes or more of VR demos. Are you running a "VR Experience" program? You will probably want to keep the talking portion of this event to a minimum, as your guests will be wanting to dive right in.

Really, the key aspect of any sort of VR event will be proper time management. If we examine a "VR Experience" program—which, honestly speaking, tends to be the more entertaining event—you will want to make sure everyone has a chance to try immersing themselves in VR. Your staff will want to go through a simple routine for each library patron that wishes experience VR:

- Clean the device before use—let the patron see you do this.
- Ask the patron if they know the risks of motion sickness and dizziness.
- Tell them to let you know if they feel any symptoms at any time during the experience.
- Tell the patron there is a chair behind them to sit on, in case they cannot stand.
- Ask them for permission to grab or hold them if they start to fall or need help putting on the device hardware.
- Have them select an experience from your preselected "VR Menu" of choices.
- If you are using controllers, explain how they work.
- Help them to put on the headset and do adjustments.
- Ask if they are comfortable.
- Help them navigate to the experience.
- As the experience starts, ask if they are ok.
- Set a timer. We recommend 10 to 15 minutes per experience.
- Assist them with removing the VR headset.
- Ask them to tell everyone what the experience was like this can be an amazing part of running the program!
- Wipe down the headset and prepare to start a new round with another library patron.

This is by no means a perfect procedure. In fact, you may want to tweak it slightly to best fit your own event needs. The time limit for the experience is important—you have to find the sweet spot. If the experience is too short, patrons will never get the chance to be fully immersed. If the experience is too long, the patrons who are waiting will get bored—quickly. Remember to try to keep the waiting patrons occupied. Tell them to look at the TV or projector screen broadcasting the experiences. Ask them their thoughts. Pass around smartphone VR devices or the "VR Experience Menu" while they are waiting.

Keep things light, fun, and funny!

Using High-End PC Hardware to Present a Virtual Reality Experience for Adults

An Interview with Katy O'Grady and Jane Kauzlaric of Sun City West Inc., an Active Adult Community

As some of our communities age, and our users with them, libraries are constantly looking for ways to better engage with their patrons. As we have seen in our other chapters, using technology to offer cutting-edge workshops that can offer attendees a unique experience is a fantastic way to get more people visiting our libraries and learning.

When we learned about Sun City West Inc. and its R. H. Johnson Recreation Center's VR activities, we had to find out all of the details regarding this special program. We approached Katy O'Grady, the general services officer, and Jane Kauzlaric, director of the R. H. Johnson Library, for a discussion about VR and how this program has impacted the community. "We are in a unique position here in Sun City West as we serve only seniors. We have about 28,000 residents age 55 and older, and we have more than $150 million in amenities that we offer them, including recreation centers, fitness centers, golf courses, tennis, pickleball, swimming, etc. There is no shortage of activities to serve our active residents. What we wanted to do with this program, though, is reach our less active residents and find a way to keep them engaged—mentally, physically, and socially. Our goal was to provide something for those who couldn't participate in most of our other activities and [that] would work for just about any limitation a person had," shared Katy O'Grady and Jane Kauzlaric.

Expanding on that notion a bit, both Katy and Jane explained that there was an opportunity for Sun City West to reinvent its library. "The library has always been the one place that works for everyone because of the nature of what it offers—more passive pursuits but a wide range of topics. Toward that end, our Library Director, Jane Kauzlaric, has reinvented our 40-year-old facility, which still boasts the state of Arizona's biggest collection of large-print books, and created more of a community center," shared Katy. It seems that many of these residents were extremely interested in technology and technology workshops. "Tech talks are always a huge draw, from how to use Instagram and Facebook to getting started with your new smartphone and cutting the cord from traditional cable and telephone service," stated Katy. Once that became clear, they wondered if VR could offer something unique and exciting.

The staff at Sun City West had an inkling that their community would be interested in VR technology. "We knew the younger Boomers and other active residents would love VR," stated Jane. But, amazingly, they saw the potential for VR to help those with accessibility issues. "We wanted to first serve those who were limited physically, visually, socially, etc. VR seemed a perfect fit! Whether someone was recovering from a stroke, used a walker, was just getting out of long-term rehab or a hospital stay, or had visual limitations, VR could reach them. Our team truly felt we could make a difference for this audience, and we were cautiously optimistic the audience would embrace VR," Katy shared excitedly.

In order to get their VR experience off the ground, Sun City West staff members carefully thought about the type of content they would use to form the basis of this event. Would they try using VR games that might require movement and quick reflexes, or should they choose something more passive? It seems they knew from the start that the material would have to vary in order to meet these specific needs, and they would have to be careful about the type of content they shared with participants. "We needed to make sure anyone could learn the technology quickly, as some titles do require handset use. More importantly, we wanted to make sure users didn't have motion sickness problems or balance issues once in the headset. We had several titles we threw out due to jumpy movement or difficulty in getting around," explained Jane. "Be sure to go through every title before offering it to your people. Make sure it is easy to learn/use, make sure you can provide verbal instructions to them when you're not in the headset yourself, and make sure they can't hurt themselves," they added by way of helpful insights.

For this program to be successful, they realized that they had to keep things simple. Could VR still provide a worthwhile experience? "One of our most popular titles is one where the participant walks on a plank, exiting the elevator of a high-rise building and looking down several stories below," they shared. They said that the effect was quite convincing. "Our residents loved this title. Unfortunately, we had a couple of people try to 'jump' off the plank, and ended up bumping into a wipe board on the wall, so we have discontinued that title." This sounds as though, while they were sort of victims of their own success, they also realized they would have to take movement in to consideration. "Our residents have embraced the roller coasters, walking the plank, going upside down in jets, shooting ghosts, and more. We've had requests for downhill skiing (cross country is too boring!), skydiving, and the like. Our residents enjoy using a lightsaber in Star Wars and boxing or playing goalie against virtual opponents," shared Katy and Jane. It seems like it may work best to introduce your audience very carefully to these different experiences, but don't be surprised if you have some thrill seekers in attendance!

Content selection is one thing, but let's take a deeper look at some of the logistics of their programming. Having some basic parameters in place for running these types of programs can help to ensure they are both effective and fun. "We have worked with groups as large as 10, but prefer four to five people at a time, with about an hour and a half per group. This allows everyone to do two to three titles per visit, without getting bored waiting for others in the group to have their turn," which is an excellent point made by Katy and Jane. With regard to the length of each individual experience, they shared that "we picked titles that were five to seven minutes long so everyone would rotate in and out without getting bored. We installed a large TV so those waiting could see what the participant was seeing, although not in the immersive way that the headset provides. It's fun to watch the audience as they react to the participant's reaction to what is happening on the screen."

Their equipment choice is notable as well: "We are using the HTC VIVE VR setup. With that and the higher-end PC we purchased, our total start-up costs were under $2,000." Katy and Jane explained that "we are making due with what we have—which is a shared break room/meeting room/VR room. We have to break down and set up part of the equipment each day we offer the program. The equipment includes a mounted TV (optional, but allows the audience to share in the experience) and two mounted base stations that are placed high on the wall. Those don't have to move in between. A PC, the headset, and the hand controls are on a moveable A/V cart, so those can be stored away safely when not in use. We also use a rolling chair and carabiners that snap onto the ceiling tile braces to keep the cords away from the users. We keep a stock of wet wipes and lens cleaners on hand to keep the equipment fresh for each user, as some of them work up a sweat!"

So, with all of that explained, how has the VR experience performed? We were curious to know how the program has panned out and what the response has been. After talking to Katy and Jane, it was clear that it was immensely successful. They had some wonderful anecdotes to share with us, and one, in particular, stood out.

> We could tell you story after story of individuals who we met in this program who were touched in one way or another. I personally worked with a gentleman who had the early stages of dementia. His caregiver daughter needed a break for him and herself, so she brought him to the library. He was stubborn and kept questioning her about why he was there. She sounded worn out but was very patient with him. He wanted to do our "Grand Canyon" program, which he did. He was moderately satisfied with it but not impressed, as he'd seen the real thing, and this didn't live up to his expectations. I made several attempts to talk him into visiting a virtual world in "Senza Peso," a visual and musical feast that requires no action by the participant other than to sit in the virtual gondola and enjoy the ride and the scenery. This gentleman who participated—I could see his face change as the program progressed. He went from grumpy to smiling, his head turning and looking all around as he got used to the new environment. By the end he had a grin on his face and exclaimed, "I couldn't tell if I was going to heaven or hell!" His daughter also had a huge smile on her face, and she enjoyed her own VR programs, providing her with a brief but much needed respite.

The program has been a hit, and they've worked hard to meet demand at Sun City West. "We have to take reservations and are booked weeks in advance. We have expanded from two days a month to two days per week—and we still can't keep up with demand!" shared Katy and Jane. They've been able to convert participants into volunteers as the weeks have passed, which is wonderful. Perhaps the best bit of information that Katy and Jane shared is that their program has not gone unnoticed by their peers and members of their larger community. "We received the Arizona Parks and Recreation Association award for Best Senior Program in 2018," they excitedly told us. Kudos!

VR SERVICES FOR YOUR PATRONS

Lending Virtual Reality Equipment

The increasing portability and decreasing cost of VR headsets combine to make a lending program viable within the public library. In particular, smartphone-powered and all-in-one headsets are attractive options.

As the name suggests, smartphone-powered VR headsets require that your patrons own a compatible smartphone in order to provide processing power. These headsets have the advantage of being fairly inexpensive, lightweight, and generally durable. That said, there are several drawbacks to lending them. In addition to your patrons supplying their own smartphone in order to use them, these headsets have limited device compatibility. A patron borrowing one would need to check their device against this list prior to checkout. As all-in-one headsets become increasingly affordable, the usefulness of smartphone-powered ones may begin to ebb.

With the arrival of all-in-one headsets, users can now engage in a fairly immersive VR experience without sacrificing mobility. Unlike the cumbersome setup and calibration of a computer-based VR system, these headsets are ready for use as soon as they are turned on and worn! These advantages do come at a cost; headsets in this category start at around $200. In order to effectively loan VR equipment, there are several steps you must take.

Determine Content

Hardware aside, one of the key components to a quality VR experience is the content itself. In the case of smartphone-powered headsets, your patrons will be loading games, videos, and other content onto their own personal devices. As such, your options for curation are limited. One method of exercising some quality control is to create annotated bibliographies of VR experiences. In addition to describing the content itself, a bibliography should also provide the following:

- **App availability:** Just as patrons will need a device compatible with the hardware you loan, they will then need to download content compatible with their phones' operating systems. List which app store they will need to visit and any special operating system requirements (e.g., iOS 11 and up).
- **Age appropriateness:** Although parents will be the ultimate arbiters of what is appropriate for their own children, you can ensure they are making an informed decision. Downloadable content from the device's corresponding app store will generally list a suggested age range.
- **Intensity of the experience:** As has been mentioned, disorientation and nausea are occasional side effects of a VR experience. Let patrons know how much motion/action they can expect within an experience.

In the case of standalone VR headsets, you will need to purchase and download content onto your device prior to loan. If the age-appropriateness of the content is a concern, you may wish to divide content among multiple devices using this criteria. Provide an annotated bibliography of experiences as we explored above. As the library will be responsible for managing content, create a mechanism for patrons to suggest a purchase, much as you would for your traditional content.

Types of Loans

As you plan to loan VR headsets to your patrons, two models exist; in-house lending and take home.

In-House Lending. In-house lending allows your patrons to check out library VR equipment to use—but not take home. This can be a formal checkout process, a sign in/out, or a matter of holding a library card or photo ID while the equipment is in use. There are several advantages to this approach. Equipment lent in-house will have a much quicker turnover, allowing for a limited number of headsets to be used by a larger number of patrons. In-house lending eliminates the concern of allowing potentially expensive equipment leave the library, possibly never to return! Finally, staff assistance can be made readily available if a patron requires it. Despite this, there are some drawbacks.

Patrons using your VR equipment inside the library will likely need space set aside for that purpose. A person wearing a headset will need a degree of mobility as they turn 360 degrees within a virtual environment. While noise within a VR headset is largely confined to the user, people may—and often do—enjoy the experience somewhat loudly. Even if the user limits their own noise, they will have difficulty hearing others while inside an experience. This can place them in a vulnerable position in a public space.

Take Home. If your library decides to lend VR equipment for home use, you will need to make many of the same decisions involved in lending other library realia. You will need to establish loan rules, including the replacement cost of the item and, potential fines if it is returned late. If you are cataloging your equipment, it is a best practice to individually list the games and experiences contained on a device (in the case of standalone equipment). Staff should be shown how to spot check equipment for damage, so they may inspect headsets for damage both before lending them out and after they are returned. Finally, if your equipment is leaving your building, a protective case is a necessary purchase!

Health and Hygiene Concerns

Whether lending in-house or for patrons to take home, there are certain matters of health and hygiene to address. Patrons borrowing your equipment should sign a document acknowledging the potential health risks of VR. To mitigate the library's liability, signed forms may be kept on file.

In addition to the risk of nausea, dizziness, and so forth, headsets can present a hygiene challenge as they cycle through multiple users. As a matter of course, libraries can provide inexpensive disposable masks for users to wear while using your headsets. Bulk purchases can run as little as 25 cents per mask, and they can prevent direct contact between skin and headset. Consider packing a small number of these with each device you loan out as the cost of doing business.

Although you'll want to place your headsets in protective cases prior to lending them out, you should avoid storing them in there for long periods of time. Without proper air circulation, mold can take hold, and headsets may develop a musty odor ("How to Clean Your Oculus," 2019). Whenever a headset is returned, it should be thoroughly cleaned before returning to circulation. If the manufacturer of your headset provides directions, follow them. In absence of that, a general cleaning process should involve a damp, soft cloth or antibacterial wipe. You should be sure to avoid the use of alcohol, heat, or direct sunlight, which can cause foam parts to become brittle and crack ("How to Clean Your Oculus," 2019).

Using VR for Library Outreach

An Interview with Melanie Davidoff of the Port Washington Public Library

As they look to create VR programming for their communities, libraries should realize that VR events do not have to take place in your building. With the proper VR setup, it is absolutely possible to take a "VR Experience" program to a remote location and use it as a form of community outreach. As for Melanie Davidoff of the Port Washington Public Library, she believed she had found the perfect way to showcase cutting-edge technology for older community members, many of whom could no longer travel to their local library.

Melanie had been running a few versions of her library's "Virtual Reality Experience" program, with some sessions geared toward teens and one toward adults. This was similar to other VR experience programs, with her programs consisting of "an open-ended version where we offer a variety of YouTube VR experiences as well as the option to sample some of our VR games and our themed offerings, where we offer a 'menu' of YouTube VR videos that share a theme (e.g., Pride celebrations around the world, space-themed videos)," shared Melanie. According to her, the entire purpose of these sorts of events was to "introduce patrons to VR technology. The themed programs also have the goal of offering immersive, educational programming."

Melanie decided that, because her library's VR hardware was rather portable, she could take this experience "on the road" and share it with those members of the community who could no longer travel easily. "One of the best experiences with the program so far has been when we brought it to The Amsterdam, an older adult community in Port Washington. We gave a brief presentation on what VR is, what it's being used for, and the consumer options that are out there, followed by a demo of the headset for eight of the residents who attended. The older adults were incredibly interested in the technology and had plenty of questions about it. Endorsements include 'it was very virtual' and 'it was just like being plunked down in this room, except I was plunked down in Bryce Canyon,'" explained Melanie. She already has plans to further provide this experience, stating, "We plan on bringing the technology to them again, in a format where residents would sign up for a 15-minute timeslot, so there's not so much waiting around."

The "waiting around" aspect of the program is important to note. Melanie seemed keenly aware that the experience can be mostly solitary, and she wishes to point out to others that "we haven't fully worked out the best way to keep patrons occupied while waiting their turn for the headset. Watching the videos on the television screen is only entertaining for so long, even if we do have only a limited number of patrons participating in the session."

We were curious about the exact setup that Melanie was utilizing to make this special VR event happen. Melanie explained the following: "We use the PlayStation 4 VR bundle and connect it to a TV. It cost around $700 for the console and VR bundle. Since the initial purchase, we have purchased a few additional games to offer. We've also since purchased some Google Cardboard headsets to circulate to patrons who may wish to experiment with VR outside of the library." Additionally, she stated that "the VR system is connected to our television, so patrons who are waiting their turn to use the equipment can still get an idea of what the patron in the headset is seeing."

So, is there anything that Melanie would change about this form of outreach, and VR programming in general, aside from working to keep attendees a bit more occupied while they wait for their turn in the VR headset? "I'd love to offer it more frequently. Every time the program is offered, patrons ask how they can go about using the equipment again. So far, we've been able to offer it once a month, but it would be great to have it available more often," she shared.

Melanie's insights proved to us that VR programming is absolutely a fantastic form of community engagement and outreach for libraries looking to do events that are both high-tech and fun!

Presenting Virtual Reality Tours of Your Library

We've spoken at length about fantastic games, VR experiences, YouTube videos, and the like for patrons to view while using VR headsets. Our hope is that they are whisked away to a virtual world or a faraway place, and completely wowed by what they see and feel. However, what if there was a way to send patrons, virtually, to your own library for a tour? Maybe there is something special about your library that you want to share with the world? A special music performance? A unique art exhibit? A fun day of arts and crafts with adults? You can use very basic hardware to create your own VR videos, similar to YouTube 360-degree videos, in a matter of minutes.

Taking a 360-degree video is actually quite simple, and there are a number of hardware solutions available to make this happen. One popular device is the Samsung Gear 360 camera ("Samsung Gear 360," 2017). This device is rather small—only the size of a baseball—and it can be mounted on a tripod, a helmet, or anything with a universal camera mount. The lenses can be set to a "fish-eye" mode or put into normal mode. It can record content in high definition, thus providing crystal clarity for playback.

Once you've created a 360-degree video that you are happy with, you have a few options for showcasing that content. Videos in this format can now be uploaded to YouTube and played back natively on VR devices. This is exactly how many of the YouTube VR experiences we had showcased earlier in this chapter were created. Videos can also be embedded on a library website, for easy finding by patrons or website visitors. They can be viewed by anyone, regardless of if they are using VR hardware or not. The only drawback will be that users will have to use their mouse to navigate viewpoint and perspective as the video plays back. Smartphone and tablet users will have to move the screen with their fingers. Google has also created a web-based interface for creating 360-degree tour videos. It is located here https://vr.google.com/tourcreator/.

This is definitely an area that is still growing, and more content is being created every day. If creating tours with your own hardware seems a bit beyond your staff's technical expertise, there are now a number of companies that will do this form of recording as a service and can ensure that the final video has a high level of quality and polish.

Teleconferencing Station for Patrons

Over the last several years, many libraries have seen and understood the need to provide teleconferencing areas for their patrons. A significant number of our community members do not have access to broadband, or the equipment, or the space needed to conduct Skype job and college interviews. We've tried to accommodate this by providing hardware like laptops, webcams, microphones, and quiet areas to facilitate video conferencing calls. One change in this area that is on the horizon is VR-based teleconferencing.

Admittedly, this technology is new and still a bit rough around the edges. We were able to identify one solution that could provide virtual spaces for people to meet, talk, and collaborate, through the use of VR hardware solutions. One vendor, MeetinVR (http://meetinvr.net), has a web presence and is rolling out an "early access" program to eventually allow users to test their service. At this point in time, there is no word on pricing. According to their website, the service is planned to support all the major VR headset manufacturers, including HTC and Oculus. From the initial teaser videos on their site, it looks like people can utilize VR to appear in virtual meeting rooms, classrooms, and other environments. Once there, they will meet other avatars, or persons, and they can engage in conversation.

Again, this is very new, and we are not willing to pass judgement on the service yet. Let's give this technology and meeting solution some time to grow and see how things progress. With that being said, it seemed very interesting and worth sharing.

CONCLUSION: WHERE IS VR TECHNOLOGY HEADED?

It is easy to see why we find VR to be such an exciting field that is full of potential for public libraries. In our own experience, and in the experiences of those we interviewed for creating this work, there was a common thread of absolute amazement among VR participants. And unlike other forms of library programs, VR seemed to have the same effect on our community members, regardless of age. We feel we can safely predict that VR will be a technology that will become more and more ingrained into popular culture and will continue to grow in usefulness as we move into the future.

But what will that future look like? While we are reluctant to make any wild predictions, we think there are some safe bets that can be made. VR hardware solutions will continue to become cheaper and faster, just like almost all other forms of technology. As headsets improve, so will display resolutions, refresh rates, and head tracking. That will surely increase the level of immersion that participants feel and will also work to reduce the potential for motion sickness. Expect to see better controllers and control mechanisms in the future. There are some very cool movement systems that can help players to better simulate walking—however, they are large and expensive at this point. Perhaps we will see a revolution in that area.

On the software side of things, there is definitely room for improvement and we know many companies are hard at work in that area. We can expect to see VR software with far better graphics and a move toward more interactivity. We may finally start to see VR software that integrates MMO (massively multiplayer online) environments where thousands of players can directly interact with each other. Social media integration may help to make that a reality. We loved Ernest Cline's "Ready Player One," the tale of future teenagers escaping their everyday lives by jumping in to virtual worlds through use of their VR headsets. Maybe that fictional reality isn't too far away. Be sure to keep tabs on this technology in the coming years, as it surely continues to improve and impress!

FIVE

Synergies

Although at first glance, 3D printing, drones, augmented reality, and virtual reality may not appear to have much in common, these technologies can have a synergistic relationship. By combining two or more technologies, libraries can offer unique experiences to our patrons!

AUGMENTED REALITY AND 3D PRINTING

As discussed in the chapter on augmented reality, the Merge Cube operates as a sort of QR code that can be held in your hand. This inexpensive, easy-to-use tool is a fantastic way to showcase how some of our cutting-edge library technologies can overlap and even complement each other.

Imagine there was a simple way to view a 3D model, in your hand virtually, through the use of augmented reality. Such a tactile experience is now possible and the results are useful for 3D modelers wishing to more thoroughly explore and analyze their creations. The "Object Viewer" app for the Merge Cube, which can be easily installed on a smartphone or tablet, will allow you to view 3D objects, virtually, through the use of your smartphone or tablet.

The "Object Viewer" app will allow users to upload files with the extensions STL, OBJ, and BLEND (*Object Viewer for Merge Cube*, n.d.). These are 3D model files and are often the result of downloading creations made in the popular and free TinkerCAD web-based software.

Figure 5.1 A patron interacting with a MERGE cube displaying an STL file.

What can be showcased for staff, after a bit of preparation work, is the ability, through the use of augmented reality, to look at 3D models that have been created before they are 3D printed. In practice, this means you can work with patrons to create 3D objects in the computer-aided design software of their choice (CAD) and then enable them to inspect the object in a much more tactile manner (see figure 5.1). Once a patron is happy that the object looks correct, you can them assist them in 3D printing it.

If you have staff members in your organization or members of your community who are already deeply interested in 3D printing and modeling, the use of a Merge Cube and the Object Viewer app will definitely create a significant "wow!" moment for them.

3D PRINTING AND DRONES

3D printing is a technology that pairs perfectly with drones! Indeed, there are numerous opportunities to develop programs and services that incorporate both simultaneously.

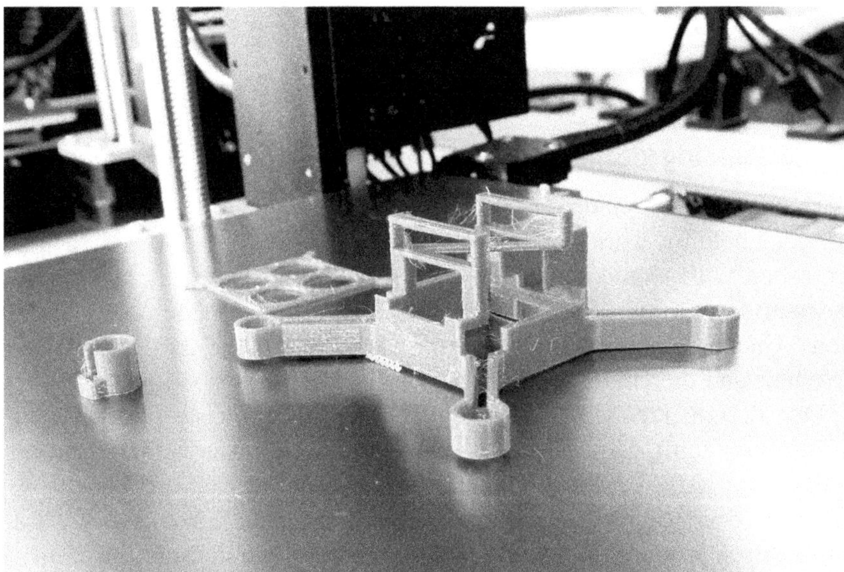

Figure 5.2 3D printed drone parts. Photo courtesy the Sachem Public Library.

Replacement Parts

One of the inherent risks of piloting a drone is breaking the equipment. Crashes can easily damage rotors, casings, and landing gear, among other parts. Even standard wear and tear can cause equipment failure. While these are the costs of doing business, it is possible to reduce this overhead, both for yourself and your patrons, using 3D printing.

On 3D repositories like Thingiverse, a simple search for drone parts will return numerous examples of free, printable schematics. As it is likely that many of the patrons who will be piloting your drones will be inexperienced, it is essential that you secure a source of inexpensive replacement parts. By preprinting those pieces most likely to suffer damage, you can manage the long-term health of your drones (see figure 5.2). Additionally, these spare parts can allow you to perform onsite repairs, limiting your downtime even during an active program!

If you want your drone owners to use your 3D printer(s), you will want to demonstrate the capabilities of your 3D printer(s). Consider printing and then displaying examples of 3D printed drone parts. Identify online communities of drone hobbyists on social media and networking sites, including Facebook and Meetup, and reach out to them.

When hosting programs on drones, provide information on your printers to attendees.

Drone-Building Workshop

Once you feel confident using both 3D printing and drone technology, consider holding workshops on building 3D printed drones. In such a workshop, staff would create kits comprising your 3D design, along with the necessary electronic components indicated within the assembly instructions. Under the guidance of an experienced instructor, participants can assemble and then flight-test a drone.

One design, the XL-RCM 10.0 PIXXY Pocket Drone (available on Thingiverse.com), can be fully assembled at a cost under $100 per drone ("XL-RCM 10.0," 2014). Although the cost may at first cause sticker shock, the price point can become increasingly manageable in the context of a multisession program. If the drones are library-owned items (rather than a take-home project), you can build the library's collection while also teaching the design process. In such a program, users can work in groups, further multiplying your investment.

3D SCANNING AND VIRTUAL/AUGMENTED REALITY ENVIRONMENTS

The following is based on an interview conducted on July 1, 2019 with Chad Mairn, the librarian in charge of the Innovation Lab at St. Petersburg College.

Chad Mairn runs the Innovation Lab (iLab), a makerspace, or what he calls a "solvespace" as the iLab is frequently is tasked with solving problems. The iLab is located on the Seminole Campus of St. Petersburg College. In addition to serving students and faculty, the iLab receives many school-age visitors throughout the year. At present, Mairn is experimenting with combining 3D scanning and then importing these objects into virtual and augmented reality environments. Regarding this work, Mairn has found several willing partners.

The first of these is the Imagine Museum of St. Petersburg, which houses a collection of studio glass artwork. As a proof of concept, Mairn has begun to scan select glass art to import into Tilt Brush's virtual reality software. In this environment, people are able to interact with the objects inside virtual reality, without worrying about dropping the pieces—an obvious concern considering the medium!

As reflective and transparent objects can be difficult to scan, this project can be challenging, but will become a rewarding experience for visitors. After demonstrating this proof of concept, the Imagine Museum is now working with a firm specializing in virtual reality to build out an augmented reality experience and companion app!

A second partner has been the Seminole Historical Society. Before going into the partnership, a little background is first required. In 2007, a Seminole High school student, Sierra Sarti-Sweeney, discovered an interesting rock that would later turn out to be the tooth of a Columbian Mammoth! This discovery sparked an archaeological dig, which would turn up a collection of fossils. Today, the results of that dig are housed at the Historical Society (http://www.seminolehistoricalsociety.org/Tour).

At the society, these fossils are displayed prominently in a glass case. That said, the public is not allowed to physically handle them. Mairn is currently working with two young students from his virtual/augmented reality club performing 3D scanning (and photogrammetry) of these fossils (see figure 5.3). The goal of this project is to import physical objects (the fossils) into a virtual environment. There are several platforms being considered. One is utilizing Merge Cubes (detailed in the chapter on augmented reality) to mimic handling the fossils. Separately, Mairn is considering the use of a third-party VR platform, particularly web-based to aid virtual learning. The intended audiences of both these approaches are elementary school children who are unable to visit the Seminole Historical Society in person.

Figure 5.3 Student scanning a fossil with the Structure Sensor 3D scanner.

Mairn employees a variety of hardware and software in the course of these projects.

Scanning hardware:

- Panasonic LUMIX DMC-FZ300K camera for photogrammetry
- (2) Microsoft Kinects
- Structure Sensor for iPad
- Matter and Form desktop scanner

Scanning software:

- Qlone iOs/Android app for 3D scanning
- ItSeez3D iOs app for Structure Sensor
- Skanect software for Structure Sensor
- MeshLab software for processing and editing 3D triangular meshes
- AutoDesk Recap Photo software for photogrammetry projects
- Sketchfab to publish, share, and discover 3D/VR/AR content

When interacting with augmented reality, virtual reality and holograms, Mairn utilizes several more expensive pieces of equipment, which he views as optional (though great to have).

They include the following:

- HTC Vive
- Magic Leap
- HoloLens

Chad notes that the majority of software is free for educational use. For a library owning an iPad, you can begin taking high quality scans using the Structure Sensor attachment or Qlone app, greatly reducing your startup costs! The iLab also benefited from a donation of Merge Cubes, VR headsets, and the aforementioned Structure Sensor, thanks to the Friends of the Library.

In terms of a learning curve, Mairn identifies photogrammetry as the most complex process. Generally, 60 to 70 photographs need to be taken from a consistent distance, with decent lighting, and with no movement from the model/object. The software stitches all the images into one 3D object and can take a very long time, depending on the captured images. Mairn has one staff person who assists with the Innovation Lab's VR/AR club for kids and has become familiar with the process, having witnessed it multiple times.

When asked about any potential policy concerns or considerations, Chad notes that 3D scanning and printing can be seen as a form of preservation, well within the established role of public libraries. His work involves willing partners and an educational purpose, rather than a commercial enterprise. Although this may be within the bounds of fair use, he recommends individual organizations perform their own prior research. When scanning a person, Mairn strongly suggests securing their permission, particularly if that file will be shared to an online repository such as Sketchfab.

The response to these adventures in virtual environments and 3D scanning has been overwhelmingly positive. Mairn notes that members of the community are blown away when they see fairly high-quality 3D scans after using the iPad's Structure Sensor and Skanect software. Even when using a smartphone with the Qlone app, the technology still provides a "wow" experience. Mairn says audiences begin imagining numerous possibilities once they witness these scans being placed in augmented and virtual reality environments.

As excited as visitors to the iLab are currently, Mairn sees an even more promising future for these technologies and is proud that he has an opportunity to share the possibilities with visitors. He expects multiple new 3D scanning applications to continue evolving, including architectural digital preservation, crime scene investigations, dentistry, real estate, art, simulated/visualized learning, mechanical engineering, and filmmaking. In the near future, 3D objects will be embedded in web-based articles, where readers will be able to drag the item into their real world (using augmented reality) and then see that object in 3D and to scale. "Picture reading about a space suit, but then being able to see it life-size in your room with all the details outlined in the article? Pretty cool," he says.

Finally, Mairn suggests we keep an eye out for volumetric video technology, a process of video capture that allows for later viewing from any angle at any moment in time (Redohl, 2019). "Just imagine getting a perfect representation of an event and being able to re-experience it decades later just like you were there at the time of the recording!"

DRONES AND AUGMENTED/VIRTUAL REALITY

A true measure of a successful fusion of two technologies is when this synergy helps achieve what neither could do alone. Such is the case in VR and drone flight. At present, the FAA severely restricts the flight of personal drones, requiring an individual to maintain line of sight (Feist, 2019). Though no such requirement exists for indoor flight, the more cramped setting essentially forces a pilot to maintain line of sight, regardless. By pairing a drone with a VR headset, an operator can effectively "see" through the eyes of the drone, using its camera. As a result, one could pilot a drone at relatively high speeds through an obstacle course or—more practical for libraries—take a slower approach through a more cramped environment (such as between stacks) in a controlled program setting. In this scenario, a high-performing system would be required, lest latency stand in the way of responsive controls.

In addition to VR, AR also interfaces quite nicely with drone technology, particularly in the realm of gaming. Take the Air Hog Drone, for instance. Some models of Air Hog can be paired via Bluetooth to an iPad or other device and then piloted through the company's Air Hogs Connect: Mission Drone app (Spin Master, 2019). As a user pilots the Air Hog drone, a virtual world is overlaid upon the iPad's screen. For example, a child using the app in their living room sees a number of buildings aflame, instead of seeing the room, and uses the drone to perform a series of rescues. Games aside, this serves as an easy introduction to drones and helps the user gain experience in making precise movements that can be difficult to master.

3D PRINTING AND VIRTUAL REALITY

Previously, we have seen how one can physically interact with a 3D file using the Merge Cube. Happily, the synergy between virtual environments and 3D printing flows in many directions, illustrated best by combining 3D printing and Tilt Brush.

An inexpensive virtual reality painting software, Tilt Brush is a near-essential purchase for libraries with computer-connected VR systems. Users can quickly create 3Dworks, which others can interact with in a virtual environment. As the output was rendered in three dimensions, these works can be 3D printed, though it can be a cumbersome process.

Ideally, the original design should be exported as an OBJ directly from Tilt Brush. If this isn't the case, a simple web search will produce a number of sites that can do the conversion at no cost. Once working in a standard format, your challenge will be making the file printable. The series of brushstrokes that make up a Tilt Brush design are often beautiful to behold, but they lack a lot of the connectivity and closed gaps that are essential for a successful 3D print (Veldhuizen, 2014). Free software, including MeshMixer and MeshLab, can be used to perform many of the necessary fixes to your model. You can target areas of "overhang" and anything that seems disconnected from the model at large and delete them. Following these fixes, you'll need to open your file in Netfabb, another free piece of software, where you will run an automatic repair and then export the file as a print-ready STL file (Crispin, 2017).

Though the process may seem convoluted, much of the conversion and repair is done automatically, rather than requiring active participation by staff or the public. The computer performing this work will need to have a good CPU, or the process may take a long time and potentially crash the computer. Essentially, the preparation of a file for printing can occur without active participation, with a staff member or patron revisiting the software on occasion to check progress. Then, your file can be sent to your 3D printer to be handled like any other print job.

FINAL THOUGHTS

Clearly, although augmented reality, virtual reality, 3D printing, and drones are their own distinct technologies, this sampling of ideas demonstrates the potential of using them in tandem. At first, your organization may wish to adopt each of these technologies individually, but as your comfort with them grows, you will undoubtedly seek new challenges. As you do so, be sure to consider the possibilities that exist in combining two or more of these emerging technologies!

Conclusion: Where Do You Go from Here?

So at last you've come to the end of our book. We hope you'll come away inspired and filled with a sense of possibility! As you seek to implement some of what you've read, we wanted to offer some humble suggestions.

HAVE A PLAN

The importance of having a plan may seem obvious, but there are times when enthusiasm can cause one to leap before one looks. Use this book as a roadmap. Decide on the technology you wish to invest in, understand the policy implications, and be sure to formally address them. Select your equipment and outline what programs and services you intend to offer. Securing funding from administration, your library board, and stakeholders is much easier when you can effectively communicate a plan for implementation.

Once you have adopted a plan of action and secured funding, you can move on to training staff. Just as having a plan can aid you in securing funding, staff training can similarly benefit from your thoughtfulness. Having a firm idea of what hardware and software you will employ and identifying which programs and services you intend to offer will allow you to specifically tailor staff training. This will ensure that you neither waste time on topics you needn't cover nor fail to include the necessary information.

START SMALL AND BUILD ON YOUR SUCCESSES

Emerging technologies embody change, and within any organization, there will be those who resist. This resistance can harden if your first few forays into an emerging technology fail to meet expectations. Conversely, if your early attempts are successful, this resistance can melt away. Knowing this, it is essential that you begin with simple, achievable program and service goals.

Outlined in this book are approaches to 3D printing, drones, AR, and VR that run the gamut from the introductory to the ambitious. Though you should endeavor to take these technologies to as far as you can in the pursuit of excellent service to your public, you should first create a stable foundation on which to build. As staff comfort grows over time, and patrons become increasingly familiar with the fundamentals of these emerging technologies, you can then seek to explore them in new and more challenging ways. In particular, the ideas outlined in the Synergies chapter requires a strong base of knowledge in several technologies as a prerequisite.

KEEP CHALLENGING YOURSELF

While you should seek to become comfortable using these emerging technologies, avoid becoming *too* comfortable. If your programming begins to feel routine, you should consider whether or not there is a new direction you can take a given technology. Just as your proficiency will grow over time, your patrons will likewise master the technologies we explored through the classes you offer. With this growing group of proficient users within your community, you have a built-in audience for intermediate and advanced classes! We challenge you to embrace a degree of happy uncertainty and begin developing the next generation of programs and services!

Appendix

The sample forms, policies, and procedures that follow do not, and are not intended to, constitute legal advice but rather serve general informational purposes only.

To advance its goal of providing free and open access to technology and information promoting literacy, education, enlightenment, and entertainment, the South Huntington Public Library offers patrons the opportunity to 3D print their own original designs or those found on various open-source websites.

Formats accepted are as follows: STL or OBJ. Patrons are permitted to submit their file for review at the Adult Reference Desk via USB flash, CD/DVD, or by emailing it to adultservices@shpl.info. Upon approval, patrons will be notified of a print price.

Prints will be priced according to the volume of material used. Prices are subject to change.

Patrons will be contacted when their print is ready for pickup. Prints that are not picked up after 30 days will become the property of the Library and unpaid charges will be applied to the patron's library account.

No project shall be printed that Library staff determines is:

- Prohibited by local, state, or federal law
- Unsafe, harmful, dangerous, or posing as a threat to others
- Obscene or offensive to the community's standards/mores
- In violation of intellectual property rights—copyright, patent, or trademark

In addition to the above restrictions, the Library reserves the discretionary right to refuse any 3D print request that it deems inappropriate or unwarranted.

By submitting content, the patron agrees to assume all responsibility for, and shall hold the Library harmless in, all matters related to patented, trademarked, or copyrighted materials. The South Huntington Public Library is not responsible for any damage, loss, or security of data arising from the use of its computers or network, or for the functionality or quality of content produced on the 3D printer.

Figure A.1 The South Huntington Public Library's 3D Printing Policy.

Mountainside Public Library

3D PRINTING REQUEST FORM

The Ultimaker 2+ 3D Printer prints 3-dimensional objects using corn-based PLA filament. It supports classroom assignments and personal creativity. To create objects for printing either use 3D modeling software or download files from thingiverse.com. **Object files must be in .stl format.**

Please use a separate form for each request.

Date of Request ______________________

Name ______________________

Contact Information:

Email: ______________________

Phone: ______________________

I have read and agree to the Mountainside Library 3D Printer Policy (Read policy on back of this page)

☐ I Agree

Item Information:

Common name ______________________

File Name ______________________

Color (Based on availability)
Please write 1 for first choice, 2 for second choice

_____Black	_____Red	_____Aqua
_____White	_____Yellow	_____Copper
_____Silver	_____Blue	_____Green

- **Cost is $2.00 per print**
  Items over 20 grams will cost an additional $.05 per gram (items will be weighed after printing)
- **File must be able to print in 5 hours or less.**
- **You must clean your own rafts and supports.**

For Staff Use Only:

Date Completed: ______________________

Patron Notified: ______________________

Amount Due: ______________________

Print time ______________________

Support ______________________

Size ______________________

Weight ______________________

Amount of material ______________________

Mountainside Public Library
Constitution Plaza, Mountainside, New Jersey 07092
908-233-0115
info@mountainsidelibrary.org
www.mountainsidelibrary.org

Figure A.2 Mountainside Public Library's 3D Printing Request Form.

DRONE
ITEM BARCODE:______________________

Longwood Public Library
Equipment & Gadgets Lending Agreement

By borrowing a gadget, I agree:

- To abide by the Longwood Public Library Equipment & Gadgets Borrowing Guidelines
- To pay an overdue fine if gadget is returned late
- To pay full repair and/or replacement costs should the gadget or components of the gadget be stolen, lost, not returned, or damaged

I acknowledge that the library is not responsible for any injury, loss, or damage that may occur from use.

I received the Equipment & Gadgets Borrowing Guidelines: ____________ (Patron's Initials)

Prior to operating the drone, I will read the Disclaimer and Safety Guidelines and follow them accordingly. _________ (Patron's Initials)

Signature: ______________________________ Date: ________________

Print name: ______________________________ Email: ____________________________

Patron barcode: ________________________ Phone number: ____________________

CHECK OUT Staff Initials	PHOTO	CONTENTS	CHECK IN Staff initials	TECH Staff Initials
		(1) Drone		
		(1) Drone Battery		
		(1) Bluetooth Controller		
		(1) Charging Cable		
		(1) USB Wall Adapter		
		(1) Disclaimer and Safety Guidelines/User Manual		
		(1) Black Carrying Case		

Figure A.3 Longwood Public Library's "Equipment & Gadgets Lending Agreement" for their drone collection.

DRONE

ITEM BARCODE:____________________

For Technical Services Use Only

Maintenance Procedures Performed:

____

____

____

____

____

____

____

Parts Reordered/Replaced:

____

____

____

____

Tech Services Staff Member Signature:____________________

Date: ________________

Figure A.3 Continued.

Port Washington Public Library

Virtual Reality (VR) and Augmented Reality (AR) Release of Liability

For the purpose of this waiver, the terms VR and AR shall be used interchangeably.

Due to the unpredictable nature of the human response to virtual reality (dizziness, nausea, seizures, fear of heights, bumping into objects, etc.), we require all participants to sign this waiver releasing the Port Washington Public Library (the "Library") from any liability regarding your (or your child/dependent/minor's) use of the Oculus Rift, HTC Vive, and/or any of the Library's VR equipment.

Oculus VR, LLC. and PlayStation VR, does NOT recommend that children under the age of 13 use the VR headsets.

A list and description of risks associated with the use of VR is available at: https://pwpl.org/vr-resources/

Please stop use of the VR equipment if you feel any discomfort whatsoever.

BY USING ONE OF THE LIBRARY'S VR HEADSETS, YOU ARE INDICATING YOUR ACCEPTANCE OF THE TERMS AND CONDITIONS OF THIS AGREEMENT.

I (or my child/dependent/minor) wish to use one of the Library's VR headsets. I recognize and understand that the use of a VR headset involves certain risks.

1. I (or my child/dependent/minor) am using the VR equipment voluntarily;
2. I am familiar with the physical, psychological, and financial risks associated with use of VR equipment and voluntarily assume same;
3. By signing, I acknowledge that I have read and understood all of the terms of this release form and that I am voluntarily giving up substantial legal rights, including the right to sue the Port Washington Public Library or its employees;
4. If the headset is being used by child/dependent/minor] I am the parent or legal guardian of the minor named below. I have the legal right to consent to and, by signing below, I hereby do consent to the terms and conditions of this Release of Liability.
5. To the fullest extent permitted by Law, I agree to defend, indemnify and hold the Port Washington Public Library harmless from and against any and all loss, liability, claim or damage arising from my use of AR & VR at the Library promises, including reasonable attorneys' fees incurred as a result of my use of AR or VR or incurred to enforce this agreement; whether caused in whole or in part by negligence of the Library

I understand that I must sign this Release of Liability before I, or the minor I am giving permission for, may use any of the VR equipment.

Participant's Name

First　　　　　　　　Last

Phone Number　　　　　　　　Email

Parent or Legal Guardian's Name

First　　　　　　　　Last

Figure A.4 A sample virtual/augmented reality waiver for use with the public. Courtesy Port Washington Public Library.

References

Abdullah, Q. A. (n.d.). "Classification of the Unmanned Aerial Systems." Retrieved March 12, 2019, from https://www.e-education.psu.edu/geog892/node/5.

"About FarSight XR." (2019). Retrieved June 9, 2019, from http://thefarsight.com/about.

ALA Office for Intellectual Freedom. (2018, January 11). "Selection Criteria." Retrieved May 8, 2019, from http://www.ala.org/tools/challengesupport/selectionpolicytoolkit/criteria.

Andriessen, C. (2019, June 22). "Review in Progress: Harry Potter: Wizards Unite." Retrieved June 23, 2019, from https://www.destructoid.com/review-in-progress-harry-potter-wizards-unite-558301.phtml.

"AR/VR Learning & Creation." (n.d.). Retrieved May 15, 2019, from https://mergevr.com/cube.

"ARia's Legacy—AR Escape Room." (2018, September 24). Retrieved June 24, 2019, from https://apps.apple.com/us/app/arias-legacy-ar-escape-room/id1359270156.

Arrighi, P. (2018, July 10). "3D Scanners Categories—Guide on the Different Types of 3D Scanners." Retrieved October 9, 2018, from https://www.aniwaa.com/3d-scanners-categories/#Desktop_3D_scanners.

"ARrrrrgh." (2017, October 26). Retrieved June 14, 2019, from https://apps.apple.com/us/app/arrrrrgh/id1299548311.

Artley, B. (n.d.). "Aerospace 3D Printing Applications." Retrieved May 1, 2019, from https://www.3dhubs.com/knowledge-base/aerospace-3d-printing-applications.

Bailenson, J. (2019). *Experience on Demand: What Virtual Reality Is, How It Works, and What It Can Do*. New York: W. W. Norton & Company.

Bardi, J. (2019, March 26). “What Is Virtual Reality? VR Definition and Examples.” Retrieved April 4, 2019, from https://www.marxentlabs.com/what-is-virtual-reality/.

Bellisle, M., & Daley, M. (2018, August 1). “Judge Blocks Release of Blueprints for 3D-Printed Guns.” Retrieved November 7, 2018, from https://www.apnews.com/0c55d778df35412dbac0be6444917bc7.

Caudell, T. P., & Mizell, D. W. (1992). “Augmented Reality: An Application of Heads-Up Display Technology to Manual Manufacturing Processes.” *Proceedings of the Twenty-Fifth Hawaii International Conference on System Sciences, II.* doi:10.1109/hicss.1992.183317.

Chowdhry, A. (2013, October 8). “What Can 3D Printing Do? Here Are 6 Creative Examples.” Retrieved April 3, 2018, from https://www.forbes.com/sites/amitchowdhry/2013/10/08/what-can-3d-printing-do-here-are-6-creative-examples/#2beb182b5491.

Computer Hope. (2017, April 26). “What Is a Walled Garden?” Retrieved July 8, 2019, from https://www.computerhope.com/jargon/w/walled-garden.htm.

Crispin, S. (2017, September 26). “3D Print Your Tilt Brush Sketches Using Meshmixer.” Retrieved May 9, 2019, from https://www.instructables.com/id/3D-Print-Your-Tilt-Brush-Sketches-Using-Meshmixer/.

Cullinane, S., & Criss, D. (2018, August 2). “All Your Questions about 3D Guns Answered.” Retrieved November 5, 2018, from https://www.cnn.com/2018/07/31/us/3d-printed-plastic-guns/index.html.

Dierkes, G. (2017, April 1). *Falvey Memorial Library Blog.* Retrieved May 28, 2019, from https://blog.library.villanova.edu/2017/04/01/falvey-pilots-first-of-its-kind-drone-delivery-service-2.

“Dig! for Merge Cube.” (n.d.). Retrieved May 5, 2019, from https://miniverse.io/experience?e=dig-for-merge-cube.

“Drone Classification and Types.” (2017, December 7). Retrieved May 29, 2019, from http://penguinengine.com/drone-classification-types/.

“e-NABLE Chapters—Get Added to the Map!” (n.d.). Retrieved December 12, 2018, from https://docs.google.com/forms/d/e/1FAIpQLSf6nr7SKFDI69X41OigZ6NIXYs-4Fys9LQ_Q0vv0EAEsKPWxw/viewform.

Fagan, K. (2018, March 4). “Here’s What Happens to Your Body When You’ve Been in Virtual Reality for Too Long.” Retrieved May 10, 2019, from https://www.businessinsider.com/virtual-reality-vr-side-effects-2018-3.

Federal Aviation Administration. (2019, May 17). "Getting Started." Retrieved May 21, 2019, from https://www.faa.gov/uas/getting_started/.

Feist, J. (2019, July 5). "AR Glasses vs. VR Headsets—Great FPV Drone Goggles?" Retrieved July 6, 2019, from https://www.dronerush.com/ar-glasses-vr-goggles-drone-accessory-10599.

Fingas, J. (2019, May 20). "Google's Next-Gen Glass Eyewear Lasts Longer and Runs on Android." Retrieved May 22, 2019, from https://www.engadget.com/2019/05/20/google-glass-enterprise-edition-2/.

Flanagan, J. (2018, November 14). "A Brief History of Augmented Reality." Retrieved April 9, 2019, from https://medium.com/datadriveninvestor/a-brief-history-of-augmented-reality-b07dcb7b4221.

Ford, J. (2019, January 7). "The History of Drones (Drone History Timeline From 1849 To 2019)." Retrieved March 15, 2019, from https://www.dronethusiast.com/history-of-drones/.

Garber, M. (2014, June 23). "At This School, You Can Check Out Drones Like Library Books." Retrieved April 28, 2019, from https://www.theatlantic.com/technology/archive/2014/06/at-this-school-you-can-check-out-drones-like-library-books/373214.

Gent, E. (2016, October 4). "Are Virtual Reality Headsets Safe for Children?" Retrieved May 15, 2019, from https://www.scientificamerican.com/article/are-virtual-reality-headsets-safe-for-children.

"Harry Potter Wizards Unite." (2019). Retrieved June 23, 2019, from https://harrypotterwizardsunite.com/.

Hoffman, C. (2018, June 12). "How to Use Windows 10's Hidden Video Editor." Retrieved March 7, 2019, from https://www.howtogeek.com/355524/how-to-use-windows-10s-hidden-video-editor/.

Hollister, S. (2014, November 19). "How Magic Leap Is Secretly Creating a New Alternate Reality." Retrieved May 20, 2019, from https://gizmodo.com/how-magic-leap-is-secretly-creating-a-new-alternate-rea-1660441103.

Horwitz, J. (2019, September 25). "Oculus Quest Will Get Hand-Tracking, Oculus Link to Play Rift PC Games." Retrieved October 17, 2019, from https://venturebeat.com/2019/09/25/oculus-quest-will-get-hand-tracking-oculus-link-to-play-rift-pc-games/.

"How to Clean Your Oculus Rift and HTC Vive." (2019, March 19). Retrieved June 18, 2019, from https://vrcover.com/how-to-clean-your-oculus-rift-and-htc-vive/.

"IKEA Place Augmented Reality App." (n.d.). Retrieved June 15, 2019, from https://highlights.ikea.com/2017/ikea-place/.

"An Introductory Guide to Selective Laser Sintering (SLS) 3D Printing." (2017, June 22). Retrieved March 12, 2019, from https://formlabs.com/blog/what-is-selective-laser-sintering/.

"isSupported." (n.d.). Retrieved April 22, 2019, from https://developer.apple.com/documentation/arkit/arconfiguration/2923553-issupported.

Karin, J. (2018, November 30). "The Future of 3D Printing." Retrieved May 16, 2019, from https://thefutureofthings.com/4664-the-future-of-3d-printing/.

Kharpal, A. (2018, July 11). "AT&T Strikes Partnership and Invests in Secretive Google-Backed 'Mixed Reality' Start-Up Magic Leap." Retrieved May 4, 2019, from https://www.cnbc.com/2018/07/11/att-strikes-partnership-and-invests-in-magic-leap.html.

Kuchera, B. (2019, June 28). "Valve Index Review: $999 Buys You the Best VR Experience Yet—When It Works." Retrieved July 1, 2019, from https://www.polygon.com/reviews/2019/6/28/18758877/valve-index-review-steam-vr-headset-virtual-reality-pc.

LaFay, M. (2015). *Drones for Dummies* (1st ed.). Hoboken, NJ: John Wiley & Sons, pp. 17–18.

LaMotte, S. (2017, December 13). "The Very Real Health Dangers of Virtual Reality." Retrieved October 17, 2019, from https://www.cnn.com/2017/12/13/health/virtual-reality-vr-dangers-safety/index.html.

Leigh, E. (2011, March 18). "The Most Difficult Plastics to Recycle." Retrieved May 7, 2019, from https://recyclenation.com/2011/03/difficult-plastics-recycle/.

Liptak, A. (2019a, February 10). "Google Is Letting Some Users Test Its AR Navigation Feature for Google Maps." Retrieved April 8, 2019, from https://www.theverge.com/2019/2/10/18219325/google-maps-augmented-reality-ar-feature-app-prototype-test.

Liptak, A. (2019b, June 2). "Here's How to Look at Life-Sized Animals in AR through Google Search." Retrieved June 13, 2019, from https://www.theverge.com/2019/6/2/18649312/google-ar-search-results-animals-3d-model-augmented-reality-lions-tigers-bears-oh-my.

Merge Headset. (2019). Retrieved June 25, 2019, from https://mergevr.com/headset.

Merriam-Webster. (n.d.). "Experience." Retrieved June 18, 2019, from https://merriam-Webster.com/dictionary/experience.

Meyer, D. (2017, October 18). "This Secretive Augmented Reality Firm Just Raised Another $502 Million." Retrieved May 4, 2019, from http://fortune.com/2017/10/18/magic-leap-502-million-google-alibaba.

"Minecraft Earth FAQ." (2019, June 4). Retrieved June 24, 2019, from https://www.minecraft.net/en-us/earth/faq.

Mlot, S. (2014, December 17). "Neal Stephenson Named 'Chief Futurist' at Magic Leap." Retrieved May 20, 2019, from https://www.pcmag.com/news/330435/neal-stephenson-named-chief-futurist-at-magic-leap.

"Model Train Scale and Gauge." (2019, February 12). Retrieved May 8, 2019, from http://rrmodelcraftsman.com/model-train-scale-gauge/.

Naudus, K. (2019, May 2). "Nintendo Labo VR review: Cute, Cardboard and Kinda Boring." Retrieved June 9, 2019, from https://www.engadget.com/2019/05/02/nintendo-labo-vr-review-cardboard.

"Nintendo Labo Official Site—What's Included, Where to Buy." (2019). Retrieved July 7, 2019, from https://labo.nintendo.com/kits/vr-kit/.

Norman, J. (n.d.). "L. Frank Baum's *The Master Key* Imagines a Kind of Augmented Reality." Retrieved April 6, 2019, from http://www.historyofinformation.com/detail.php.

Object Viewer for Merge Cube [PDF]. (n.d.). San Antonio, TX: Merge.

Oculus Go. (n.d.). Retrieved July 7, 2019, from https://www.oculus.com/go.

Oculus Quest. (2019). Retrieved July 8, 2019, from https://www.oculus.com/quest/.

Oculus Rift S. (n.d.). Retrieved July 7, 2019, from https://www.oculus.com/rift-s.

Owen, J. (2017, October 1). "About Us." Retrieved March 19, 2019, from http://enablingthefuture.org/about/.

Pollard, C. (2017, December 7). "Why Visual Content Is a Social Media Secret Weapon." Retrieved March 26, 2019, from http://www.huffingtonpost.com/catriona-pollard/why-visual-content-is-a-s_b_7261876.html.

"Product Comparison." (n.d.). Retrieved June 9, 2019, from https://www.vive.com/us/comparison/.

"Product Safety Information." (n.d.). Retrieved July 8, 2019, from https://vr.google.com/cardboard/product-safety/.

Rainey, K. (2015, April 7). “Special 3-D Delivery from Space to NASA’s Marshall Center.” Retrieved April 7, 2019, from https://www.nasa.gov/centers/marshall/news/news/release/2015/special-3-d-delivery-from-space-to-nasa-s-marshall-space-flight-center.html.

Redohl, S. (2019, January 10). “Volumetric Video Is So Much More Than VR.” Retrieved May 4, 2019, from https://www.immersiveshooter.com/2019/01/10/volumetric-video-means-so-much-more-than-vr/.

Reichental, A. (2018, January 23). “The Future of 3-D Printing.” Retrieved May 11, 2019, from https://www.forbes.com/sites/forbestechcouncil/2018/01/23/the-future-of-3-d-printing/#402be29d65f6.

Robertson, A. (2016, April 28). “The *New York Times* Is Sending Out a Second Round of Google Cardboards.” Retrieved July 8, 2019, from https://www.theverge.com/2016/4/28/11504932/new-york-times-vr-google-cardboard-seeking-plutos-frigid-heart.

Robertson, A. (2019, April 30). “Oculus Rift S Review: A Swan Song for First-Generation VR.” Retrieved July 7, 2019, from https://www.theverge.com/2019/4/30/18523941/oculus-rift-s-review-vr-headset-price-specs-features.

Rogers, S. (2019, June 21). “2019: The Year Virtual Reality Gets Real.” Retrieved June 28, 2019, from https://www.forbes.com/sites/solrogers/2019/06/21/2019-the-year-virtual-reality-gets-real/#30614da66ba9.

Rogers, T. (2015, October 7). “Everything You Need to Know about Polylactic Acid (PLA).” Retrieved May 8, 2019, from https://www.creativemechanisms.com/blog/learn-about-polylactic-acid-pla-prototypes.

Ross, P. (2015, February 17). “Native Facebook Videos Get More Reach Than Any Other Type of Post.” Retrieved April 8, 2019, from http://www.socialbakers.com/blog/2367-native-facebook-videos-get-more-reach-than-any-other-type-of-post.

“Samsung Gear 360.” (2017). Retrieved July 8, 2019, from https://www.samsung.com/global/galaxy/gear-360.

Smith, S. L. (2017, April 20). “Samsung Gear VR Review (2017): A New Way to Play.” Retrieved July 10, 2019, from https://www.tomsguide.com/us/samsung-gear-vr,review-3248.html.

Spin Master. (2019). “Products.” Retrieved May 8, 2019, from https://www.spinmaster.com/product_detail.php?pid=p21006.

"10 Best iPhone iPad AR Apps and Games for Kids." (2017, November 27). Retrieved May 20, 2019, from https://arcritic.com/947/10-best-iphone-ipad-ar-apps-and-games-for-kids-2017/.

"3D Printing in Automotive." (n.d.). Ultimaker. Retrieved April 25, 2019, from https://ultimaker.com/en/explore/where-is-3d-printing-used/automotive.

"2018 Best 3D Printer Guide." (2018). Retrieved January 8, 2019, from https://www.3dhubs.com/best-3d-printer-guide.

"Valve Index." (n.d.). Retrieved May 8, 2019, from https://store.steampowered.com/valveindex.

Varotsis, A. B. (2019). "Introduction to FDM 3D Printing." Retrieved April 4, 2019, from https://www.3dhubs.com/knowledge-base/introduction-fdm-3d-printing#/what.

Veldhuizen, B. (2014, November 3). "3D Print a Model Downloaded from Sketchfab." Retrieved May 8, 2019, from https://sketchfab.com/blogs/community/3d-print-a-model-downloaded-from-sketchfab.

"Video Length and Loops on Facebook." (n.d.). Retrieved April 4, 2019, from https://www.facebook.com/business/help/1160942077279936.

Virtual Reality Society. (2017). "What Is Virtual Reality?" Retrieved June 30, 2019, from https://www.vrs.org.uk/virtual-reality/what-is-virtual-reality.html.

Weinberger, M., & Shontell, A. (2019, February 24). "Microsoft Reveals the HoloLens 2, Its New $3,500 Holographic Headset That Seems to Improve on the Original in Every Way." Retrieved April 28, 2019, from https://www.businessinsider.com/microsoft-hololens-2-price-details-hands-on-2019-2.

"What Are the System Requirements?" (n.d.). Retrieved May 8, 2019, from https://www.vive.com/us/support/vive/category_howto/what-are-the-system-requirements.html.

"What Is a QR Code?" (n.d.). Retrieved April 10, 2019, from https://www.qrcode.com/en/about/.

"What Is Augmented Reality?" (n.d.). Retrieved June 22, 2019, from https://www.realitytechnologies.com/augmented-reality/.

"What Is 3D printing? The Definitive Guide." (2019). Retrieved February 23, 2019, from https://www.3dhubs.com/what-is-3d-printing.

"Which Design?" (2018, June 6). Retrieved March 22, 2019, from http://enablingthefuture.org/which-design/.

"XL-RCM 10.0 PIXXY: Pocket one/FPV quad by 3dxl." (2014, March 15). Retrieved February 10, 2019, from https://www.thingiverse.com/thing:272234.

Yeap, M. (2019, March 5). "The Future of 3D Printing—A Glimpse at the Next Generation." Retrieved April 22, 2019, from https://all3dp.com/2/future-of-3d-printing-a-glimpse-at-next-generation-making/.

Zavala, M. (n.d.). "The DM Workshop." Retrieved May 3, 2019, from https://www.shapeways.com/shops/dmworkshop.

Zibreg, C. (2017, January 26). "Google Translate's Augmented Reality Feature, Word Lens, Now Works with Japanese." Retrieved June 13, 2019, from https://www.idownloadblog.com/2017/01/26/google-translates-augmented-reality-feature-word-lens-now-works-with-japanese/.

Index

About the Authors

CHRISTOPHER DECRISTOFARO received his master's degree in Library Science in 2001. He is currently a technology librarian and team leader of *The Studio*, Sachem Library's makerspace in Suffolk County, New York. He is also past president and member at large of the Computer and Technical Services Division (CATS) of the Suffolk County Library Association (SCLA). Chris moderates the Technology Information Forum, a place for library technologists to discuss issues and advances in library technology. He is also the creator and cohost of "The Library Pros," a podcast that discusses libraries and technology with guests from all around the world. He has also spoken at various library and technology association conferences and webinars.

JAMES HUTTER is a technology librarian, currently serving as head of Computer Services at the Port Washington Public Library and as vice president/president-elect of the Nassau County Library Association. A graduate of the CUNY Queens College School of Library and Information Studies, James had previously worked as an information technology manager before making the leap into librarianship. Throughout the years, James has presented seminars, workshops, and webinars on behalf of the Port Washington Public Library and the Nassau County Library Association. Covering topics such as digital privacy, video gaming in libraries, 3D printing design, and general technology trends, he is always anxious to share knowledge and experience with others in the field and members of his community.

NICK TANZI is the assistant director of the South Huntington Public Library. A technology enthusiast, he has spoken in the United States and abroad on topics ranging from social media marketing to 3D printing. He is the author of *Making the Most of Digital Collections through Training and Outreach*, which received a starred review from *Library Journal*. He writes "The Wired Library" column for *Public Libraries Magazine*. Tanzi was named a 2017 Dewey Fellow by the New York Library Association, and he currently serves as president of its Making and STEAM Round Table.

CPSIA information can be obtained
at www.ICGtesting.com
Printed in the USA
LVHW051727161120
671836LV00005B/303

9 781440 869280